Networks of Democracy

Lessons from Kosovo

for Afghanistan, Iraq, and Beyond

Anne Holohan

STANFORD UNIVERSITY PRESS

Stanford, California 2005

Stanford University Press
Stanford, California
© 2005 by the Board of Trustees of the
Leland Stanford Junior University

Library of Congress Cataloging-in-Publication Data

Holohan, Anne.
    Networks of democracy : lessons from Kosovo for
Afghanistan, Iraq, and beyond / Anne Holohan.
        p. cm.
    Includes bibliographical references and index.
    ISBN 0-8047-5190-0 (cloth : alk. paper) —
    ISBN 0-8047-5191-9 (pbk. : alk. paper)
    1. Kosovo (Serbia)—History—Civil War, 1998–1999.
2. United Nations—Serbia and Montenegro—Kosovo (Serbia).
3. Communication and technology. 4. Intervention
(International law). I. Title.
DR2087.H65 2005
949.7103—dc22

                                        2004024576

Printed in the United States of America
Original Printing 2005
Last figure below indicates year of this printing:
14   13   12   11   10   09   08   07   06   05

Typeset at Stanford University Press in 10/13 Sabon

TO ANURAG

Acknowledgments

Thanks to everyone who was part of this research in Kosovo, internationals and Kosovars, with admiration and best wishes. Many, many thanks for your openness, honesty, and hospitality. If not for all of you, there would be no book.

I would like to thank my PhD committee at UCLA, Professor William Roy, Professor Steven Clayman, and Professor Lynne Zucker for their constant and continuing encouragement and mentoring. Thanks to Laura Miller, formerly at UCLA and now at Rand, for opening up many of the opportunities in this research over the years since Haiti and for being a great traveling companion on that first trip, and to Charles Moskos of Northwestern University for his kind mentorship. Thanks to Professor Antonio Chiesi and all my other colleagues at the University of Trento for great feedback and a welcoming, intellectually stimulating environment in the Dolomites. Thanks to Kate Wahl at Stanford University Press for her encouragement, patience, and vision, and thanks to everyone else at SUP who helped with the publication of this book. Thanks to Peter Dreyer for his meticulous editing. For permission to reprint parts of chapter 5, I thank the *Journal of Information Technology and International Development*. Going way back, I'd like to express my appreciation to Hilary Tovey at the Department of Sociology at Trinity College, Dublin, for early intellectual inspiration, and to John Barnes in the Department of Government at the London School of Economics, who combined excellent scholarship with a wonderful kindly wry view of the world. My research in Kosovo was funded by the University of California's Institute for Global Conflict and Cooperation (IGCC) Dissertation Fellowship, 2001–2.

In Los Angeles, thanks to Elham Gheytanchi, Julie Eisenberg, Steve Sherwood, Gwen McEvoy, Jodi Finkel, Pepper Glass, Vishwas Karve, Martin Griffin, Philip Leeman, Donal Ryan, and Gabriela Fried for friendship, collegiality, and support during the PhD process and after. Thanks to friends and fellow sociologists and writers in England: Jessica Jacobson-Gaffar, Sarah James, and Jenny Winters. Thanks to my LA and London buddy Stacy Pollard for opening up the world of business and innovation. A special thanks for everything to my dear parents, Mai and Peter Holohan. Thanks to my wonderful siblings and brother-in-law, Beth, Mike, Aideen, and Fergal, in Dublin. Thanks also to my family in India, and especially to the memory of Nanaji. Most of all and always thanks for everything to you, Anurag, my partner in everything!

Throughout this book, the names of all people and places in Kosovo, except Pristina, Racak, and Kacanik, have been changed to protect confidentiality.

Contents

Figures and Table

Acronyms and Abbreviations

CIMIC   civil-military cooperation

CivPol   UNMIK civilian police in Kosovo (international)

DMA   deputy municipal administrator

EU   European Union

ICT[s]   information and communication technology [technologies]

IT   information technology

KFOR   Kosovo Protection Force

KLA(UCK)/
KPC(TMK) Kosovo Liberation Army (UCK in Albanian)/Kosovo Protection Corps (TMK in Albanian), a civil defense force incorporating the demobilized KLA. These acronyms were used interchangeably by people in Kosovo in 2001.

KPS   Kosovo Police Service (local)

LDK   Democratic League of Kosovo (a moderate-centrist political party)

MA   UN municipal administrator—the most senior person in UNMIK in each municipality

NATO   North Atlantic Treaty Organization

NGO   nongovernmental organization

OSCE   Organization for Security and Cooperation in Europe

PDK   Democratic Party of Kosovo

UNCA   UN Civil Administration in Kosovo (under the auspices of

Acronyms and Abbreviations

the UN Secretariat in New York). UNCA is not an official acronym but I use it for the sake of clarity when talking about the UN Civil Administration.

UNMIK   UN Interim Administration Mission in Kosovo

UNV   UN volunteer (contracted junior UN staff)

Networks of Democracy

Lessons from Kosovo for
Afghanistan, Iraq, and Beyond

Introduction

The task before the international community is to help the people in Kosovo to rebuild their lives and heal the wounds of conflict.

—UN Secretary-General Kofi Annan

I don't think there's anybody out there who has ASKED the questions we're trying to answer. Who do I talk to?? If you talk to Americans, anybody who created democracy in America is dead. I reckon my job is to walk out of here, turn over whatever I'm doing to the municipality, and this thing will run by itself. We have to build 5,000 odd houses, get everything working again, get a reconciliation between the Serbs and Albanians . . . the brief has not been written on how to do this.

—Terry Peterson, UN municipal administrator,
Banshik, Kosovo, 1999–2001

The tasks facing any international intervention are huge. To get an idea of the coordination and cooperation required of both international organizations and local populations in an intervention such as those in Kosovo or Afghanistan or Iraq, picture a place where decades of corruption have been followed by war, uprooting what normal life there had been. A place where many houses and public buildings are heaps of rubble, where electricity is constantly cutting out, where running water is only sporadically available. A place where roads are potholed disaster areas at best, rutted dust tracks at worst; where if you have cancer, treatment is not an option. A place where unemployment levels reach 75–90 percent, where the streets of small towns are thronged with teenagers at the end of each school shift (schools typically run several shifts a day because the demand exceeds the facilities), where there are no jobs to absorb the thousands leaving school each year. A place where the taxation and banking system is nonexistent, where government departments either did not exist before or were run by members of a regime that has been ousted, where records of titles to property have been destroyed or stolen by the departing regime, or simply lost in the chaos that followed that departure.

These challenges overlie the ethnic divisions and vividly remembered political mistakes that produced the conflict. The marks of neighbors killing neighbors and stealing their belongings, and the brutalization and disappearance of family members, leave a bitter legacy. The regime that has been ousted and the prior local opposition to that regime (usually the armed wing), who are frustrated about their loss of power, tolerate the international organizations comprising the intervention at best and threaten them and target them for assassination at worst. The local populations in the middle, usually represented by the supporters of what had been the peaceful or constitutional opposition, as well as the members of the same ethnic group as the former regime who had never endorsed its means or ends, struggle to be heard above the din of threats from factions that are defeated or disarmed in theory but very much armed in practice. This has been true of extremist elements both among the Serbs remaining in Kosovo and in the former Kosovo Liberation Army; in Afghanistan, of the Taliban and the Northern Alliance, as well as various warlords and their factions; and in Iraq, of the former Baathist regime and Shiite cleric-politicians with Islamic state ambitions. The international intervention in each case has to try to get past the legacy of hatred, to persuade all ethnic groups to participate in the rebuilding of society, both the physical reconstruction and the building of local and national institutions. The international intervention also has to figure out how to do this, how to coordinate the efforts of all the organizations involved, both international and local. As Terry Peterson says, "the brief has not been written on how to do this."

Kosovo, Iraq, and Afghanistan are among the territories struggling to democratize and develop economically at lightning speed in the early twenty-first century under the auspices of an international intervention, sometimes sanctioned by the United Nations, sometimes not. All can usefully gain from lessons gleaned from the efforts of participants in this process in the other countries or territories. Kosovo was a bold initial foray by the international community and the local populations into a cooperative drive toward democracy. It is on an unprecedented scale: effectively, Kosovo has become a territory under temporary international authority. Given the earlier start in time, and hence the opportunity to make mistakes that other interventions can learn from, the experiences of the people and organizations involved in the intervention in Kosovo have an increasingly practical importance for those working in Iraq, Afghanistan, and other countries involved in democratization and postconflict reconstruction. The origins of the problems may differ, as may the agencies and nations involved, and the situations on the ground may vary in the degree of chaos, but in all of these places, organizations and populations are struggling to coordinate reconstruction and democratization. A close look at the reasons for successes and failures of the interorganizational and interpopulation efforts in Kosovo yields lessons that may be useful elsewhere.

The Origins of the Book

This book originated in observations I made in Haiti and Kosovo between 1997 and 2000 on the relationships among civilian organizations (NGOs, international police, and UN agencies) and between those organizations and military units participating in the intervention. I went to Haiti in the summer of 1997 as a research assistant to a professor studying the effect on the U.S. military of participating in Military Operations Other Than War (MOOTW).[1] Through a personal connection, we stayed with an Irish nongovernmental organization (NGO), Concern Worldwide. We took the opportunity to interview its personnel and those of other NGOs active in Haiti at this time, such as CARE International and World Vision, about their perceptions of and contact with the U.S. military. During this trip, I also met with members of a UN police mission and military personnel from Canada working under the same UN mandate as the U.S. military contingent.[2] There was, however, minimal actual cooperation among the international agencies in Haiti. Most of the NGOs there were barely aware of the existence of the international peacekeeping mission, and when it was pointed out, they did not feel that it had any relevance for their work. The U.S. military in turn responded to the occasional requests for help (transport or logistical) from individual NGOs but did not see this as in integral part of their mission. They had next to no contact with local people or organizations, including the UN personnel. There was considerable disgruntlement about being part of a UN mission among the U.S. military personnel, who were unhappy about being under a non-U.S. command and questioned their suitability for this type of mission. Communications between different organizations were also hampered by the lack of a communications infrastructure. There was no common phone system—landline or mobile, no use of e-mail between organizations, and no common space on the Internet.

Three years later, in 2000, as part of the same ongoing project looking

at the effects on the U.S. military of participating in peace-building operations, I spent ten days at Camp Bondsteel, the home base of the U.S. military in the U.S. sector of Kosovo. In stark contrast to Haiti, the military
leadership there viewed their joint operations with civilian organizations
as *the* key factor in the success of their mission. The soldiers themselves
were enthusiastic about the opportunity to help people, to get good training experience, and to travel. A visit to Novo Brdo, a municipality in the
U.S. sector, which had a U.S. company based in a building in the center
of the town, demonstrated a remarkable shift from Haiti. "We're soldiers, police officers, firefighters, drivers, mediators," the soldiers reported, and they participated in weekly councils of all the organizations
involved in the UN mission in Kosovo—the UN civil administration
(UNCA), the local government, the Organization for Security and Cooperation in Europe (OSCE), and NGOs—and worked with them in a coordinated and conscious fashion. At the end of the research trip, we went
to the airport outside Kosovo's capital, Pristina, to fly home. At the entrance to the airport, the head of the team encountered an old acquaintance, Terry Peterson, who was working as a municipal administrator for
the UN in a municipality in the north of Kosovo. During the ensuing conversation, I expressed an interest in coming back to further investigate the
interorganizational cooperation, and limits to cooperation, that I had
witnessed. Peterson was enthusiastic about the idea and gave me his business card, telling me to get in touch when I was ready to come back. A
year later, I landed at Pristina Airport to begin an intensive period of research in two municipalities, based with the two UN teams but with rov-
ing access to the militaries, NGOs, OSCE, and EU in both locations.

Map of the Book

In Kosovo, the United Nations embarked on a massive undertaking, unprecedented in both its scope and structural complexity. This was the first
intervention that had been designed so that other multilateral organizations were full partners under UN leadership. Interventions in the twenty-
first century require more than just one organization or a handful of organizations working independently. They call for a multiplicity of
organizations of different sizes, styles, and purposes working together in
a coordinated way. This book, among other things, compares the fate of
the two municipalities, or localities, of Banshik and Thezren in Kosovo in
2001, two years after the intervention got under way in 1999. Although

similar in demographics, geography, and socioeconomic status, the two municipalities were heading down different paths by 2001. Banshik had made progress toward the goals of the intervention—institution building, democratization, and reconstruction—while Thezren was stagnating. The crucial difference was in the ability of the international organizations in Banshik to cooperate as if part of one organization, as what is known as a "network" organization. In a network organization, a number of traditionally hierarchical, bureaucratic organizations come together to temporarily form a single organizational entity to pursue specific goals. Once those goals are attained, the temporary network organization disbands. The organizational integrity of the participating organization is not harmed by this temporary organizational cooperation with other organizations. To operate effectively, the boundaries of the network organization need to be fluid. The network organization's constituents, the people and organizations that are the focus of its efforts, must also be included. Banshik managed to make considerable progress toward pulling local organizations and populations into the process of institution building and reconstruction. Indeed, one might argue that this very process of cooperation was itself the content of democratic institution building.

In contrast, in Thezren, the international organizations stayed behind their traditional, hierarchical organizational walls. They functioned reasonably well as individual organizations alongside other organizations. But they did not cooperate in a meaningful, interdependent way with the other international organizations and local populations. In an environment that was so complex, with every organization dependent on others to carry out its own job, and with the task of pulling hostile populations together, this focus on a traditional, bureaucratic, hierarchical approach resulted in a very poor level of cooperation.

This book deals with Kosovo, but it has relevance for interventions anywhere in the world, including the challenging situations in Afghanistan and Iraq. Most scholarly and policy books and articles on interventions have been written from far away, by academics and policymakers steeped in theory and history, content with producing a macro analysis. In the process, it is easily forgotten that it is flesh and blood people working who are in the interventions and are on the receiving end of interventions. An account based on fieldwork in an intervention that grounds those experiences in theoretical perspectives yields insights that are not specific to any particular intervention but are relevant anywhere organizations are trying to cooperate. This is an account of the everyday behavior of both the internationals (a term used to denote any non-Koso-var working for UNMIK or KFOR) and the local people, and of its impact on the intervention. As such, I hope it will contribute to our understanding of how human behavior helps create organizations and institutions such as those in UNMIK.

① The first key argument in the book is that in a situation with several different types of organizations, the network organizational form is the best way to organize a coherent mission. For a network organization to be effective, it must produce an institutional culture, or a shared identity and understanding of how things are done, that will serve it throughout its existence.

Four factors that shaped the institutional culture of the network organization of organizations in both Banshik and Thezren—the type of leadership, the degree of formality in the organizational network, the degree to which work relationships were embedded in social ones, and the degree to which behavior reflected transparency and accountability—were produced by everyday acts. They were critical in fostering a network institutional culture where trust was continually produced, people identified not only with their own organization but with the mission as a whole, information was freely shared, and problems were tackled in a collaborative way.

② The second main argument of the book is that the use of information and communication technologies (ICTs) is a key variable in the workings of international interventions. ICTs, which include the Internet, e-mail, mobile telephones, satellite technology, and radio communications, play an essential part in any interorganizational effort at democratization, institution building, and reconstruction.

In Chapter 1, I introduce Banshik and Thezren and discuss how the flag issue captured the differences between the international organizations' approaches in the two municipalities—and the consequences. An intervention comprising diverse organizations requires leadership and an organizational or institutional culture that is all about generating trust and inducing participation. In Kosovo, this proved to be an essential addition to the traditional, bureaucratic leadership typical of international organizations, particularly the United Nations. The municipality of Banshik did generate an institutional culture that was appropriate for the network of organizations working together, but Thezren had great difficulty in doing so. In this chapter, I also give a brief history of the background to the intervention in Kosovo and describe the setup of the international intervention itself.

The second chapter is theoretical and can be skipped by nonacademic readers or readers who want to go straight to the substantive findings of the book. (However, it might be useful!) The complexity of international interventions requires an interdisciplinary approach, because it is impossible to understand a modern international intervention from the standpoint of a single discipline. I use organizational sociology, economic sociology, symbolic interactionism, and cultural sociology to throw light on issues usually studied in international relations, political science, or in political sociology. I explain the great need for and, with the advent of new communication technologies and accompanying changes in organizational form, greater capacity for interorganizational cooperation, using the idea of a network organization. I focus on the parallels between the use of this organizational form in the private sector and in interventions. In both the private sector and interventions, traditionally hierarchical, bureaucratic organizations are in a process of shifting from only working inside their own organizational walls to having to cooperate together on particular projects. They have to come together temporarily to form a network organization, disbanding once the goals of the project (or intervention) are achieved.

In Chapters 3 and 4, I document and compare daily working life among the international workers and organizations in the two municipalities of Banshik and Thezren. The personnel and organizations in the former aspired to a networked intervention; the personnel and organizations in the latter were persistently traditionally hierarchical in working behind individual organizational walls with traditional institutional cultures. The processes and consequences of both approaches are very significant for understanding institution building and democratization. The international intervention in Kosovo was attempting to grope toward developing the characteristics of a network organization: where expertise, not rank or status, gets precedence; decisions are decentralized to the local level; cooperation with other organizations is a priority; communication channels are not prescribed, but it is possible to communicate with anyone inside the organization or beyond its boundaries, as needed; the culture of the organization is more informal than formal; and identification is not just with your own organization but with the network organization—in this case, the intervention—as a whole. The network of organizations in Banshik produced an institutional culture appropriate to the network organizational form; Thezren did not. I explore the factors—appropriate leadership, informality, social embeddedness, accountability—that produced the network institutional culture in Banshik and show how these factors did not exist in Thezren, leading to an institutional culture that was inappropriate to the network organizational form.

Chapter 5 looks at the role of information and communication technologies (ICTs) in the international intervention in Kosovo. ICTs play a critical role in network organizations, but our knowledge of the interaction of technology and people and organizations in this type of environment is very limited. I look at what did happen and at the potential of such communications. How did ICTs assist the network organization of UNMIK? Did they contribute to forming a distinctive mission culture? How important was face-to-face interaction in a technologically enabled environment? Traditionally hierarchical, bureaucratic organizations such as the UN Secretariat, militaries, and police forces are struggling to use ICTs and new organizational forms stemming from technology to streamline their organizations and make them more responsive, while at the same time retaining control both within the organization and of their immediate environment in an international intervention such as Kosovo. Chapter 6 is a salutary reminder of the importance of face-to-face communication in building trust. Such personal interaction cannot be replaced, but can certainly be complemented, by the use of ICTs.

In the last section of the book, Chapters 7 and 8, I examine each of the organizations working in the intervention in Kosovo and show how at least some of them transformed themselves into successful hybrids, part hierarchy, part network, capable of maintaining their hierarchical integrity while simultaneously participating in a network organization.

This book addresses the questions everyone wants answers for: How do you get from the chaos of a postconflict society to one with functioning institutions based on cooperation? What role do international organizations and actors play in this? How is the necessary cooperation between all the participants—international and local—achieved? How can the idea of a network organization contribute to democratization efforts in international interventions? What difference does globalization and the information and communications revolution make to the processes of democratization and postconflict reconstruction? The interventions in Afghanistan and Iraq are evolving in ways that are different from that in Kosovo. But the basic challenge of cooperation between the international organizations and between those organizations and the local populations remains critical.

PART I

The UN Mission in Kosovo as a Network Organization

CHAPTER ONE

Democratizing Through Networks

A Tale of Two Municipalities: Banshik and Thezren

Kosovo in the fall is filled with fields of golden wheat and corn, blue skies, green pastures, and smoky blue hills. Banshik and Thezren are adjacent municipalities in this bucolic setting. They occupy either side of a range of hills and are of similar size (approx. 350 sq km). The overall population of each is between 80,000 and 100,000, and in each case, approximately 10,000 of the inhabitants live in the main town and the remainder in the agricultural hinterland. Each municipality has a postwar Serb population of less than 5 percent. Both had limited industrial bases before the war. They were two of the most heavily damaged municipalities of Kosovo, with just under half of all houses in each destroyed.

But Banshik and Thezren have fared differently since the end of the bombing in 1999. By the second half of 2001, they were following divergent paths. Banshik was a bustling, thriving market town. Interethnic tensions were still high, but the active hostility between the populations had been reduced to skirmishes over stolen cows. There were no ethnically motivated killings in Banshik during 2001. No families were living in tents as winter approached, reconstruction was progressing rapidly and in line with the UN Mission in Kosovo (UNMIK) requirements, and the schools had fuel for the winter. The five factories were working again, although at partial capacity (30–50 percent). Albanians and Serbs in the municipal administration and elected bodies worked uneasily with each other but well with the international civil administration. The elected Municipal Assembly had representatives of all ethnicities, who met and worked together. There was a weekly interorganizational meeting that was part of ongoing meetings and activity between the international organizations. A general feeling of normality prevailed, and there was a sense of hope about the future.

In Thezren in 2001, the town had the same abandoned feeling as in 1999, with no thriving weekly market or feeling of normality. There were high levels of active hostility between the Albanians and Serbs, with two ethnically motivated fatalities occurring while I was there in the fall of 2001. Potholes several feet deep scored the main road through the town. Water had been unavailable for most of the summer, the sewage system was not working, and reconstruction was far behind UNMIK guidelines. Hundreds of families were still in tents as winter bore down, and heating fuel had not been ordered for the schools. None of the three prewar factories were working, despite a $7 million donation in 2000 for their rehabilitation. Members of the local municipal administration consisted only of Kosovar Albanians, who walked around with pistols openly tucked into their jeans, uneasily sharing a building with the international UN administration. The shared governance occurred in a relationship characterized by distrust and frustration. The internationals had uneasy relationships with both Albanians and Serbs in this municipality. The elected Municipal Assembly had representatives of all ethnicities, but security issues regularly precluded ethnic minorities, including Serbs, from attending. The international actors met once a week at the "four-pillar meeting," but it was clear at these meetings that they did not work together actively the rest of the time.

In short, Thezren was like a negative image of Banshik. Why was this so? The two municipalities were adjacent and very similar socioeconomically, demographically, historically, and geographically, and had similar experiences during the war. The amount of money poured into both municipalities after the war was the same, and the same set of international actors were present: the UN civil administration (UNCA), European Union–funded nongovernmental organizations (NGOs), the international police (CivPol), and the militaries comprising the Kosovo Protection Force, or KFOR. The Democratic Party of Kosovo (PDK), the political party of the former Kosovo Liberation Army, was more powerful in Thezren and this was often cited as the reason why there was such a puzzling discrepancy between Thezren and Banshik in 2001, but its power had increased since the arrival of the international mission, and the PDK had also attempted to dominate in the early days of the mission in Banshik. The response of the international actors to this political party and its backers in each municipality made a difference in the form ethnic relations took locally and was indicative of the problem-solving styles that were appropriate or otherwise for this situation.

Realizing that disgruntled armed factions are a lot less trouble within the fold than outside it, Banshik's UN civil administration gave the former KLA, also referred to as UCK or TMK (and henceforth referred to as UCK/TMK), and its political arm, the PDK, a real role, while making sure that it did not overreach itself. In Thezren, the PDK became much more powerful because, intimidated by its armed wing, the UCK/TMK, the UNCA did let it overreach its entitlement and acquiesced in the UCK/TMK's seizure of land and demands for money. This further strengthened its sense of entitlement, and in the crucial early days of the intervention, authority slipped out of the hands of the internationals and into the hands of armed factions disgruntled at having to share power with the internationals and moderate Albanians, and aghast at the prospect of working with Serbs.

Banshik's ability to deal with this problem was a direct result of how the organizations worked together and with the local populations at the local level. The leadership of the network organization around the hub of the United Nations recognized the importance of maintaining full and equal participation—and recognizing the interconnectivity—of all organizations and populations in the mission. The organizations involved—the UNCA, militaries, the Organization for Security and Cooperation in Europe (OSCE), and police—are all traditional hierarchical, bureaucratic organizations, used to operating behind the walls of their respective organizations. The ability to work effectively in UNMIK required each organization to retain its organizational integrity while simultaneously adapting itself to function as a networked organization under a network umbrella organization such as UNMIK. The organizational design of UNMIK was a hybrid of the hierarchical organizational form and the network organizational form. It was a combination of each organization having a hierarchical chain of command, from the local through the regional to the center, and simultaneously working together as a network organization at each level.

In the fall of 2001, the international intervention in Kosovo had been under way for over two years. The organizations in the intervention—the UNCA, the militaries, CivPol, the NGOs, and the OSCE—had been thrown together on the ground in Kosovo in a hastily devised plan. Each

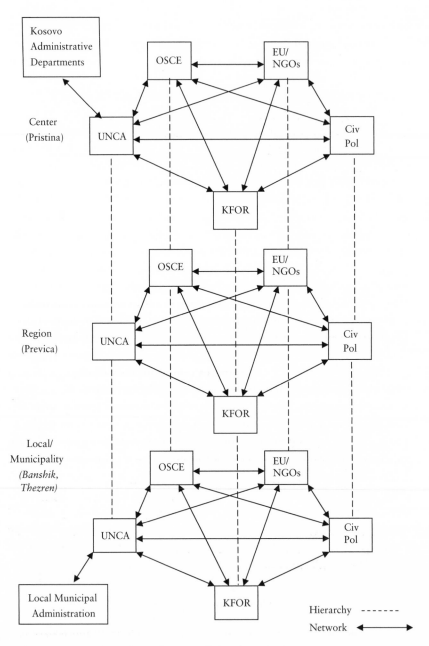

Fig. 1. UNMIK Hierarchy and Network Organization
KEY: CivPol = UNMIK civilian police in Kosovo; EU = European Union; KFOR = Kosovo Force; NGOs = nongovernmental organizations; OSCE = Organization for Security and Cooperation in Europe; UNCA = UN civil administration.

had its own chain of command, from the local municipal level through the regional level to the center in Pristina, and beyond that to their head-quarters in New York or some other city outside Kosovo. But in the twenty-nine local municipalities of Kosovo, these organizations were re-quired to work together almost as if they were part of a single organiza-tional entity. Lacking any guidance from the center beyond a minimal or-ganizational blueprint, these interorganizational entities in the municipalities had developed in different directions around the hub of the leader organization, the UNCA. The divergent directions taken by the or-ganizations in the two municipalities provide valuable lessons for any team of organizations working together in any postconflict reconstruc-tion and nation-building project. The organizations must work together to reestablish social order and build democratic institutions. In one of the municipalities I studied, Banshik, the UNCA wove the participating or-ganizations into an active network and addressed the need, in such a rag-tag collection of differing organizations, to generate trust, effective flows of information and communication, working relationships embedded in social ones, and creative and collaborative or collective problem-solving capabilities among all the participating organizations.[1] And beyond—the local municipal structure and local organizations were seen as a necessary part of this drive for participation. An important factor in this municipal UNCA's ability to persuade people to participate and cooperate was lead-ership "from behind," with an informal culture emanating from the UNCA and radiating through the interorganizational entity in Banshik. The second municipality I investigated, Thezren, had the skeletal interor-ganizational design, but the UNCA did not forge a cooperative working culture between the organizations. No other organization was as well placed to do so, and the result was a disparate collection of organiza-tions, both international and local, that were characterized by a lack of trust, a lack of good information flows, a lack of socially embedded working relationships, and consequently a lack of creative and collective problem-solving capabilities.

The Flag Question

The network organizational ability to solve problems in innovative and cooperative ways was demonstrated in the issue of the flag. Shortly after the start of the mission, almost every municipality in Kosovo, including Banshik and Thezren, was faced with the desire of the local majority Al-banian population and their leadership, which in the initial stages in both municipalities was dominated by self-appointed PDK members, to fly the Albanian flag beside the UN flag over the municipal building. UN regulations expressly forbade the flying of any flags except the UN flag or an authorized municipal flag over public buildings.[2] In both Banshik and Thezren, not only was there a strong push for the Albanian flag to fly along with the UN flag but there was also overwhelming opposition to putting up the Serbian flag as a balancing measure. The UNCA in Banshik devised an alternative strategy, getting schoolchildren to participate in a competition to design a flag for Banshik municipality that did not refer to any ethnicity. The result was a flag depicting the old Turkish bridge in Banshik town with a sheaf of golden wheat indicating the dominant industry in the municipality, agriculture. In fall 2001, it flew beside the UN flag over the municipality's front entrance. The Albanian flag was flown on a small flagpole at the side of the building.

In Thezren, the same struggle with the Albanians resulted in a defeat for the UNCA. Thabo, the UN utilities officer, who had been there during the struggle, recalled: "That was a big fight here also. It's in the Regulations so there is no way it could go up alone. . . . Orders were sent by [the central UN office] in Pristina [not to allow it]. Jon [the MA] did have a big fight about it here, but he lost the fight. We told them they could not put up the Albanian flag outside if no Serbian flag went up too." But the UN administration was ignored, and only the Albanian flag went up beside the UN flag. The issue was one of several at a critical time when the culture and institutional nature and authority of the UNCA and its relationship with the municipality were being established. The consequences for authority were clear: "Because we didn't stop them, now it's too late . . . now it is out there next to the UN flag. . . . All these things send a message to the people," Thabo said. "It set a pattern by which they could get away with a lot," Henry Ghosh, the UN local community officer in Thezren, confirmed. "For instance, all the documents are in Albanian, but not all are in Serbian. They say they haven't been able to find translators. Almost nothing has been translated into Serbian. The minutes of the municipal assembly are translated from Albanian into Serbian, but [the minutes of] all other meetings are not . According to the regulations, everything is supposed to be translated into both, but it's not. Part of the reason is that it's a logistical nightmare, but part of it is political. It's frustrating . . . faxes don't get faxed, that kind of thing."

Banshik's UNCA, although also working with the same two opposing ethnic groups, managed to increase trust through creating a sense of cohesion by emphasizing the identity of both Serb and Albanian residents as citizens of the municipality and flying a flag that was symbolic of membership in the municipality and not of an ethnicity. Banshik was the Albanian name for the town—all towns and places in Kosovo have both Albanian and Serbian names. Because of this, the flag was launched with a new name, or rather a very old one—Bianum, which is the old Latin name for the town. It never really caught on in daily usage but was effective in generating the idea that the town and municipality belonged to everybody. Thus the municipality of Banshik, unlike Thezren, was able to build and draw on trust based on citizenship, not ethnicity.[3]

Bianum

Understanding the importance of the symbol of the flag emerged from my theoretical and methodological orientation—the social construction-ist approach. This emphasizes how organizations are socially constructed out of recurrent behaviors that happen at the face-to-face level.[4] Organizations are generated and sustained out of the patterns of common behavior and language use. Social and organizational realities undergo a continuous process of enactment and reaffirmation at the face-to-face level. Theorists of what is known as symbolic interaction and eth-nomethodology argue that, as Harold Garfinkel puts it, we must give "the most commonplace activities of daily life the attention usually accorded extraordinary events";[5] that by so doing we may be able to understand these mundane activities as substantive social phenomena in their own right. This theory and method pays attention to what occurs as people interact, their use of symbols (in the example above, flags) in communication and interaction, and the flexible, adjustable social processes that result.[6] The interactionist sees humans as active, creative participants who are continuously constructing their social world.

methodology

Learning from the Private Sector

The challenges of cooperation and coordination among organizations in Kosovo are not unlike the challenges that have faced business organizations since the early 1990s. The idea of a network organization has been primarily used to understand developments in the economic field, particularly the adaptation of business firms to new information and communication technologies. But democratization, governance, and peace building share many of the concerns and issues of cooperation and coordination that are faced by economic organizations in the new networked global marketplace.[7]

Just as information and communication technologies allow for-profit firms to continually and effectively come together around short-term projects, organizations with diverse cultures can now come together to participate in international interventions that require them to use their resources in overlapping ways. Temporary network or virtual organizations allow for-profit firms temporarily to overcome their divergent interests with their competitors in the business sector.

Similarly, in interventions, organizations with diverse inner cultures understand and appreciate one another's contributions enough to work together on particular projects. Each organization contributes interactively to a goal that they could not achieve without the exchange of information, the creation of knowledge, and efficient utilization of shared resources. Each participating organization brings something different to the table, and success depends on the efficient utilization of resources, nonduplication of tasks, and coherence in conceptualization and application. In Kosovo, the militaries, the UNCA, NGOs, and democratization organizations such as the OSCE are enmeshed in alliances and linkages that eschew centralized control and correspondingly enhance flexibility and adaptability to local situations.

Information technology is central to the ability of organizations to be networked and to participate in network organizations. Just as new information technologies allow entirely new, less centralized, and flexible production arrangements, they enable less centralized and flexible democratization. The ICT revolution has produced new organizational forms, specifically the network organization. Electronic media and infrastructure allow employees working on the same project but in different places and time zones to interact remotely.[8] The advantages these confer give rise to new, flexible modes for organizing work and new organizational forms.[9] Silicon Valley's success, for example, is based on a regional industrial system organized around small, flexible companies that do one part of the supply chain extremely well and are constantly coming together with other companies around distinct projects—forming a temporary network organization—without damaging their own organizational integrity and disbanding once the project is completed.[10] Instead of each organization being independent and responsible for a well-defined and complete portion of the supply chain, they are now part of a web of firms that are strongly connected, and market opportunities trigger combinatorial processes that result in ad hoc forms of cooperation.[11] Instead of competition, you have what is known as "co-opetition."[12] "Co-opeti-

co-opetition

tion" is when firms engage in a virtual form of interaction where they both cooperate *and* compete with their counterparts.

In each of the twenty-nine municipalities of Kosovo, attaining the goals of the intervention also required innovation and responsiveness, only possible through cooperation with other organizations. The turbulent environment, the temporary nature of the mission, and the goals of the mission required all the international organizations to work together with the local community to maintain peace and build sustainable democratic institutions. These organizations, each with a distinctive organizational structure and culture, with very different forms of authority structures and standard operating procedures, needed one another in unprecedented ways and to an unprecedented extent.

On the one hand, one hierarchical organization could not do it all, because each of the organizations had unique resources and capabilities that the others could not duplicate. On the other hand, the transaction costs of these organizations getting together to solve discrete or minute crises only were too high. They needed one another constantly. For example, the military established a secure environment for all the organizations to work in, the European Union funded NGOs to oversee construction projects, the OSCE organized elections in cooperation with the international police, and the UNCA worked with all the other organizations and the local municipality overseeing the setting up and running of municipal departments of economic development, utilities, housing, and health. The unique challenges of such a mission could only be met by an overarching organization that brought all the participating organizations together. It had to be an overarching organization that was horizontal rather than vertical in structure, that facilitated cross-boundary communications between organizations, and where resources flowed to expertise. Ideally, these organizations would temporarily become part of one organization while working toward specified goals with the intention of disbanding that temporary organization once the goals were achieved. This is what has become known in the private sector as a network organization, organizations coming together around a project as each of them focuses on one part of the supply chain, typically, the part it does best, and then disbanding once that project is completed.[13]

The UNMIK and KFOR mission in Kosovo was an example of nonprofit organizations coming together to form a network organization. The hierarchical (vertical) procedures and organizations' capacity to work independently—behind walls—were being supplemented if not replaced by horizontal structures that are crucially facilitated by formal and informal linkages and networks—webs—between the organizations. In order to work together, they had to acknowledge that they were all part of one temporary organization, to trust one another enough to exchange information, and to solve problems in a collaborative or cooperative way.

Interventions

Why is this attempt to understand organizational behavior in interventions so critical? The turbulence in the global economy is mirrored by the turbulence in international politics. The huge increase in number and scale of international interventions since 1990 means that cooperation among organizations in international interventions and local organizations and populations has become a central issue. Since the establishment of the United Nations in 1945, there have been fifty-six UN peacekeeping operations; the Security Council has created forty-three of these operations since 1988. There are currently thirteen UN peacekeeping operations in the field.[14] However, since the end of the Cold War, the changes have not only been in the number but also in the nature of these missions. Peacekeeping has given way to peace building or enforcing, and there has been a move toward a prominent role for the United Nations as an agent of democratic transitions. In all of this, it has become increasingly clear that militaries are not the only type of organization essential to such missions and that cooperation with the other organizations is an integral part of the job. The mission in Kosovo was designed to be cooperative; although the militaries were not under the same umbrella as the range of civilian organizations, in practice, they were inextricably involved, and their functions and activities are governed by the UN mandate. There has been a growing recognition that "in order for the military and other agencies to succeed, they need to move beyond their own organizational culture," as one commentator noted.[15]

The increase in peacekeeping, and peace building—involving a military intervention followed by institution building and governance—is evidence of an increasing interconnectedness in international affairs in the wake of the end of the Cold War and the end of bipolarity in international relations, the ensuing breakup of former socialist states, and the outbreak of ethnic conflicts.[16] It has also grown out of the increasing concern with human rights and willingness by nations to activate Chapter 7 of the UN Charter, which provides for the overriding of sovereignty when genocide is threatened or human rights are egregiously imperiled. These changes, and, more immediately, the shame of not having intervened in Rwanda and having done so only belatedly in Bosnia, led to the NATO action to stop the ethnic cleansing of Kosovar Albanians,[17] followed by the multilateral, multiorganizational reconstruction and democratization mission.

September 11, 2001, and the subsequent realization that lack of democracy, economic development, and conflict inside countries can breed terrorism and tacit support of terrorism led to the launching of an (as yet very inadequate) intervention in Afghanistan. The intervention in Iraq, although instigated for different reasons, now faces the challenges of any intervention. Only democratic institutions and a functioning economy will prevent the postwar chaos and instability from developing into a petri dish for extremist activity.

The extent of the cooperation between organizations and countries required in these interventions would be impossible without another transformation that has occurred since 1990—the massive growth in the development and application of information and communication technologies (ICTs). The ICT revolution has facilitated the use of communication technologies to directly connect and organize around issues transcending existing organizations and nation-states. Besides creating a new type of organization based on this coming together as needed, a temporary network organization, ICTs have also brought about a transformation in how existing organizations work. Traditional large, powerful hierarchical organizations have found themselves challenged in efficiency and influence by small, flexible organizations organized around and enabled by the new technologies.

Traditionally hierarchical organizations such as the UN Secretariat and militaries from around the world are racing to catch up. But they are realizing that incorporating the new technologies is not just a matter of "plug and play." Interconnectedness is not just electronic. An interconnected world requires interconnected thinking and strategy. Thinking that is based on working in hierarchical "closed" organizations and behind national borders won't work. What is required is an embracing of a new organizational culture and networking competence that will allow organizations to both work together and engage effectively with democratically oriented constituencies, particularly the constituencies in those areas that are the focus of international interventions. This requires recognition that such a coordinated and cooperative approach is the most effective and appropriate response. The imperatives of the contemporary world mean one thing: *only cooperation and coordination can yield successful results in today's interventions.*

Kosovo

The governance and reconstruction part of international intervention in Kosovo began in 1999 when the United Nations established an interim international administration in Kosovo (formerly part of Yugoslavia, but part of Serbia since April 2002), following the end of NATO air bombings and the withdrawal of the then Yugoslav forces. The UN Security Council vested in the UN administration unprecedented authority over the territory and people of Kosovo, including all legislative, executive, and judiciary powers. Under the umbrella of the United Nations, the EU, OSCE, NATO (as KFOR), and UNCA embarked, along with the people of Kosovo, on a mission to create a functioning, democratic society, with substantial autonomy within Serbia.

To democratize a nation that has experienced war and ethnic conflict, a knowledge of and appreciation of both the populations involved and the events that led to the need for democratization and reconstruction are essential. In Kosovo, the international intervention followed more than a decade of high tensions and conflict between the majority Kosovar Albanians and the Serbs in Kosovo. But there had been a time when the two populations lived in uneasy but de facto peaceful coexistence. The conflict was ignited by a reinvigoration of a centuries-old Serbian nationalism after the death of the communist leader Tito in 1984. Serbian nationalism led to violent ethnic conflict in Bosnia, Croatia, and finally Kosovo during the 1990s. Kosovo had long been immortalized as the site of the 1389 battle on the Field of the Blackbirds, in which the Turks had defeated the Orthodox Christian Serbs, ushering in five centuries of Ottoman rule. The sense of identification forged from this defeat kept Kosovo enshrined as a special place in the mythology of the Serbs. However, the proportion of the Kosovar population that was Serbian was in a state of continuous decline during the second half of the twentieth century, sliding from 24 percent in 1948 to 10 percent in 1991.[18]

As in Iraq and Afghanistan, in Kosovo, the current divisions in the population are to a great extent a result of old prejudices and hatreds reheated for recent political purposes. Tito had granted full autonomy to Kosovo within Yugoslavia, but after his death, an undistinguished Ser-

bian apparatchik named Slobodan Milosevic turned himself into a national leader by exploiting nationalist public sentiments on the issue of
Kosovo. His popularity soared, and once he had succeeded in taking over
the Communist Party machine, he removed Kosovo's autonomous status.
Milosevic went on to oversee new measures decreed by the Serbian assembly in March 1990 that shored up the position of Serbs and excluded
Albanians. These decrees created new municipalities for Serbs, concentrated new investment in Serb-majority areas, and provided for the building of new houses for Serbs who returned to Kosovo. They also encouraged Albanians to seek work in other parts of Yugoslavia, annulling,
retrospectively, sales of property to Albanians by departing Serbs. The Al-
banian-language newspaper was suppressed, the Kosovo Academy of
Arts and Sciences was closed, and many thousands of state employees
were dismissed. State schooling for Albanians was abolished, and the
Serb police presence in Kosovo was expanded.

In Kosovo, as in Iraq and Afghanistan, there was opposition to oppression, but in Kosovo, it took a primarily democratic institutional
form. After the dissolution of the Kosovo assembly and government,
many of the Albanian delegates met in secret in the little town of Kacanik
on September 7, 1989, and proclaimed a constitutional law for a "Republic of Kosovo," which provided for a new assembly and an elected
president of the republic. It deemed laws from Serbia and Yugoslavia in-
valid unless in harmony with the constitution. In September 1990, the Albanians managed to hold a referendum that supported a decision taken
by the underground assembly that Kosovo be a sovereign and independent republic. Kosovo-wide elections followed in 1992 for the underground assembly and government, with private houses used as polling
stations.

The president of the Association of Writers of Kosovo, an academic
named Dr. Ibrahim Rugova, became the leader of this political movement, known as the Democratic League of Kosovo, or LDK. It was a
mass movement as well as a political party and enjoyed widespread support, more than any other party. The majority of the elected members of
the assembly were LDK members, as was the assembly's president, Rugova. The party and movement had a tripartite policy: to prevent violent
revolt, to get international political mediation, and systematically to deny
the legitimacy of Serbian rule by boycotting elections and creating at least
the outlines of the state apparatus of a Kosovo republic. In the face of extensive repression and human rights abuses during the 1990s, the LDK

and its followers largely achieved the first and third aims, organizing their own parallel system of clinics and schools, mostly on private premises; the doctors and teachers were paid by the "Republic" out of an income tax of 3 percent levied on a voluntary basis on the Albanian diaspora.[19]

The networking or cooperative ability demonstrated by the outreach to the diaspora and the coordination on the ground, and the substantive expertise inherent in this underground government and the groundwork it laid were unfortunately ignored by the international organizations when they were establishing the framework for the intervention. The consequences were significant both in terms of cost and in participation by the local populations. Failure of internationals to listen to local leaders and to learn about the Kosovar parallel society led internationals to overlook its potential as an efficient network for coordination of volunteer efforts, distribution of public goods, and development of human rights values. The parallel administration not only had a wealth of human resources and ideas, it also had a participatory ethos. Properly capitalized upon, it would have given legitimacy and effectiveness to the international intervention.[20]

The international community also did not take the time or trouble to distinguish the different strands of opposition to the Serbian onslaught. The one that loomed largest for the internationals was the opposition that took a nonpeaceful form—the Kosovo Liberation Army (KLA). This emerged later than and was dwarfed at all stages by the scale and depth of peaceful opposition. However, the KLA did play a significant role, which was not properly understood in its complexity by the international community.

After the international intervention, most KLA members laid down their arms or wanted to be part of a new Kosovo army, but a handful employed their weapons in organized crime after the cessation of hostilities, and their numbers steadily increased. This was in part because of the reluctance of the international community to engage with the KLA as an organization and then to challenge it when its underground criminal power grew rapidly. They continued and continue to fail to separate out the differing factions within the KLA and have moved from tainting it as a terrorist organization to calling it a criminal organization. Perceived as an unarmed civilian force by the international agencies, the UCK/TMK—the Albanian and English acronyms for the new organizational form of the demilitarized Kosovo Liberation Army—was marginalized and excluded from participating in the mainstream reconstruction effort. The frustration this caused yielded more problems than inclusion would have brought. The struggle of UCK/TMK members to be recognized as having played an important role grew into a determination to get the recognition and rewards they felt they deserved, an aim they pursued through the PDK.

Indeed, the international community had played a direct role in creating the space where an armed response emerged. At the negotiations in Dayton, Ohio, in the wake of the NATO bombing of Bosnia, Western diplomats affirmed Serbia's territorial integrity and did not broach the subject of restoring Kosovo's autonomy. The resentment generated by this failure to act, in the wake of continuous and increasing oppression for almost a decade, contributed significantly to the rise of action and support of the Kosovo Liberation Army. The KLA had enjoyed mainly émigré support until March 1998, when the massacre by Serb forces of fifty-eight members of the family of Adem Jashari, a KLA leader, produced a surge of support for the KLA among Kosovar Albanians. It also produced a series of shootings of Serb police by the KLA and more mass killings by the Serb forces. In 1998, journalists and human rights groups, including the OSCE Kosovo Verification Mission, descended on Kosovo. After the massacre of forty-five civilians in the village of Racak, Ambassador William Walker, the head of the mission, called for military intervention to stop the attempted genocide of Albanian Kosovars. Supported by European diplomats, the U.S. government convened a conference at Rambouillet, outside Paris, which called for Serbia to remove most of its troops from Kosovo, restore Kosovo's autonomy, and allow an international peacekeeping force to be deployed in Kosovo.

NATO and UNMIK

The NATO air campaign began in March 1999 after the failure of negotiations on the status of Kosovo between Serb officials and representatives of the Kosovar Albanians at Rambouillet. The Serbian government began to drive all Kosovar Albanians out of Kosovo, destroying property and identification documents so as to ensure their stateless status. On May 6, the Group of Eight (G–8) foreign ministers adopted a set of "general principles on the political solution to the Kosovo crisis," which included an immediate and verifiable end to violence and repression in Kosovo; withdrawal from Kosovo of Serb military, police, and paramilitary forces; and the deployment in Kosovo of effective international civil and security presences to keep the peace and to begin the reconstruction of the province's physical, administrative, and governing infrastructure and institutions. These principles were endorsed and adopted by the United Nations and ultimately accepted by the Federal Republic of Yugoslavia (FRY) as a basis for ending the Kosovo conflict.[21]

After the end of the NATO campaign in June 1999, the 800,000 Kosovars who had fled or been driven out of the province, and as many as 500,000 others who had been internally displaced, returned to their homes. Many found their homes and possessions destroyed or stolen.[22] The returnees were faced with an economy that had been destroyed by Serb repression over the previous ten years and the damage caused by the war. The events of the 1980s and 1990s, culminating in the Serb actions during the NATO bombings, did great damage to the relations between the Albanian and Serb residents of Kosovo. There were widespread reprisals by Albanians against Serbs, as well as looting and seizure of homes and other property, with no functioning law enforcement system to provide justice.

The international community had to establish an effective security system and a system of governance, at least for an interim period. Without such a system of governance, the chaos in Kosovo would constitute an ongoing threat of escalating violence and instability in the region, not to speak of being a serious humanitarian crisis. UN Resolution 1244 called upon UNMIK to perform basic civilian administrative functions; promote the establishment of substantial autonomy and self-government in Kosovo; facilitate a political process to determine Kosovo's future status; coordinate humanitarian and disaster relief of all international agencies; support the reconstruction of key infrastructure; maintain civil law and order; promote human rights; and assure the safe and unimpeded return of all refugees and displaced persons to their homes in Kosovo. Working closely with Kosovo's leaders and people, the mission was to perform the whole spectrum of essential administrative functions and services, covering such areas as health and education, banking and finance, post and telecommunications, and law and order. In January 2000, joint interim administrative departments were created; in October 2000, local elections took place in Kosovo's twenty-nine municipalities; in May 2001, the new Constitutional Framework of Kosovo was adopted; province-wide elections were held in November 2001.

To implement its mandate, UNMIK initially brought together four "pillars" under its leadership. At the end of the emergency stage, Pillar I (humanitarian assistance), led by the Office of the United Nations High Commissioner for Refugees (UNHCR), was phased out in June 2000, and in May 2001, a new Pillar I was established in its place. In 2001, the pillars were:

—Pillar I: Police and Justice, under the direct leadership of the UN
—Pillar II: Civil Administration, under the direct leadership of the UN
—Pillar III: Democratization and Institution Building, led by the OSCE
—Pillar IV: Reconstruction and Economic Development, led by the EU

The head of UNMIK is the special representative of the UN secretary-general for Kosovo. As the senior international civilian official in Kosovo, he presides over the work of the pillars and facilitates the political process designed to determine Kosovo's future status. However, each participating organization has its own chain of command. In addition to the four pillars, KFOR, comprising NATO and a small number of non-NATO militaries, undertook the security mission in Kosovo. It was not under the command of UNMIK; nor was UNMIK under KFOR command. They were to work in cooperation with each other.

CHAPTER TWO

Theoretical Background

Theory from sociology proved to be unexpectedly useful for understanding international interventions in an era of organizational change. Although the ideas explained here will enable readers to get more out of the substantive part of the book, those whose interest is more in the events themselves may wish to skip ahead to the next chapter.

The culture of the network of organizations in Banshik was open, flexible, responsive, and based on the need to know. The institutional mechanisms that make this possible are informality, the appropriate kind of leadership, social embeddedness, and accountability. These factors generate an atmosphere of identification with the mission, and of trust and openness, because organizational boundaries are blurred in the pursuit of the goals that pull rival factions together, such as the "superordinate goal" of getting Banshik working as a democratic, accountable, peaceful city and municipality.[1] The UNCA in Thezren in contrast lacked appropriate leadership and exhibited a high degree of organizational imperialism,[2] that is, competition for resources, responsibility, and status between organizations pursuing similar goals in a circumscribed environment such as Kosovo. Organizational imperialism led to very poor levels of identification with the intervention, poor levels of trust, and poor information exchange. Formal organizational boundaries were highly visible, the local people and institutions were alienated from each other and from the international organizations, and there was no sense of pursuing the same goals.

There are pivotal organizational qualities that need to be generated by the network to enable information and knowledge exchange and cooperation. The mechanisms for producing these qualities include not only the organizational design and communication/information systems but also, and critically so, the appropriate <u>leadership</u>, <u>narrative</u>, <u>doctrine</u>, and <u>culture for such a network organization</u>. You can bring an organization into a network (noun), but you can't make it network (verb).

<u>But what is a network organization? In answering this, I begin by placing it in the context of organizational theory</u>. I then show the development of the concept of network organization in economic sociology, including the business and management literature, and thereafter consider networks from a social constructionist and cultural perspective.

Organizational Theory

<u>The idea of a network organization builds on and in fact synthesizes previous perspectives that dominated organizational theory for most of the twentieth century.</u>

The <u>classic rational perspective on organizations emphasized the importance of a formal division of labor based upon specialized knowledge and a system of coordination based upon hierarchical supervision and well-defined rules.</u>[3] This approach was <u>tempered by the social relations</u>, or <u>"people without organizations,"</u>[4] perspective, which argued that the informal or social organization of the firm was at least of equal, if not greater, significance for understanding how organizations function, and that individuals had social and psychological needs above and beyond material interests and those of the organization.

<u>But contrary to the assumptions of both the dominant traditions, organizations do not exist in a vacuum</u>. Both perspectives <u>overlook how</u> "the environment sets conditions that help shape the organization even as the organization shapes and influences its environment."[5] In the <u>environmental approach</u>, the organization's formal structure is no longer given *ex ante*, but rather is a dependent variable, whose variations are to be explained, at least in part, by the operation of external forces not completely under the control of organizational participants. The focus is on the behavior *of* organizations within their environments rather than behavior within organizations.[6]

<u>Institutional theory, on the other hand, combines both the structural and social system perspectives and takes account of the environment by postulating a more encompassing practical actor (organization) model.</u> Institutions are rules and shared meanings that define social relation-

ships, help define who occupies what position in these relationships, and guide interaction by giving actors cognitive frames or sets of meanings to interpret the behavior of others. Action is constrained not only by structural position but also by the organization's cognitive and normative orientation.[7] New institutionalist theories concern how fields of action come into existence, remain stable, and can be transformed.[8] While an organizational practice may have its origins in certain rational principles, it can become institutionalized over time and continue to be used even though it may no longer be beneficial to the organization.[9] In turbulent times or environments, rules can be made from laws in intended or unintended ways or can be borrowed from other fields to create new institutions. Individuals with appropriate social skills can create new social orders or "fields" through their ability to get others to cooperate with them.[10]

From an environmental and institutional perspective, network theorists overcome the limitations of the structural and social perspectives by arguing that action is guided by utility maximization within structural constraints, and that innovations are diffused by the imitation of a focal actor. Actors (organizations), if driven by status conformity pressures, follow the behavior of their rivals, identified by their structural equivalent position in the network of ties.[11] If driven by imitative pressures, the focal actor tries to reduce uncertainty in a given situation by imitating other actors with whom it has close ties.[12] The interorganizational ties tend to be historical in nature and include a variety of formal and informal interorganizational relationships, each of which serves as a medium for exchanging both resources and information. It is not just the organization's direct ties but also their position within a wider network of ties that is crucial.

All of these perspectives have contributed to our understanding of how organizations work and still do so today. Indeed, a structural perspective and a view from the social system within the organization are crucial dimensions for exploring organizations changing from traditional hierarchies to organizations capable of participating in a network organization. The institutional perspective is intrinsic to this study, because I view the network organization as comprised not only of its organizational design or structure but also of the institutional rules and practices that develop in response to the challenges of working cooperatively with other organizations. The environment is crucial both for the hierarchical organizations within the network and also for the network itself, because it operates in an environment where the local population has a tremendous impact on the working and achievements of the network and must be considered as part of the network organization sphere or system.

[handwritten margin notes: The "intellectual" authors of the network theory; Annalee Saxenian; Manuel Castells]

Hierarchies, Markets, and Networks

The increasing importance of linkages and networks in organizations has been recognized in the literature on the role of networks in the economy.[13] Much of the discussion, such as Annalee Saxenian's work on Silicon Valley, centers on how open networks of communication and exchange of information across companies are crucial for successful cooperation, which in turn is crucial for sustained growth and successful organizations.[14] Manuel Castells argues that this networking is based on and enabled by information technology. In fact, he sees the organizational forms that grew out of the second industrial revolution being superseded by a networked form of organization created by the imperatives of information technologies.[15] Or, as expressed by John Arquilla and David Ronfeldt, "The network appears to be the next major form of organization—long after tribes, hierarchies and markets—to come into its own."[16]

The literature on the network as a distinct form of organization is primarily in the fields of organizational and economic sociology and in business schools. The first time the concept of a network organization was raised was in an early business-oriented analysis by Tom Burns and G. M. Stalker in 1961 that distinguished between mechanistic (hierarchical, bureaucratic) and organic (networked but still stratified) management systems. The organic form was deemed more suited to dealing with rapidly changing conditions and unforeseen contingencies, because it has "a network structure of control, authority, and communication" along with a "lateral rather than a vertical direction of communication."[17]

Besides this article and despite a few significant efforts to develop ideas on network forms of organization,[18] it was not until a seminal paper by W. W. Powell in 1990 that a school of thinking began to emerge in a coherent form. That paper looked beyond informal social networks to argue that formal organizational networks were gaining strength, especially in the business world, as a distinct design—distinct in particular from the "hierarchies and markets" that economic transaction theorists, some other organizational economists, and economic sociologists were accustomed to emphasizing. "The familiar market-hierarchy continuum does not do justice to the notion of network forms of organization," Powell asserted. "[S]uch an arrangement is neither a market transaction nor a hierarchical governance structure, but a separate, different mode of exchange, one with its own logic, a network."[19]

Networks

Although the concept has had an enormous impact on organizational design and culture, there is still much work to be done to clarify the meaning of "network." There are three prominent usages, all of which I incorporate into my understanding of what is meant by "network organization." First, there is the technical meaning of communication grids and networks; second, social networks or organizational networks; and third, the argument made by Powell and Castells for a network as an organizational dynamic, even though it requires appropriate social and technological dynamics to work.

The first usage is self-explanatory. The second has long dominated network research in the social sciences. It holds that all social relationships, including in organizations, can and should be analyzed as networks, that is, as sets of actors (nodes) and ties (links) whose relationships have a patterned structure.[20] Sociological studies in this tradition have observed that networks often come in several basic shapes: chain or link networks, where the members are linked in a row and communications must flow from an adjacent actor before getting to the next; hub, star, or wheel networks, where members are tied to a central node and must go through it to communicate with each other; and all-channel or fully connected networks, where everyone is connected to and can communicate directly with everyone else. All of these "shapes" were present and are relevant to understanding the emergence and workings of the network organizations in Kosovo.

However, social network analysis's concept of the network is limited; it has conceptualized the network as the role of the formal and informal networks that gird a hierarchical bureaucracy or a market system in making that social organization or system work the way it does.[21] In this perspective, power and influence depend less on one's personal attributes than on the location and character of one's ties in and to the network. This model's "unit of analysis" is not the person or organization but the network. The issue is whether an actor's power and prestige depend on his "centrality" in a network or whether he has greater autonomy and potential power if he is located at a "structural hole."[22] Other analysts have stressed the importance of the links between the actors: whether the ties are strong (tightly coupled) or weak (loosely coupled), and what difference this may make for acquiring and acting on information about what is happening in and around the network.[23]

For understanding the organizational challenges in Kosovo, social network analysis is limiting. The resulting analyses tend to be intricately methodological, putting a premium on mathematical modeling and visualization techniques. These analyses are generally not normative or prescriptive, in the sense of observing that one kind of network structure may be better than another for a particular activity, such as a humanitarian organizational network like in Kosovo. The "static" nature of much network analysis, looking at the "before and after" existence of networks, has reached its limits. To investigate what the dynamics of networks are and how they function, a serious investment in ethnography is needed.[24] Only with ethnography can the elements that constitute and produce a network institutional culture be discovered.

Moreover, these analyses are not evolutionary in the sense of observing that the network may be a distinct form of organization, one that is now coming into its own: not market, not hierarchy, but a network organization.

I am primarily concerned with the network as a distinct form of organization, one that is predicated on and gaining strength owing to developments in communications and information technologies that exponentially increase the network organization's flexibility, adaptability, and speed of response. For social network analysts, almost any set of nodes (actors) that have ties amount to a network. But for organizational analysts, that is not quite enough. I want to ask, for example, (a) whether the actors recognize that they are participating in a particular network, (b) whether they are committed to operating as a network, and (c) what they are doing to build the institutional basis of the network form. Operationally, by network organization, I mean the entity resulting when several organizations come together to form a temporary quasi or virtual umbrella organization, with each organization subordinating itself to the umbrella organization, but without losing its integrity. Economic sociology literature captures the dual nature of this phenomenon in the term "co-opetition" (i.e., cooperation and competition combined). In practice, most network organizations are hybrids of hierarchies and networks, because they are made up of existing organizations, often of long standing, with established hierarchical structures.[25]

From Business to Interventions

Until now the application of these concepts has been limited to economic and business relations or conventional human service providers.[26] They have not yet been applied to nonprofit organizational and interorganizational activity in crisis management or humanitarian interventions. Indeed, there has been a dearth of analyses of the evolution of the organizational forms that constitute such interventions. This is all the more surprising given the far-reaching nature of the interventions of the past decade—from the increase in the size and complexity of humanitarian operations to the possibilities opened up by new ICTs. The need to understand the challenge of organizations working together in such environments is all the more pressing because September 11, 2001, raised the stakes in interventions. Establishing and maintaining peace, establishing participatory democracies, rebuilding ruined nations, and establishing accountable democratic institutions are all vital in countering the conditions that breed an extremist militant form of Islam.

Economic sociology and organizational theory, specifically network organizational analysis from an institutional perspective, are very useful in this arena, because crisis management shares many of the concerns and issues of cooperation and coordination that are faced by economic organizations in the new, networked global marketplace, whose success depends on their ability to function as overarching networked organizations. Each participating organization brings something different to the table, and success depends on the efficient utilization of resources, avoidance of duplication of tasks, and coherence in conceptualization and application. Among government and nonprofit organizations, large is being replaced by small, and mass deployment by flexibility, just as M. J. Piore and C. F. Sabel argued that smaller organizations or firms and greater specialization and flexibility have begun to replace giant corporations in the economic arena.[27] Militaries, the UN, NGOs, and democratization organizations like the OSCE are now enmeshed in alliances and linkages that eschew centralized control and correspondingly enhance flexibility and adaptability to local situations. Just as new information technologies allow entirely new, less centralized, and flexible production arrangements,[28] they enable less centralized and flexible crisis management.

Both in the initial setup period and later, with constant rotation of personnel in and out, organizations have to cultivate an environment that facilitates swift learning, because not all the knowledge they need is internally available. Research on the development of successful start-up companies stresses the importance of networks in obtaining quick access to external resources and know-how.[29] This is especially true in interventions because of the high turnover of personnel.

Networks Embedded in Social Relations

The notion of "embeddedness," although conceptualized initially for economic exchange, is very useful for capturing the mechanisms required to produce trust, a sense of identification, information transfer, and collaborative problem-solving capabilities, all of which are essential for communication and cooperation in international interventions. W. W. Powell[30] and Mark Granovetter[31] developed the notion of "embeddedness" as the role played by socially embedded personal relationships in economic exchange.

Based on loyalty, network organizations in the economic sphere routinely violate the assumption that price is the primary factor in purchasing decisions, preferring instead to favor suppliers with whom they have established relations.[32] In Kosovo, where the issue was not economic exchange or technically a contractual one, but one of exchange, coordination, and cooperation with respect to resources and personnel, trust plays a much greater and more critical role. In fact, trust is *the* element that needs to be constantly in production to optimize the networked organization. In the absence of a market exchange of resources and information, and in the absence of one giant hierarchy, what brings people and organizations from diverse organizations together in an effective way is trust. Trust is intrinsic to greater identification with the mission, greater exchange of resources and information, and greater cooperation in problem solving.

Most generally, trust is heuristic, a predilection for putting the best interpretation on the motives and actions of others. From an economic exchange perspective, the primary outcome is that it promotes access to privileged and difficult-to-price resources that enhance competitiveness

Trust

but are difficult to exchange in the absence of personal ties.[33] This is equally true of the resources used by the organizations in UNMIK. There is also a strong element of reciprocation. Trust begets trust: "I trust because you trust." As cooperation based on such trust succeeds, the trust is increased, which in turn promotes success, and so on.

It is helpful for my purposes to distinguish between forms of trust arising from different sources as different mechanisms are implied in the creation of each form. Lynne Zucker has identified three forms.[34] First, there is characteristic-based trust, which is formed in a group on the basis of factors such as ethnicity; second, there is process-based trust, which results from past and expected future exchanges; and finally, there is institution-based trust, which stems from embedded social practices.[35] All three are relevant for Kosovo and not always in immediately obvious ways. For example, in Banshik, the UNCA created a group that could use characteristic-based trust—namely, citizenship of and loyalty to Banshik, the municipality itself. The second and third types of trust, by their presence or absence, were, however, of equal importance in attaining the goals of the mission, as I shall show.

Trust in hierarchical organizations does not have the same importance as trust in network organizations. Trust is the base upon which the network rests. In terms of organizational design, there are five levels above trust that affect one another and that determine the effectiveness of the network. The five levels are

1. the organizational design
2. the narrative—the story being told
3. the doctrinal level—the collaborative strategies and methods
4. the technological level—the information systems in use, and
5. the social level—the personal ties that assure loyalty and trust (superordinate goals, propinquity, norms)[36]

The first and fourth levels are the least affected by management. In Banshik and Thezren, the organizational design was roughly comparable, as were the technological information systems in use. However, the narrative, doctrine, and social levels differed dramatically, producing two very different institutions. I found that the strongest networks will be those in which the organizational design is sustained by a winning story and a well-defined doctrine, and in which all this is layered atop advanced communication systems and rests on strong personal and social ties at the base.

The ability of leaders in organizations to get people to trust them and

Trust

one another and cooperate is what Neil Fligstein calls "social skill."[37] He argues that this is of critical importance at times of institutional change. When new fields of endeavor are being established or transformed, socially skilled individuals can play a role in shaping the emerging institutional form or culture in a way that they cannot do in established fields. The turbulent and unprecedented environment of interventions, along with the emergence of the network organizational form and the greater connectivity enabled by information and communication technologies provided one such emerging field and the leadership in Banshik had the social skill to shape this.

The "driver" behind network organizations ICT[s]

Embedded Virtual Networks

Changes deriving from information technologies are at the basis of the design of the network organization.[38] Most of the research exploring this claim has been in the business and organizational management literature, and it tends to take a technological determinist position. Without going to the opposite pole and assuming a social determinist position vis-à-vis information technology in organizations, I show how the use of information technologies is embedded in the institutional environment of the organization.

Electronic media and infrastructure allow employees working on the same project but in different places and time zones to interact remotely.[39] The advantages these confer give rise to new flexible modes for organizing work and new organizational forms.[40] The literature on organizational change in business and traditional business models assumes that each organization is responsible for a well-defined and complete portion of the supply chain. This relative independence is being transformed into a web of firms that are strongly connected. Market opportunities trigger combinatorial processes that result in ad hoc forms of cooperation.[41] Each organization contributes interactively to a coherent, aggregated performance that individual organizations could not achieve. This intricate connectivity implies exchange of valuable resources like knowledge and information and an increased formation of quasi organizations comprising individual organizations that have overlapping interests. However, this doesn't preclude them from also having interests that are partially divergent.[42]

These technological and organizational changes are also applicable to large nonprofit organizations such as those working together in the

And in what other arenas? ✱

peacekeeping arena. Just as technological developments allow for-profit firms to come together effectively around short-term projects, in human-itarian interventions, organizations with diverse cultures can now come together to participate in an intervention that requires them to use their resources in overlapping ways. Just as these quasi or virtual organizations allow for-profit firms temporarily to overcome their divergent interests with their competitors, so they allow organizations with diverse inner cultures to understand and appreciate each other's contributions enough to work together on particular interventions, whether in Kosovo, Afghanistan, or Iraq. Each organization contributes interactively to a goal that could not be achieved without the exchange of information, the creation of knowledge, and efficient utilization of shared resources.

Although information technology is critical to the management of information exchange and knowledge transfer that is at the heart of the network organization, the technical limitations of the environment in Kosovo and the organizational imperialism of several of the larger participating organizations resulted in a picture that does not quite conform to this theoretical ideal.

Creating Shared Knowledge

strategic knowledge

Creating knowledge that can be shared between organizations that are very different in purpose and style is challenging to say the least. Research on strategic knowledge management has predominantly focused on cognitive processes *within* a firm's boundaries but not processes transcending them.[43] These processes include creation of knowledge, making tacit knowledge explicit,[44] the transfer of knowledge,[45] and the integration of knowledge.[46] Knowledge sharing has been defined as "the transfer of useful know-how or information across company lines."[47] Research on interorganizational sharing recognizes the fact that firms are nowadays involved in multiple temporary or more permanent agreements for cooperation in the form of information sharing.[48] As it is in the private sector, so it is in interventions.

It is also useful to distinguish between explicit and tacit types of knowledge.[49] Explicit knowledge refers to concepts, information, and insights that are specifiable, and that can thus be formalized in rules and procedures.[50] Access, storage, and transfer of this knowledge are achieved by corporate documents and information systems like databases. Implicit or tacit knowledge refers to less specifiable insights and skills that are car-

Strategic Knowledge (handwritten margin note)

ried in individuals' minds or embedded in an organizational context.[51] Employees collectively develop and refine routines to achieve orga niza- tional adaptation and learning.[52] J. G. March and H. A. Simon call these routines "programs" and say that most of them "are stored in the minds of employees who carry them out, or in the minds of superiors, subor- dinates, or associates."[53] Understanding and transferring this type of knowledge depends on direct participation and inclusion in the context where it resides.[54] Exchanging tacit knowledge across organizational boundaries is supposed to exacerbate these issues, because professionals lack a set of commonly shared concepts and values provided by an orga- nization's culture.[55]

Face-to-face interaction is crucial for achieving this exchange of knowledge. However logistically (number of organizations, lack of infra- structure, multiplicity of goals, geographic considerations), this is not al- ways possible. In addition, sometimes face-to-face interaction might ac- tually inhibit coordination and cooperation, because it confronts the participants with real representations of an organizational culture in some ways at odds with their own. Information technology provides one means of overcoming the limitations of time and space and of turning interper- sonally shared information into situated and valued knowledge in a neu- tral space. A new type of "virtual organization" has emerged via new me- dia and communication technology with consequent reconceptualization and modification of organizational roles and norms. In this new virtual organization, "mediated, virtual forms of communication and interaction play a central role within the organization and substitute direct, face-to- face communication to a large extent, while its structure reflects this con- stitutive quality of organizational relationships and resembles a virtual, heterarchical network."[56] However, for this to work, for successful recip- rocal interaction, there must be approximately identical interpretation by all partners of the interactive process. For this to happen in practice, a vir- tual relationship or organization needs to be embedded in a face-to-face relationship, with a face-to-face meeting on at least one occasion.[57]

Shared meaning (handwritten margin note)

Common Interpretation

Cultural sociology can provide theoretical assistance in understanding how this process occurs. For example, drawing on Edmund Husserl, Max Weber, and Peter Berger and Thomas Luckmann, Daniel Diemers applies the dialectical relationship between the subjective reality of the individual

Shared meaning
and the "transfer
motion of organization to os.
structures to communitos.

and the objective reality of the society to the sharing of knowledge on-line.[58] He describes how objectifications—the "bricks of knowledge" out of which our daily life world is made—are jointly created and sustained to the point where we can speak of an objective social reality. Alfred Schutz argued that the most efficient way of doing this was habitualizations—we sediment a knowledge or skills of how to do certain things.[59] Once several actors share these habitualizations, we can speak of a social institution. Institutions have their own reality, and every institution has a corresponding set of knowledge, which constitutes its semantic content. But our knowledge of these institutionalized habitualizations is confined to a temporal and cultural specificity and is subject to change. Information's situation value resides in intersubjective configurations of meaning between two or more individuals within organizational boundaries.

A common interpretive space can be constructed that is a specific set of signs, shared meanings, norms, and values of individuals in "co-presence" with each other. The historical line of their interaction will become part of the common interpretative space and at a certain point socio-emotional contents—trust, friendship, tradition, bonds, and so on—may become part of the common interpretative space.

In common interpretative spaces, information is transformed into knowledge in three steps, according to Diemers:

1. It must be "fit for use," that is, in a familiar language and syntax. For example, UN and military documents available only in English pose difficulties for those who do not speak English.

2. There must be a commonly established interpretative space, with a synchronized semantic interpretation and overlapping sets of typifications. This is really reciprocal learning about the other's stock of knowledge, its historical line of acquisition, and especially its actual self-interpretation by the owner, because past experiences are constantly re-interpreted and modified in order to fit into the currently established system of relevancies. The aim is to achieve large overlapping of stocks of knowledge. Also through constant repetition in a social context, we are eventually able to create meaningful rituals, which achieve internalization through the process of habitualization and institutionalization.

3. Finally, any face-to-face situation is important in an attempt to synchronize associations and establish common interpretative space.[60]

Empirical work in this area has concentrated on online communities.[61] I propose to apply it to nonprofit organizations and to look at face-to-face interaction *and* online interaction, because with the establishment of an interactive space where there is common interpretation and understanding of information and behavior, organizations can segue into communities. Charles Handy identifies trust, a sense of mutuality, and reciprocal loyalty as inevitable requirements for virtual organizations and proposes a "community membership" that abandons the traditional notion of organizations as a means to an end, where members work in exchange for some sort of payment.[62] This concept calls for a transformation of organizational structures into communities, where individual efforts and commitment are rewarded with a sense of belonging, mutual trust, and identity. This could not have come about without the media and communications revolution—but now the two concepts of organization and community are no longer theoretically opposed to each other and may enter combined discourses. My examination of the interaction of the differing organizations both face-to-face and online will shed some light on the type and degree of shared discourse and interpretation that is occurring in a real-life situation.

A Logic of Compromise

In the process of contributing to network organization theory and literature, the use of electronic media, and economic sociology, this book contributes to the literature on the United Nations and institution building.[63] The empirical and theoretical constructs here will contribute to our understanding of the United Nations and the organizational challenges it faces in the twenty-first century. Since the end of the Cold War, there has been a massive increase in the number of peacekeeping operations. There have also been great changes in the nature of such operations. Kosovo was the first intervention where the UN moved into the area of democratic transitions. The UN and the organizations working in partnership with it and the local populations are all involved in building the political conditions for a sustainable, democratic peace, in addition to enforcing peace between two hostile populations, the Serbs and the Albanians.

The challenge facing the UNCA in Kosovo is manifold and principally arises from the organizational structure and culture of the UN itself. The parameters of peace building remain vague and ill-defined in UN doctrine, even though, as Eve Betram observed, "at root, full scale peace-building efforts are nothing short of nation building; they seek to remake a state's political institutions, security forces, and economic arrangements."[64]

In questioning the UN's ability to create the necessary conditions for peace, Betram raises three concerns, two of which are relevant here. The first is that the local actors may have an incentive to cling to a logic of conflict and not move on to the logic of compromise. Second, Betram questions the capacity of local institutions, describing them as all too often "underdeveloped, deeply biased, rife with internal conflicts and competing interests, or simply corrupt." And because they naturally tend to institutionalize patterns of behavior, she notes, "they are invariably and deeply resistant to precisely the type of transformation that is the object of UN peace builders."[65]

This book provides an opportunity to see if these claims hold true on the ground. What Betram describes may prevail and determine the outcome, but it is not inevitable. Through the contrasting experiences of two municipalities, we can see that there are mechanisms for dealing with these challenges effectively.

Organizational Design of a Network

For UNMIK to function successfully as a network organization, it had to have a network organizational design for the constituent organizations to be part of and to know which organization to work with on what. In theory, all the activity of all organizations was governed by the UN mandate. Each organization was part of the hierarchical chain of command from the local to the regional to the central level. Simultaneously, at the local, regional, and central levels, each organization was part of a network organization incorporating all the other organizations at that level (see fig. 1). UNMIK and KFOR required a weekly meeting of the constituent organizations of this network organization in each municipality and in the five regions and at the center—the "interagency meeting."

However, the network design was weakened by three factors. First, organizations had trouble understanding that the mission's effectiveness was dependent on interorganizational sharing and cooperation. There was a high level of organizational imperialism, that is, each hierarchical organization wanting to control its environment and to protect its own interests against possible interference by other organizations. A frequent strategy was to hoard resources, information, personnel, and equipment that could be useful to other organizations. When an individual hierarchical organization's interests appeared to conflict with the interests of the mission, the resolution of this dilemma was usually in favor of the individual organization. Second, the omission of the local municipal administration from the interagency meeting excluded a key partner in the democratization and reconstruction process. Third, beyond the bare design and the mandate, there was little or no guidance on how to implement cooperation or operationalize a network organization. Most of the large organizations were traditional bureaucratic hierarchies. Beyond knowing that they were to cooperate, there was little organizational guidance on or knowledge about how to actually do this. For the UN Secretariat, there was little or no guidance from the headquarters in New York to the local head office in the Kosovo capital of Pristina, or from the region to the local or municipal level. Each level struggled to adapt to this new reality. How this combination network and hierarchical design worked in the municipalities of Thezren and Banshik demonstrates how all of these weakening factors were perpetuated and how they could be circumvented.

The Electronic Network

A network organization typically has an electronic network that contributes to and underpins the organizational design. In a network organization, information technology is critical to the management of information exchange and knowledge transfer and the building of a sense of identification with the overall project (or in the case of an international intervention, the goals of the mission). The technical limitations of the environment in Kosovo and the organizational imperialism of several of the larger participating organizations resulted in a picture that did not quite conform to this ideal of a network organization whose design *is* the electronic network. However, this model of a virtual organization is useful as an "ideal-type"[66] against which to assess the functioning of the network organization of UNMIK and KFOR.

In the "virtual" organization, virtual forms of communication and interaction play a central role and substitute for direct, face-to-face communication to a large extent. However, for this to work, there must be almost identical understanding by all partners of what is going on. The actors involved must build a recognizable reality for all involved. This means expressing knowledge in a common language and not in the jargon of an organization that may be incomprehensible to members of other participating organizations. The meaning of speech and writing must be clear. The aim is to build knowledge that is meaningful for all involved. An initial and occasional face-to-face encounter helps to make sure meanings are shared.

The history of people's interaction will become part of the common interpretive space, and at a certain point, socioemotional content—trust, friendship, tradition, bonds, and so on—becomes part of that common interpretative space.[67] To be optimally effective, UNMIK needed to be able to morph from an organization into a wider community of the kind proposed by Handy.[68]

The Common or Institutional Culture of the Network

In order for the diverse constituent parts of UNMIK to share a basic organizational identity and understandings, a shared institutional culture was essential. Individuals had to identify not only with their own "home" organization but also with UNMIK. They had to be able to work with people from other organizations on complex issues on a daily basis. This required a level of shared understanding equivalent to what they had with colleagues in their home organization or institution.

Institutions are rules, and shared meanings that define social relationships help define who occupies what position in these relationships and guide interaction by giving actors cognitive frames or sets of meanings to interpret the behavior of others.[69] Every organization is also an institution, but the formal rules and the institution's rules are not necessarily the same. Institutions emerge, evolve, and change over time.

As the consequences in Banshik proved, at key times in organizations' histories, individuals can have tremendous impact in shaping the institution. Fligstein argues that at times of transition, particularly when institutions are emerging, socially skilled individuals who know how to get others to cooperate can play a key role.[70] Skilled social actors relate to the situations of other people empathetically and in doing so provide these people with reasons to cooperate. They understand how the sets of actors in their group view their multiple conceptions of interest and identity and how those in external groups do as well. They use this understanding in particular situations to provide an interpretation of a situation and frame courses of action that appeal to existing interests and identities. Key international actors in the municipality of Banshik demonstrated such social skill and were able to establish a new institutional base that all other personnel and organizations, both international and local, could buy into.

Local Participation in a Network Organization

UNMIK's task was governance, and its goal was to establish the institutions of a democratic, multiethnic, peaceful society. But in Kosovo, as in Afghanistan and Iraq, the organizations wouldn't get very far with either this task or goal without the participation of local populations of all ethnicities. To build a civic society that would be the basis of democracy, UNMIK had to figure out how to get people and organizations to truly participate in an interconnected way. The degree to which this happens is the degree to which the goals of the network organization are attained, because without them, the mission is meaningless. Traditional hierarchical organizations control from the top down and limit their outside influence to controlling the environment for its own benefit. Network organizations are more fluid. When a gap in the supply chain becomes apparent, a firm or firms move in to fill it. There is an overarching goal or set of goals, but there is little control from the center, and fluid boundaries and inclusivity are key.

The UN mission in Kosovo failed to assess the situation on the ground objectively. There was a logic of compromise already in place. Kosovar Albanians had adhered to a philosophy and practice of nonviolent passive resistance to Serb repression, organizing a "parallel" system of government and administration during the 1990s. It was only in the latter part of the 1990s, when the international community refused to do anything, that the KLA began resorting to armed resistance. However, its membership remained small, and the bulk of the population remained firmly in support of Dr. Ibrahim Rugova and his LDK.

The international community's peace-building plans in Kosovo conflated the two and ignored the tremendous resources and capabilities for reconstruction, both practical and political, proffered by the functioning parallel system. Kosovar personnel offered both a wealth of experience and knowledge of the issues and a practical willingness to work together in a cooperative fashion in a difficult environment, but UNMIK employed them only as drivers and interpreters. Not only did the internationals not avail themselves of these resources, but their attitudes and actions also had a strong negative effect on the mission. The goals of the mission required the participation of the local populations, but the resentment and frustration generated by the subordination of the local population into second place or a second tier was a major impediment to progress.

The cohesion and initiative of the Kosovar Albanians in the 1980s and 1990s in the face of Serbian repression was a local example of the thinking that cooperative nation building requires. The UN leadership in Banshik, the municipal administrator, Terry Peterson, and his deputy, Orash Fatoohi, fitted in well with this culture. Sharing this "we can do it" attitude certainly contributed to the UN's success in Banshik. Banshik UNCA respected the remnants of the parallel structure, choosing to recognize and work with existing groups in the process of incorporating them into the new structures. The local municipal administration was largely in the hands of the PDK (the political wing of the former KLA), which had rushed in to fill the positions just before the arrival of the UN. In spring 2001, the UN decided that to ensure fairness, all positions had to be terminated and the posts reassigned based on merit. This caused a lot of tension, because the PDK felt that the more electorally successful Rugova-led party, the LDK, was going to push its own people into the posts, and the PDK threatened to pull out of the municipal assembly. The UNCA and the OSCE worked together to monitor every step of the hiring process, making it fully transparent, with the OSCE producing a report. The PDK agreed that the process was objective, and the new hires were accepted.

Beyond setting up the requisite weekly meetings, Thezren UN chose to shut the local structures out, with the result that Kosovars viewed the internationals as opposition and as something to fleece rather than as a cooperative, participative partner in reconstruction. This approach inadvertently generated a logic of conflict, but this was hidden—or ignored—under the empty rhetoric of compromise from the internationals. Particularly in the case of the former members of the KLA, many of whom joined the PDK, the frustration this caused yielded more problems than inclusion would have brought, because their struggle to be recognized as having played an important role grew into a determination to get the recognition and rewards they felt they deserved. Peterson and Fatoohi recognized that disgruntled and excluded armed factions are a lot less trouble inside the camp than outside it, and they took care to give them a real role, while making sure that they did not overreach themselves.

PART II

Two Municipalities in Kosovo

CHAPTER THREE

Leadership in Networks

The focus of this section of the book is the UN Civil Administration (UNCA) in Kosovo, which was in practice the hub of the network of organizations at the local, regional, and central levels. In theory, the network organization at each level was an all-channel network, in the sense that anyone could contact anyone in any organization. But inasmuch as the UNCA at each level was usually where interagency meetings took place, and a UN mandate and UN regulations were the legal framework for the mission, and thus governed the actions of the other three pillars and KFOR, it also had a hub-and-spokes aspect.[1] The local municipality's work and culture were also directly affected by the UNCA's organizational design and culture (see fig. 2).

The UN Interim Administration Mission in Kosovo (UNMIK), consisting of several different traditionally hierarchical, bureaucratic organizations, was attempting to grope toward developing the characteristics of a network organization, defined by the degree to which expertise, not rank or status, gets precedence; the degree to which decisions are decentralized to the local level; the priority accorded to cooperation with other organizations; the ability to communicate with whomever you need and not have to go through prescribed channels of communication; and the degree to which personnel identify with both their own organization and the network (in this case, UNMIK).

The classic perspective on organizations emphasizes the importance of a formal division of labor based upon specialized knowledge and a system of coordination based upon hierarchical supervision and well-defined rules.[2] The network perspective emphasizes fluid and flexible patterns of working based on communications networks, yielding innov-

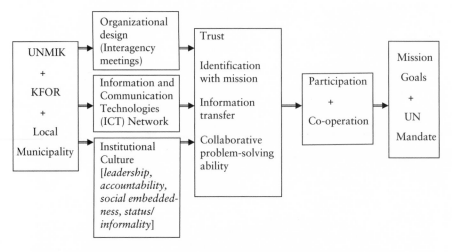

Fig. 2. A Model of a Network Organization for Achievement of the Goals of a
UN Peacekeeping, Reconstruction, and Democratization Mission

ative contexts for interactions and collaborative work that spans traditional organizational boundaries. Point-to-point communication between
groups, often supported by information technology (e-mail, mobile telephones, the Internet), integrates them. Expertise, not status, is the basis
of personnel advancement and recognition.[3]

The other pillars and KFOR, although parts of the network organization and not technically under the authority of the UNCA, recognized its
central role in view of its intricate linkage with the local government and
population, and hence with every aspect of the municipality's affairs. The
chief representatives of the UNCA at the local level were the UN municipal administrator (MA) and deputy municipal administrator (DMA),
who were thus perceived by the local municipality and the local population to be the overall leaders. The MA was seen as the ultimate authority
to appeal to on the local level. "When push comes to shove, we have to
go to the local UN civil administration," Harry, the EU political affairs
officer in Pristina, said apropos of the introduction and enforcement of,
or noncompliance with, EU policy by departments in local municipal administrations. Leadership, the degree of formality and accountability, and
the social embeddedness of the network organization contributed to producing different degrees of trust, identification with the mission, information transfer, and collaborative problem-solving capabilities within
each of the two municipalities, Banshik and Thezren.

In Banshik, the MA was Terry Peterson, and the DMA was Orash Fa-toohi. "I think his [Peterson's] team does a very good job," a representative in Banshik of the Organization for Security and Cooperation in Europe (OSCE) said. "We need the collaboration of the municipality. We can say he is the one who connected all the elements of local authority. He is the 'guider.' All the people know they have access to one international [representative (i.e., Peterson)]. . . . UNMIK is setting the goals or strategies of the whole mission at the senior level. Then at the local level, it is the municipal administrator" (Carolina, OSCE, Banshik).

The institutional culture of the UNCA in Thezren was that of a classic hierarchy, and the MA, Khalid Shamon, a retired diplomat who had spent his career in highly status-conscious, bureaucratic contexts, was a classic "hierarchical" administrator. Shamon was thoughtful and responsible, but under his leadership, the UNCA focused on its own tasks, within its own organizational boundaries, largely independent of the other organizations present in the municipality. Shamon had been there since July 2001. His predecessor, Jon, who had been MA from June 1999 to June 2001, had drawn on a background of traditional hierarchical business organizations.

Unfortunately, the effects of these two hierarchical leadership styles were cumulative. Although Shamon had been there for almost half a year when I was in Thezren, the other UN workers felt frustrated with lack of progress on key issues and did not think much was changing. Most of the Thezren UNCA team had been there for much longer, on average a year and a half, and the DMA had been there since the beginning. Shamon's leadership was formal and bureaucratic, and he viewed his leadership as encompassing only the international UN staff immediately under his command. The previous MA had had a less bureaucratic style than Shamon, but neither fostered an institutional culture that forged networks and linkages with other organizations and the local municipality or population.

Every type of organization has its own institutional culture, and the institutional culture of a hierarchical organization has certain personnel requirements. A network institutional culture requires different personnel characteristics—which can be inculcated and transmitted in training, just as bureaucratic culture can be. It is much bigger than any one person. This type of organizational strategy and institutional culture is also to be found in other contexts. The firms in Silicon Valley and the new globalized hi-tech economy think like this—not just pioneers like Jeff Bezos and

Peterson and Fatoohi

Larry Ellison, but thousands of business people. However, Bezos and Ellison and other pioneers in this area helped delineate what characteristics
are necessary for success in the new interconnected world of business.

In Banshik, Peterson, Fatoohi, and their team were representative of a
more "networked" model of thinking and helped delineate the appropriate leadership for the intervention. Other municipal administrators frequently asked Peterson and his DMA for advice on how to implement the
organizational requirements of the mission. Peterson had arrived in Banshik in August 1999 and had been MA since then. Orash Fatoohi, his
deputy, had arrived three months later and had been DMA since then.
Together, they developed and practiced a form of leadership that yielded
an organizational culture that proved to be innovative and effective in the
context of UNMIK. Their style of leadership, based on trust and persuasion, went beyond the boundaries of the UNCA to encompass the other
organizations in the network and the local populations. Their backgrounds were eclectic, noncareer UN. Peterson had a military and academic background. Fatoohi had been a diplomat, banker, and academic.
Both were in their late fifties.

Peterson and Fatoohi were no doubt talented individuals in the right
place at the right time. However, their ability and success is more significant than that. Their success is important because at times of change in
institutions, or when new institutions are forming, individuals can assume an importance they do not have in times of organizational and institutional stasis. Peterson and Fatoohi possessed the qualities that happened to be appropriate for the situation in which they found themselves
and so became "institutional pioneers." They often commented on how
it was all trial and error, but that they built on what seemed to work, and
they were willing to try new ways of solving problems, even if it meant
going against the bureaucratic inertia of the United Nations. Their methods and style were emulated by other municipal administrators in
Kosovo, and it is possible to delineate them to some degree here with a
view to helping others recognize the appropriate institutional culture of a
network organization and what facilitates and cultivates such a culture.[4]

An examination of the leadership styles prevalent in the UNCAs in the
two municipalities involves looking not only at day-to-day strategy and
style but also at key challenges to their authority and the goals of the mission in the first two and a half years of the intervention and how the municipal administrators led their teams' responses to these challenges.

Each of the organizations in the network at the local level had its own leadership, and formally their chain of command ran directly up through their hierarchies to the region and then the center. Formally, the MA was only leader of his or her own staff, but the MAs did not have a clear job description, apart from the goals (laid out under the UN Mandate 1244 and subsequent regulations) they had to attain, and the fact that they not only had to cooperate with the other organizations but also to be instrumental in bringing them together on issues like security. This required them to work as part of a network organization, but without specific guidelines as to how to do this. "They need to create a policy for different issues, guidelines for different issues," Fatoohi explained. "I mean, you have an American administrator here, a Persian administrator somewhere else, and there is not any uniform approach. Things are being done differently, through actions rather than being a concrete structure and approach which has been identified and [in which] everybody can follow policy. So things are very dependent on individuals."

Recruitment by the UN for the MA and other positions was haphazard and was not done based on the qualities required in such a mission and situation, mainly because it was new and the UN did not itself know what would be required. Thus the type of people thrown together was coincidental. The applicants' CVs were screened in New York, then sent to the UN office in Pristina, the capital of Kosovo. Peterson and Fatoohi recalled that there was little knowledge of what qualities and experience the position of MA required in general, or in particular municipalities, and successful applicants were assigned wherever there was a vacancy. It was done at speed, which further minimized the degree of planning and forethought. The range of backgrounds in the leadership in Banshik and Thezren alone indicates that there was no coherent policy for recruitment and assignment. Research has shown that leaders accountable to those outside the operating environment may have been selected based on criteria having little to do with knowledge of—or motivational connection with—constituencies within that environment. Moreover, leaders selected bureaucratically are more likely to possess skills and motivations compatible with bureaucratic success than with the creative networking and innovation that the environment of a humanitarian intervention would require.[5]

Given that the networks are in practice a hybrid of hierarchies and networks, the network organization is not leaderless, and leadership is still important.[6] In Kosovo, it was evident that with diverse organizations, each of which had its own leadership structure, leaders of the network organization at each level could not rely on traditional bureaucratic authority but rather had to lead through persuasion and social skill, defined as a person's ability to induce cooperation. Such an individual does not act as commander but is in charge of shaping the flow of communications, the "story" expressing the mission, and the doctrine guiding its strategy and tactics. Above all, he or she must generate an atmosphere of trust.[8]

Trust is particularly important for institution building, because the constituencies for such an endeavor are much wider and more diverse, and administrative fiat or authority will not suffice. How successful leaders are at shaping these qualities greatly influences what Marshall Ganz calls the "strategic capacity" of their leadership,[9] that is, the extent to which they gain access to salient information about the environment, the heuristic use they make of that information, and their motivation. Strategic capacity is greater if a leadership team includes insiders and outsiders, strong and weak network ties, and access to diverse, salient repertoires of collective action. It is also critical for an organization to conduct regular, open, authoritative deliberation, draw resources from multiple constituencies, and root accountability in those constituencies.

Access to Salient Information about the Environment

The UNCA leaders had to know their environment in order to know what communications were needed and how to facilitate communications. The better one's local knowledge of the domain within which one is working is, the more likely one is to know how to deal effectively with problems that arise within that domain. Since environments change in response to actors' initiatives, regular feedback is crucial to evaluating responses to initiatives.[10] To know the environment requires commitment in time and energy. But a traditional, hierarchical concept of leadership will not necessarily see such "local knowledge" as relevant, and working habits will flow from this. In Thezren, the MA's schedule was 9 A.M. to 5 P.M. He was not accessible outside those hours, because he was driven from where he lived in Pristina (although officially the UNCA requires that its staff live in the municipality they work in) each day and left at 5 P.M. or earlier. Adherence to this schedule both led to and was indicative of a general lack of flexibility on the part of the UNCA in Thezren.

The MA's forays into the town and surrounding areas were infrequent and only included meetings on the KFOR base or in the OSCE office or the police station. He was also rarely seen inside the municipality build-

Shamon

ing, because he remained inside his own office, receiving only scheduled visitors. There were two large offices each occupied by three UNCA officers and another one used by the language assistants and drivers and one UNCA officer. The DMA, Cole Thedy, had his own office on a different floor. Since Shamon had begun working in Thezren in July 2001, he had been in the offices used primarily by the internationals only once and had never been in the office used by the language assistants. His own office door was kept closed, and no one, including his staff, could enter without making an appointment. Thedy did live in the municipality, but like the MA, he kept to a 9 to 5 schedule, rarely working in the evening or on weekends. The MA's contact with the leadership and directors of the local municipality—also in the same building—was irregular and did not concern day-to-day activities.

In Banshik, the leadership was more aware of the need for local knowledge, and work habits reflected this. Peterson and Fatoohi's offices *Peterson and Fatoohi* were two of six offices opening off a main area. Their doors were open all the time, and they were constantly in and out, interacting with the international and national staff. The local staff had one office exclusively for their use, but apart from Peterson and Fatoohi, each UNCA officer had a local language assistant working at an adjacent desk. Both the MA and the DMA worked each day till 8 or 9 P.M., and they also came into the office on weekends. They were deliberately and consciously accessible all the time. Both lived in the municipality and ate most of their evening meals in one of two restaurants in the town, where they constantly met and interacted with other internationals and local leaders.

The Leadership Team

The ties, particularly of leaders, in a network organization need to go beyond the boundaries of one's constituent organization. Half of each day, Terry Peterson was out in the municipality, attending meetings with other organizations, going into the field to check on Serb enclaves, going to town hall meetings, networking vigorously the whole time. "It's not a 9 to 5 job," he insisted, and he stressed, "We're neither bureaucratic nor structured." His ability to do this and to make this claim was critically dependent on DMA Fatoohi's willingness to take on the more administrative and bureaucratic aspects of the leadership role, because the UNCA was still also part of the hierarchical chain of command from local to region to center of the UN mission as a whole in Kosovo.

At the local level of the network organization, Peterson and Fatoohi's

duties were self-consciously divided up to match their abilities and capabilities—expertise, not status, determined their work allocation. Peterson
was the networker par excellence, while Fatoohi ran the internal Banshik
UNCA and acted as a liaison with representatives of the municipality. Although there was a great deal of overlap in the people they dealt with,
they had agreed to focus on certain areas. Fatoohi, for example, met the
mayor, or president of the municipality, Xarvet Mehmeti, for forty-five
minutes every morning. He was in constant contact with municipal staff
during the day, in particular the municipal lawyer and municipal CEO,
who worked in the same building, on the floor below the UNCA. His
close working relationship with them meant that he knew the details of
all briefs, and important decisions were always discussed in detail.

It is important to emphasize that in a network of hierarchical organizations, leadership requires not only the ability to generate the appropriate institutional culture for the network as a whole but also to attend to
the needs of the leader's "home" hierarchy. Peterson and Fatoohi complemented each other in their ability to combine to fulfill these needs. Peterson without Fatoohi or Fatoohi without Peterson would not have been
able to generate the appropriate institutional culture for a network made
up of hierarchies. Peterson excelled at creating a culture of open informality and socially embedded relationships in both the UNCA and beyond, and Fatoohi took care of finance both inside the UNCA and in
consultation with the municipality and the other organizations. He ran a
highly accountable and efficient office. The awareness of this comple-
mentarity, their shared appreciation for a networked style of operating,
and the threat of losing each other kept Peterson and Fatoohi's working
relationship on a very balanced footing.

Peterson concentrated on external links or ties. Banshik had French
and United Arab Emirates KFOR troops; Peterson attended a weekly
breakfast meeting with French KFOR and dropped in on the United Arab
Emirates' two bases on any pretext. He had regular meetings with the
TMK (the demilitarized Kosovo Liberation Army, KLA, also known as
UCK, which had been given the role of civil defense force by the UN). He
visited each of the six Serb enclaves frequently, the two largest at least
once a week, and set up meetings with individual Albanians or Serbs who
needed to see him. Usually, they were village leaders or coordinators, but
as Adlije, one of the language assistants said, "Terry will see anyone." He
was constantly on the road and out and about. He also regularly picked
up hitchhikers and was always working to make sure he knew everybody

who might be helpful in the municipality. His view was: "It's all goodwill in the bank; you never know when I might have to call on it."

Teamwork strengthened Terry Peterson and Orash Fatoohi's ability to lead in a network organization. Network theory emphasizes that teams that combine "strong" ties and "weak" ties will have greater strategic capacity than those that do not. Leaders with "strong ties" to constituencies are more likely to possess salient information about where to find resources, whom to recruit, what tactics to use, and how to encourage these constituencies to identify with the organization.[11] On the other hand, leaders with "weak ties" to diverse constituencies are more likely to know how to access the diversity of people, ideas, and routines that facilitate broad alliances.[12] Paul Holmes, the commander of the UNMIK civilian police, or CivPol, in Banshik, when asked how he contacted OSCE people, replied, "When I have information to send out, I contact Terry [Peterson]. He usually gets a hold of the correct people."

Fatoohi had strong ties both with intelligence sources in KFOR and with key people in the municipality. When members of the municipality received death threats before the elections in late 2000, Fatoohi responded by using this combination of local knowledge and connections (which were not even visible to others in UNMIK or the municipality). In the process, he demonstrated that for the UNCA in Banshik, cooperation was based not on formal position or role but on capability: the police were not up to the task, so he went to the people who were, even though it was not formally part of their job. In an interview, Fatoohi explained:

> I didn't talk with the police, as the police are very much infiltrated by unsound people. They are not qualified or they are from the UCK. There is a screening in the hiring process, but I don't think it's perfect. The interpreters especially serving the international police force [are unsound]. Through contacts I know this. The police are a peculiar structure that [consists of] many people from different cultures and different styles, and it is not an army and it is not efficient. I shared my information with some of the intelligence officers in the French Army when I needed assistance to protect the people before the election. They did the job themselves. The police is not benefiting from a high reputation among the military because of the fact that they are very heterogeneous: you have highly disciplined German police and then police without adequate training. The military provided discreet protection for the persons from the elements of the UCK . . . it's very difficult to keep information confidential if you ask something from the police. It depends on the importance of the issue. If higher authorities were in danger, I would not contact the police.

Peterson combined strong and weak ties, because the division of labor with Fatoohi enabled him to focus his energy and time on this task.[13] Af-

(handwritten margin notes: mini-riot of Serbs and mobilization of social capital "Palaj" "riot" patrons of)

ter a Serbian farmer was attacked and his tractor stolen from the Serbian enclave of Palaj in Banshik, there was a mini-riot when the Serb villagers protested against the ineffectualness of the police. The police, as indicated by Fatoohi, were universally regarded as "the weakest link" (as UN Deputy Regional Administrator Marlene Royce put it). Peterson, who was summoned on the radio by the police and went down to the Serbian enclave at 8 P.M., as the riot was subsiding, protested that it had taken the police six hours to let him know what was happening. As MA, he felt it was absolutely a matter that concerned him. The military had things under control, but Peterson went into the crowd, met with the village leaders, and set up a meeting for the villagers with the UNCA, OSCE, police, and KFOR the following afternoon. His personal acquaintance not only with the key personnel from each of the organizations but also with the local villagers enabled him to do this. He also persuaded the police and KFOR to invite their regional commanders to the meeting, which took place as scheduled the next day. It lasted four hours, with complaints presented by all sides—the police objected that the local population would not cooperate with them—and eventually it was agreed that a working group made up of all the organizations represented and village leadership would meet weekly. The purpose was to improve communications and to be aware of and try to resolve security issues. The main complaint of the Serbs was that they were being ignored and their complaints were not being taken seriously, but crucially they trusted Peterson and knew that he had the contacts to at least bring people together, however pessimistic they were about what such meetings could achieve. One tangible achievement was that the villagers agreed that there would be no more violent protests—they now had a forum in which they could air their grievances with all the key parties and know that they would be heard.

Peterson's interaction with the villagers in the past had created a resource, social capital, to draw on in the future. He explicitly said that was why he frequently visited the Serb villages and made sure that he knew all the key personnel there. This built up social capital not only for him as municipal leader but also for the collectivity, UNMIK and KFOR. Proportional to the value, positive or negative, of intensity of prior interaction, this social capital can be somewhat transferable. If A and B have a history of positive interaction, and B and C have as well, then A and C can have transferred social capital. Thus in the Palaj incident, the Serbs (A) had a strong relationship with Peterson (B), and Peterson also has a strong relationship with the police (C), so the Serbs and the police (AC) had shared social capital and were at least willing to sit down and hear each other out. In a network organization, this can be of critical importance, because the transferability of social capital can prevent violence and provide the basis for a consensual outcome.

Strong local knowledge coupled with strong and weak ties leads to greater participation by the organizations, the local municipality, and the population, because the combination of strong and weak ties links access to commitment, just as they are associated with innovation because they link information with influence.[14] Thus, Peterson and Fatoohi could access strong ties or contacts they could trust, and the organizations and individuals who had ties to Peterson and Fatoohi equally knew that it was worth sharing information with them, because they knew how to act and could be relied upon to do so. Thus, when a dispute arose between French KFOR and Albanian villagers in a mixed Serb-Albanian village, the Albanian village leader traveled into the municipality immediately—wearing his house slippers, he had left in such haste—to find Peterson and get him to come and intervene in the situation. Peterson's response was to drive the Albanian leader directly to the site of the dispute, where Peterson instructed the arguing KFOR soldiers to sit on one side of the field and the Albanian villagers on the other. French KFOR had begun constructing a pipeline that diverted most of the local spring's water away from the majority Albanian population to the Serb end of the village. The Serb villagers had begged them not to do so without consulting the Albanian villagers, but KFOR had failed to do this, and the Albanians predictably got very angry. Peterson spent the next two days bringing all parties—the French KFOR soldiers, the Albanian villagers, the Serb villagers, the UN utilities officer, and the local public utilities company representative—together to come up with a solution. Peterson saw it as a "marvelous opportunity to get the two sides [Serbian and Albanian] talking," because they had not spoken since the war, although they lived within 100 meters of one another.

In Thezren, the MA's bureaucratic style and misconception of the UN's role in Kosovo led to his failure to cultivate strong and weak ties among the various constituencies around him. Shamon did invite the highest-level people to meet him (e.g., the KFOR commander for Previca North), but these were occasional visits of personnel outside the municipality and did not cover the spectrum of people needed in a network organization in his own municipality. He got together with the local municipal leaders once every week or two weeks for a formal sit-down meeting, but when I questioned him, he had little knowledge of concrete issues they were working on—he said that the discussions he had had with the CEO and municipal president were of an abstract nature, about moral courage and political principles, which he felt it was the task of the UN to impart (interview, October 15, 2001).

Shamon also had few weak ties in other organizations and the wider community, because his daily routine was based on being at the head of a chain of command that necessitated little or no contact with people not immediately connected to him. He only occasionally attended the weekly interorganizational meeting, held in the municipal building, even when he was on the premises. Nor did he usually attend the monthly local municipal assembly meetings. He went to KFOR once a week for a security meeting, but this was the only regular time he left the municipal building. On very rare occasions, he went to a special event in one of the Serbian enclaves. No member of the public could access the MA in Thezren, and since he rarely left his office and the building or interacted with the international organizations or local municipality, he was set apart from everybody except his immediate international staff and a handful of local language assistants. As head of the hierarchical organization of the UNCA in Thezren, he held a weekly staff meeting for the UNCA officers. This was conducted in a formal manner, with each officer giving an update for that week on his or her portfolio.

This staff meeting was one meeting that the UNCA office in Banshik did not have, to the disgruntlement of some of the UN officers there, who felt it would have been good for morale and important for cohesion in the team to have a regular time set apart to have a weekly interface with one another and Peterson. This was an instance where the network organization emphasis of the UNCA in Banshik could usefully have retained this particular tradition of hierarchical organizations. The weekly staff meeting did help to forge relationships between the UNCA officers in Thezren.

In Thezren, Shamon's deputy, Thedy, had been in the municipality for over a year and had strong ties with some of the local municipal staff. However, his ties with the personnel from the other organizations were weak or nonexistent, and his ties in the local community were practically nonexistent. He too was a not a regular attendee at the weekly interorganizational meeting. Thus, the UN leadership in Thezren lacked knowledge of what was going on under the roof they shared with the local mu-

nicipality and access to a diversity of people, ideas, and routines that facilitate broad alliances. This paucity of ties, especially of weak ties, was
problematic when it came to information flows and cooperation. Leaders
who must obtain resources from constituencies must devise strategy to
which constituents will respond.[15] Leaders who draw resources from
multiple constituencies gain strategic flexibility, because they enjoy the
autonomy of having considerably more room to maneuver,[16] as Peterson
demonstrated with the Palaj riot.

The Thezren municipality faced a problematic situation in which land
owned by a state-owned enterprise, Produktion,[17] had been illegally
invaded by nearby villagers. Absent strong or weak ties in multiple constituencies, the UNCA's room for maneuver was very limited. The in-
vasion was explicitly against UNCA regulations, and the director of Produktion appealed to the UNCA for help. The local elected municipal
assembly had the authority to tell the villagers, "If you go on the land,
you'll be arrested," and the UNCA had the authority to compel the assembly to do this. The UNCA could also request that the police arrest the
trespassers, but neither the municipal assembly nor the UNCA did anything. DMA Thedy said in a staff meeting prior to the UN-monitored assembly that the municipal CEO had agreed that the issue be taken to
court. This was at least an official response to the situation, although this
request, made by politicians who backed the villagers in hope of getting
the latter's votes in the upcoming elections, was going to stalemate the situation.

But as Thabo, a UN officer in Thezren, commented in an aside while
observing the municipal assembly discussing the issue: "He [the CEO]
won't say anything now [i.e., in the assembly]." Indeed, he did not. DMA
Thedy did not press the issue, but merely lectured: "If the international
community sees this, they will not invest." The issue was not solved, and
the villagers got away with illegal occupation of the land. Timely intervention was critical in this instance, since the period for winter planting
was almost over and while the land was occupied, Produktion could not
go ahead with planting. The UNCA had known about it for several
weeks but had done nothing to solve the issue in a timely manner. The
police and KFOR both had representatives at the municipal assembly lis-
tening to proceedings, but they also made no comment. There was no effort to set up a working interorganizational body to sort out the situation. The consequence was further erosion of trust and a demonstration
of the absence of any, let alone collaborative, problem-solving capabili-

ties in Thezren. The lack of awareness of being part of a hierarchy that
was part of a network organization, and of the different working patterns
required by that, precluded a satisfactory outcome.

A similar lack of communication and cooperative problem-solving
ability led to the deaths of two Albanians during the time of my research
in Thezren. The incident demonstrated both the strength of organizational boundaries in Thezren and the fact that the UNCA neither saw itself nor was seen by the other organizations or the local populations as
the hub of a collective problem-solving network organization. All woodcutting in Kosovo required a permit, but illegal woodcutting was ram-
pant. The Serbians in Pluska, one of the enclaves in Thezren, alleged that
Albanians were cutting wood illegally in a forest beside the Serb enclave,
which they said was Serb property (although they had no documents to
prove ownership). KFOR, which had permanent checkpoints in the enclave, contacted Henry Ghosh, the UNCA officer responsible for the enclaves, and asked him to meet with KFOR officers and the village leaders
when he was in the enclave for one of his regular visits.

Ghosh commented in a later interview that he was very keenly aware
of the lack of ties between the organizations and had personally tried to
develop a relationship with KFOR and other organizations. His efforts
ensured that KFOR did turn to him when the issue of the illegal woodcutting came up. However, Ghosh was limited in the resources that he
could draw on in the UNCA; he later lamented its lack of connection
with other organizations and the resulting limited room for response in
any problematic situation. Getting the MA or other UNCA officers involved was not mentioned as a possibility in this particular situation. In
the meeting, Henry heard that the situation had been a source of tension
in the enclave for several weeks. However, no immediate plans to remedy
the situation came out of that ad hoc meeting, and there was no discussion of getting other organizations involved to brainstorm a collective solution. Instead, there were plans to make plans: Ghosh would see if an inspector from the regional or central forestry department could be
brought in to enforce the ban on woodcutting, and KFOR mused over
cutting off various routes into the wood. The clearly impatient Serbs expressed frustration and muttered about taking matters into their own
hands. The UNCA community officer, although very effective in his job,
was clearly an isolated actor, and he did not interpret the situation as one
that he could do something about or one that needed the input of all the
international organizations in the municipality. KFOR interpreted it
solely as a security issue and not an urgent one.

Two days later, I was interviewing international police officers in the police station in Thezren when news came in of a double homicide in the wood in question beside the Serb enclave. One Albanian woodcutter had been found dead, and another was missing. The police responded effectively, flying the body out and instigating a search and security operation. They did not contact any of the other organizations apart from KFOR, whose troops were already present in the enclave. The UNCA became aware of the incident two days later, and when the topic came up at the staff meeting on the Friday of that week, the MA said that it was a terrible thing to have happened and that he would discuss it at the interorganizational security meeting. It was spoken about as an incident "out there" and was clearly not perceived as something that the UNCA should have been aware of, had any role in, or could do anything about. Ghosh did not attend that staff meeting. The problem that led to the killings had been percolating for several weeks, but each organization was doing its own job inside its own organizational boundaries, with very limited communication or cooperation between them.

The task of cultivating strong and weak ties was an ongoing one and thus malleable to a certain degree. Because of the high turnover in personnel due to the nature of these missions, the location of an actor, either an individual or an organization in the network organization, is not static. In the absence of an established doctrine or strategy to follow, the location in the network organization of any person and the amount of networking between people and organizations depends to a great extent on the person in the location, and on the amount of effort put in by other actors in the network. Fatoohi's strong ties were mostly within the municipality and not subject to the high turnover rate of the mission, but Peterson constantly had to work at maintaining old ties and creating new ties. His ongoing willingness and ability to do this was crucial for maintenance of an effective network of ties. However, it was a function of the amount of time and effort he put into it, and of his social skill—that is, his ability to induce cooperation among others by empathetically relating to the situations of the other people and, in doing so, providing them with reasons to cooperate.[18] Peterson's ability to use whatever resources he had to establish links with people at every level in the municipality and to seek innovative solutions translated into a capacity to constantly maintain and yet transform his and the UNCA's position in the network organization.

The lack of an effective network of ties in Thezren was a manifestation of what happens when the absence of a conception of a network organi-

zation and the appropriate leadership for a network results in an absence
of flexibility and no investment of time and energy in establishing or
maintaining ties. Of course, the other organizations and members of the
network were also crucial, but because the UNCA was seen as, and was
in practice, the hub, its institutional culture greatly influenced the ability
of other organizations to network.

Heuristic Problem Solving

Leadership, particularly in a network organization, entails the ability of
the actors, both individuals and organizations, to solve nonroutine complex problems. In turbulent situations such as Kosovo, this is particularly
important, because there was no guidebook. Heuristic problem solving is
particularly suitable, because it uses experimental and especially trial-
and-error methods and involves a degree of feedback to improve performance. Heuristic processes permit actors to use salient knowledge to
devise novel solutions by imaginatively recontextualizing their understanding of the issue. This enables them to make alternative pathways
and solutions conceivable, facilitating analogical thinking and brico-
lage.[19] At the most basic level, the greater the number of ideas generated,
the greater the likelihood there will be good ones among them.[20] Knowledge of diverse domains not only offers multiple solutions from which to
choose but contributes to mindfulness that multiple solutions are possible.[21]

Problem solving in Thezren was within the respective hierarchies, and
within the UNCA, it followed the traditional bureaucratic model of division of responsibilities between officers and departments, with each officer reporting to the MA at the weekly staff meeting. The UNCA did not
perceive the larger problems in the municipality as problems for it to
solve. Problems in the municipality were not discussed at the UNCA-
chaired Thezren four-pillar or interorganizational weekly meeting; instead, there was a series of reports on what had been done by the respective organizations. Given that the problems facing the municipality were
very complex and required multiple and innovative perspectives, this was
very problematic for the attainment of the goals of democratization and
reconstruction. The hierarchies in Thezren did not draw on the resources
they had with other organizations in the community or on the resources
that existed in the local populations. Most crucially, the UNCA did not
activate its position as hub of a network and generate an institutional cul-

ture for the intervention in Thezren. In this situation, it was much easier for particular interests to outmaneuver the intervention's organizations in Thezren, and the outcomes on several key issues were diametrically opposite to the goals of the intervention. The institutional culture in the intervention in Thezren remained that of hierarchies working alongside each other, with the local populations "out there."

The conflict around what flags to put up in the municipalities was one issue in defining the institutional culture of the intervention, as discussed in Chapter 1. The second critical issue that contributed significantly to defining the identity and the institutional culture, not only of the network organization in both Banshik and Thezren (UNCA and municipality combined), but also of the people of the respective municipalities, was the issue of the municipal day. The Albanian majority in both municipalities wanted to decide on the day—both wanted it to commemorate the "liberation" of Kosovo on the day the KLA arrived back after the NATO bombing (although, as Peterson and Fatoohi pointed out, that was the day *after* NATO troops and the civilian population got there) and to give it a patriotic Albanian name.

In Thezren, the last part of a municipal assembly meeting I attended was devoted to a discussion about the establishment of a historical day in each month when a date of significance to the KLA or a martyred family would be remembered. These discussions were on top of the decision previously taken that the day of the municipality would be Liberation Day. The municipal utilities organization was called June 26, the day the Albanian politicians in Thezren deemed to be Liberation Day. Thabo said of this struggle: "Municipality Day—same thing [as the outcome of the controversy about what flags to fly over the municipal building]. Jon [the UNCA MA] and UNMIK defeated." He went on to say: "Maybe he didn't realize the importance of these symbolic things. Peterson is an ex-military guy and had experience working with the Albanian army; he realized the importance of these things. Jon was from the private sector." Consequentially, characteristic-based trust in Thezren remained ethnically based; trust only existed within ethnic communities (if there), and the international staff were thus inevitably excluded. The international staff talked constantly about how the Albanians did not trust anyone but their own ethnic group; although there was distrust and fighting within that group, its ranks were closed against outsiders, whether Serbs or internationals.

Fatoohi recalled of Banshik's struggles with the issue. "In Banshik, they wanted the same thing. But I wrote it into the statute that there would be *one* day, Banshik Day, not a martyr's day or anything identifiably Albanian, and that this would be decided on by consensus, and . . . once it is in the statute, it is difficult to change."[22] Despite opposition from the Albanians, Fatoohi's decision prevailed.

Heuristic solutions were particularly necessary in a situation where there were physical risks. Demolition of illegally constructed buildings was an issue throughout Kosovo. KFOR did not want to be perceived as being involved in destroying rather than reconstructing buildings. The issue was important, because it sent a strong message regarding the authority of the government and the rule of law. In Thezren, UNMIK, the UNCA, and the police refused to enforce the demolition of illegally constructed houses. Banshik faced the same problem. Peterson's initial response (half in jest) was "Give me a stick of dynamite and I'll do it myself!" He and Fatoohi wrote to the UNCA in Pristina and after much persistence eventually got the UNCA to agree with KFOR that the latter would provide security for a private company to demolish buildings built on public land. Peterson and Fatoohi were sufficiently motivated to face the possible physical threat from local interests and to persist through the bureaucratic inertia of the UNCA until they got a satisfactory result. Many issues in Kosovo were similar—with opposition from all sides, only determination and persistent motivation on the part of the UNCA at the municipal level would achieve results.

Heuristic problem-solving requires domain-specific knowledge and skills. This can require the expenditure of extra time and physical effort and sheer persistence in the face of indifference. The long hours included, for example for Peterson, a regular 7:30 A.M. Monday breakfast meeting with a commander of one of the KFOR battalions assigned to Banshik. Inasmuch as the French rotated in and out every four months, this entailed establishing a new relationship every sixteen weeks, often with somebody who could not see why he was working to establish links beyond those required by the organizational design. The following is my account of one of Peterson's breakfast meetings with the captain of the Reconnaissance Unit and his deputy.

> I accompanied Peterson to the French base one Monday morning. It is where the Engineering Battalion has its HQ, and they have notices posted at the gate that no cars, including white UN vehicles, were to be allowed in without a confirmed appointment. Peterson grumbles at this—it is a new notice put up by the new French commander of the base. We are asked to stop, and Peter-

son gets out of the car to present his credentials and the gate sergeant phones ahead to confirm we are on the list of visitors that morning. We are allowed in and drive to the officers' mess tent. The French captain and his lieutenant come in wearing their workout gear—they are relaxed and informal. We all drink coffee from bowls and eat croissants. Peterson's military background undoubtedly helps as he is totally comfortable in the military environment and partakes like he had breakfast here every day of the week. Peterson does most of the talking, because the officers are new, having arrived the previous week. The previous Monday's meeting was the handover, where the outgoing captain and the incoming one were both there with Peterson. I ask Peterson after we leave the base, is this meeting his initiative? He says yes, absolutely. If it weren't for him, there would be almost no contact between KFOR and UN-MIK. He doesn't think their role is that crucial here, except in the Serb enclaves [in Banshik], but he thinks it is important that he be able to call on them in a crisis and vice versa, or if either needs to know something really crucial. But he says: "There are no guidelines for municipal administrators. You make it up as you go along, which is what I like." He gives a copy of the daily report for the past seven days to the captain as a way of putting them "on the same sheet of music," as Peterson says. It is a good way for them to see UNMIK's perspective and concerns. If this is the introduction to the municipality's work, it is more likely that they too will read from that sheet of music. Peterson is informal and in relaying the week's news conveys a lot of information—not just information, tacit knowledge.

Peterson's establishment of such personal ties increased the amount of process-based trust available to Banshik municipality.[23] Process-based trust results from past and expected future exchanges. This was particularly important with KFOR, which was outside the UNMIK umbrella but had to work in cooperation with the organizations in UNMIK.

The Story/Narrative and Framing of the Mission

Hierarchical, bureaucratic organizations have clearly defined goals and programs of steps to get there. Network organizations, comprising diverse organizations, may not have these; network leadership is as much a function of framing a story or narrative to motivate people as it is implementing known steps in a program. In terms of the leaders' own motivation and the motivation of their team and network, the strength of their motivation was determined partly by the "story" they told themselves about what they were doing in Kosovo in the first place. Hierarchical organizations typically have rules, not stories, and in the absence of such a story, as in the hierarchical organization that was the UNCA in Thezren, the work was seen as the implementation of the UN mandate and regulations. These regulations were invoked by the UNCA in meetings as the reason why certain decisions should be made. The response as with the flag and municipal day issues was generally negative, in that actors felt pushed and pulled rather than being motivated.

In the Banshik UNCA, a story was generated that captured the goals of the intervention. It was presented as an ongoing story or narrative in which the whole of the municipality was engaged, a story of democratization and shared institution building that was the solution to the problems facing Kosovo. Peterson invoked it constantly in various settings, in a form that communicated itself almost as a verbalization of his own stream of consciousness. The open-endedness of the project and its newness were part of the narrative and generated a sense of being involved in something that was new and exciting and larger than the mandates and regulations. At the same time, Fatoohi, as the bureaucratic defender, did watch the mandates and regulations closely and ensured that they were followed.

"I think my mission is to ensure that democratic government is the solution," Peterson mused. "I don't think there's anybody out there who has ASKED the questions we're trying to answer. . . . We have to build 5,000 odd houses, get everything working again, get a reconciliation between the Serbs and Albanians . . . the brief has not been written on how to do this." Having such broad goals made it possible to extend the mission conceptually and concretely well beyond the organizational boundaries of UNMIK and KFOR and in effect to include everyone in the municipality. Peterson often invoked these goals—in his words, "getting everybody on the same sheet of music." He communicated his conception of the mission to the general population, for example, in his speech at the public ceremony inaugurating the municipal assembly.

In Thezren, the story was a legalistic one. The constant question was "Is that against the mandate?" and invariably the issue under discussion with the local municipality was against the mandate. When discussing the land dispute between Produktion and the Albanian villagers, the language used was legalistic, and there was a negative consequence inferred—"No international investors will come if you do that"—rather than a positive narrative or story that included everyone. Framing one's everyday actions in terms of getting people to talk to each other and to work together was a positive motivation for the team, and was something anyone could do; it assumed that there was something positive to work with, however small or embryonic. It was fundamentally optimistic.

Framing one's everyday actions in terms of making sure laws were not broken was a negative motivation and implied a fundamentally pessimistic view of the population.

Doctrine

Traditional hierarchies have established strategies and methods. In Kosovo, because there was very little doctrine in the sense of established collaborative strategies and methods, an important component of leadership in the municipalities was to come up with such doctrine or strategic routines and methods. Fatoohi recalls: "At the beginning Terry and I did things and we weren't sure how they were going to turn out. Then the other municipalities, if it worked, did what we did. . . but all of us have to confront this situation, which is not a rational situation. Mostly we are inventing the solutions, improvising the solutions." Sometimes the center did not respond well to ideas coming from lower down in the hierarchy. Part of the civil administration's job was to issue travel documents to Kosovars, but Peterson and Fatoohi did not want to use "Kosovo" as state of origin, because technically it was still a part of Former Republic of Yugoslavia, but for political reasons, they could not use FRY either. Instead, Fatoohi wrote on the travel documents that the carrier was a "Citizen of Territory Currently Under UN Control." Pristina criticized them heavily for taking such initiative, then three months later issued a memo designating the formulation suggested by Fatoohi instead of Kosovo as the official formulation.

The center did not acknowledge Banshik or Fatoohi or Peterson. Banshik's success in establishing doctrine, although unacknowledged by Pristina, was, however, enthusiastically received by other municipalities. Milo, the chief language assistant in Banshik, talked about how after the intervention started, he had attended a regional meeting for all the MAs in the Previca region. After the meeting, the other MAs pursued Peterson to find out how he had done his organizational chart and wanted a copy of it. Eventually, all of the other municipalities in the region modeled their own organizational charts on the Banshik chart.

The municipalities faced several challenges, in particular from the TMK/UCK. The doctrine held the potential to deal with the challenges posed by these actors, but teasing out that potential required leadership and the ability to develop further appropriate doctrine. Fatoohi cited the flag and municipal day issues and then described a meeting with a UNCA worker who had been assigned to Thezren, was not happy with what she saw, and came to ask advice from Fatoohi. "If I remember correctly, she wanted to know about the rights and obligations of the MA and how they can run their business. Especially we talked about the allocation or redistribution of land. I told her my general feeling that things were not going as well as they should in Thezren, the TMK were running the business rather than UNMIK. They do whatever they want." Banshik did face the same challenges, but a consistent response had helped curb the challenges. "They're doing the same thing here but with some precautions. It is not as general, there are one or two persons who have occupied the land who have forced the people to give the land, but we know the cases, legal procedures have started. In Thezren, I don't think they care about it, it's more about survival . . . here [the TMK] wanted the money from UNMIK, and we did not permit them to do this. In Thezren, they give money, land, everything."

There was a crucial period in both municipalities when the institutional culture was being established. The flag, the national day, money; how these were handled sent strong messages about authority and accountability. If that period was handled poorly, it was difficult, but not impossible, to reestablish authority. Fatoohi muses: "How did we gain authority? We never tried to oppose them strongly. But at that time they were also not very certain about their authority, they thought they needed our expertise, experience. That helped us control the situation a little bit." The former KLA wanted more rewards and support than they got after the end of the war, including land for families of martyrs and money. To cede on claims to property and compensation that the bulk of the local population believed were not rightfully theirs was to reduce the authority of UNMIK itself.

A realistic acceptance of the existence and appraisal of the KLA and its new incarnation as the UCK or TMK was the most appropriate response in this situation. There were claims by several local interpreters that the membership of the UCK/TMK had changed substantially since the war; now organized crime was trying to muscle in on the organization. The interpreters were adamant that the population was grateful for the protection the KLA had offered during the war but said that new elements were now muddying the waters and could not be allowed to claim what was not theirs.

Appropriate Leadership for a Network Organization

Appropriate leadership of a network organization was an important mechanism for establishing trust, creating a sense of identification with the mission, and facilitating information transfer and cooperation between the organizations. By examining how the leadership in Thezren and Banshik handled issues of authority, of doctrine, of establishing linkages with other organizations, of communicating what the "story" of the mission is, the importance of leadership as a mechanism for promoting the institutional culture that facilitates information exchange and cooperation is clear. Bureaucratic leadership is very limited in this environment, and consequently an additional type of leadership is needed. The organizations in Thezren, including the UNCA, functioned as hierarchical organizations, although they were all supposed to work together with the UNCA as their hub. Thezren's UNCA did not perceive itself as a critical hub, and interorganizational cooperation was limited.

Actors like Peterson and Fatoohi were helping to establish the type of institutional culture appropriate for a network organization of UNMIK. They displayed an unusual level of social skill, which enabled them to pioneer the emergence of an institutional culture that supported the network organization design in Banshik. Such leadership is particularly important when there is little guidance given from the organization, as was the case with the UNCA in Kosovo, because the UN itself was embarking on an organizational arrangement that was new to it. Leadership is one of four factors that are important for understanding the differences between the institutional culture of hierarchical organizations and network organizations. Chapter 4 is about the other three: the degree of formality, social embeddedness, and accountability. The degree to which these were appropriate for a network institutional form determined how much trust was generated, which influenced information exchange, identification with the intervention or mission overall (as opposed to just the hierarchical organization with which one had come to Kosovo), and collaborative problem-solving abilities.

CHAPTER FOUR

Formality, Social Embeddedness, and Accountability

Trust is the most important quality in a network institutional culture and contributes directly to the production of the other most desirable three qualities: identification with the mission, information transfer, and collaborative problem-solving capabilities. Leadership is a significant factor in the production of these qualities, as are factors that form the focus of this chapter: the degree of formality, social embeddedness, and accountability in the organizations in the network.

Trust among the organizations in UNMIK and KFOR, and between them and the local population and local organizations, had to be continually produced on the ground. To make the network (noun) network (verb), there must be trust. The demand for trust is high in temporary collaborations between individuals or organizations. Where new members share common backgrounds and experiences with members of other organizations, there is likely to be a substantial congruence in the members' interpretive frameworks,[1] and hence the common framework of the collaboration (e.g., UNMIK) can provide the independent basis for trust among collaborators.[2]

However, if, as in Kosovo, and indeed in Afghanistan and Iraq, most of the different organizations do not share one another's interpretive frameworks, and joint action and teamwork are required to fulfill the mandate of the intervention, additional social construction of trust has to be undertaken. It is not costless—it takes significant amounts of time and energy—as formal impersonal structures and informal social relations have to be developed. In short, "pre-existing common culture and the demand for trust within the collaboration strongly affect how much formal and informal trust is produced in . . . collaborations."[3] This formulation views social embeddedness as a variable, not as a universal.[4] Social embeddedness is much less necessary if the different organizations' tasks are quite separable and independent. If they are not, it must be socially constructed, because the more social ties bind together the diverse organizations or the more socially embedded the system is, the more people and organizations will participate.

The network organization can include more than the organizations that constitute it. In a situation where the goal is not profit but the establishment of the institutions of a democratic, peaceful multiethnic society, the network necessarily extends beyond the network organization to include the local municipality and the local population. Thus the network goes beyond the network of organizations. When the goal is not profit, a key question becomes: How do you get people and organizations to truly participate in a network? The degree to which this happens is the degree to which the goals of the network organization are attained, and the degree to which people participate is dependent on the levels of trust, identification with the intervention, exchange of information, and collaborative problem-solving capabilities. These in turn are dependent on institutional mechanisms. Besides having the appropriate leadership, the network organization's institutional culture has to be informal, socially embedded, and accountable.

Formality

The degree of formality or informality contributed directly to the level of trust, sense of identification with the mission, information transfer, and collaborative problem-solving capabilities in the organizational culture of the UNCA and, to an influential degree, in the network organization. Network organization theory holds that the more informal the environment and the greater the sense of trust and identification, the more communication of information there will be, and hence greater ability and effectiveness at cooperation and problem solving. Organizations faced with uncertain, turbulent environments,[5] or with uncertain means-ends relations requiring nonroutine problem solving,[6] are more likely to develop informal interaction orders.

Uncertainty could conceivably lead to more formality as organizations seek to reduce uncertainty through contingency planning and procedures. This might be feasible within an organization like the military, but even then the degree of turbulence in the environment of an intervention such as that in Kosovo, the wide range of possible problems, and configuration of problems makes it impossible to cover all or even most possible situations or outcomes. Network organizations are more vulnerable to conflict than hierarchies, because the personal dimension has a greater visibility and role. However, awareness of the interdependency of the organizations provides a counterbalancing pressure. In addition, in a network there is usually more than one person or organization one can go to or work with. For instance, when Peterson did not get on with a particular French major, he went to the other liaison officers instead and also asked the other military force present, the UAE detachment, to do things that he ordinarily would have asked the French to do. Moreover, given the turnover of staff in such a temporary network organization, even if there is interpersonal conflict, it is not a permanent feature of the interorganizational relationship. Thus, the flexibility and trust engendered by informality outweighs the costs of the uncertainty inherent in having an informal culture. The costs of being formal are much higher in the reduced sense of trust and identification, the strictures on the communication of information, and hence poorer cooperation and ability to solve problems.

Formal patterns are integral to the production of the social order and interpersonal ambience characteristic of more bureaucratic, regimented organizations.[7] The detachment of the person from the office is enacted by such things as the separation of home from work, the setting of a regular schedule, having separate financial records, and avoiding intimate relations with co-workers—all seen as necessary for the effective working of a bureaucracy. Conversely, in network organizations, informality has become associated with organizational effectiveness. The terms "informal" and "casual" are repeatedly invoked by contemporary authors to describe prevailing modes of interaction in innovative companies.[8] The implication is that such modes of interaction are critical to the success of cutting-edge firms in contemporary environments.

In Kosovo, both Banshik and Thezren faced an uncertain turbulent environment. However, the work practices in Thezren adhered to the bureaucratic structural design, institutional culture, and norms of the United Nations, a bureaucratic, mechanistic organization defined by structural features such as hierarchy of authority, centralization of decision making, division of labor, and formalization of duties. But in Kosovo, the UNCA, as part of a network organization, had to be more decentralized in decision making, participate in more lateral communication, and have fewer status distinctions if it was to cooperate and coordinate successfully with other organizations and the local population.

In the UNCA office in the municipality of Banshik, the office of Terry Peterson, the municipal administrator (MA), was overflowing with stacks of papers and books, and the walls were covered with photographs, cartoons, lists of phone numbers, contact information, and maps. There were flower boxes in the window. Outside the window was a nest covered in bird droppings, of which he said proudly: "Three generation of turtle doves have been raised there." His typical clothes were khaki pants, striped shirt or plain blue shirt, woolly sleeveless sweater, mud-spattered soft black pull-on walking shoes. He had glasses and a beard, frequently smoked a pipe or cigar, and constantly had dirty fingernails. He quite literally got his hands dirty and always drove himself around the municipality and beyond in a mud-splattered UN vehicle, disobeying UN rules about picking up hitchhikers by frequently stopping and offering rides (usually to the delight of the locals, not only at not having to walk, but at the idea of the nominal head of the municipality acting in such an informal way), making himself personally known to a wide swathe of the municipality in the process. His staff and local people who had come to speak to him could walk directly into his office, the door of which was always open. The other offices in the UNCA building followed suit, and people came and went all day. The local language assistants had desks next to their international colleagues in the respective offices of Utilities, Housing, Local Community, Finance, and Agriculture.

In a neighboring municipality, Thezren, the office of the municipal administrator, Khalid Shamon, was out of bounds to everyone except the MA himself. It was large and bare, with a desk that had nothing on it apart from a computer and an empty in-tray. There were a few file boxes in the glass-fronted cabinet beside the desk, but most of these were empty. Shamon dressed in expensive tailored suits and was always impeccably groomed. He never carried his own bag; his driver transported it to and from the car. He was extremely courteous and gracious in manner but was only available to select UN personnel and senior figures from other organizations, and then only by appointment. In the Thezren UNCA office as a whole, there was an absence of background noise and the atmosphere was hushed, partly because there was not a large amount of human traffic. The internationals and the language assistants had separate offices, and the doors were kept closed.

Why is this so important? In interventions like the one in Kosovo (and those in Afghanistan, Iraq, Sierra Leone, and elsewhere), diverse organizations with different organizational structures and cultures, such as the military, police, aid, and electoral organizations, have to work together with one another and with their local equivalents and local populations. They need one another, and to play their own parts in the intervention successfully, they need not only to be able to access one another but to understand how the other organizations function, which requires sharing of information, resources, ideas, goals, and purpose. A formal environment, such as that in Thezren, will inhibit the free flow of information, because status differentials are seen as more important than what individuals can contribute. The more formal the organizational culture, the less likely it is that there will be emotional identification with the other participants in the mission, making it more difficult to establish social ties, which in turn would facilitate the exchange of information and cooperation. An informal environment has the opposite effect: it promotes identification and feelings of equality with the other actors and the goals of the mission, thereby increasing the levels of trust and facilitating free flow of information and collaborative problem-solving capabilities. Such creative and collaborative problem solving is what is most frequently required of the organizations involved, because no problem affects only a single organization—the other organizations and the population are affected by every decision that is taken or not taken.

The consequence of a formalistic culture and environment is the enactment of status relations. E. H. Schein observes of the association between formality and status:

> Formality is symbolized by . . . obvious deference rituals among people who meet each other in the hall; many status symbols . . . frequent use of academic and other titles, such as Dr. So and So; a slower, more deliberate pace, and much more emphasis on planning, schedules, punctuality, and formal preparation of documents for meetings. Managers . . . come across as much more serious, more thoughtful, less impulsive, more formal and more concerned about protocol. . . . Rank and status thus clearly have a higher value.[9]

In Thezren, when Thabo proposed an innovative and well-thought-out plan for developing local tourism at a staff meeting, the MA's response lacked any emotional component (even though Thabo was visibly excited); he did not ask any questions about it and merely said, "Write it up in detail in a report." Thabo looked disappointed and raised an eyebrow at me. We had discussed the project as he was putting his ideas together, so he knew that I would understand his disappointment. The MA had responded in a conventional bureaucratic way to a subordinate's innovative idea—put it in writing and we'll process it. A network organization response would have seen the innovative value of the project and the emotional investment and expertise that Thabo had in the project (he said at the meeting that he had been involved in something similar in Saint Lucia in the Caribbean) and "gone with it," regardless of how it fitted into Thabo's formal portfolio or the office's list of things to do.

Even though superior-subordinate relationships exist in all organizations, the degree of perceived relative inequality may vary. In informal culture, Geert Hofstede notes, "hierarchy means an inequality of roles, established for convenience," whereas in formal cultures, "hierarchy means existential inequality."[10] Inequality inhibits the number of people who can participate freely in brainstorming and freely exchange information. Establishing an atmosphere of equality can be done in small but significant ways. In Banshik, MA Terry Peterson and DMA Orash Fatoohi discovered that the tea lady couldn't read or write, so they decided that three hours of her working day each day were to be dedicated to literacy classes, which they paid for. Peterson was usually the first arrival each morning, and his first action was to "crank up the coffeepot." In Thezren, Shamon's habits were that of the head of a status-conscious hierarchy. He habitually summoned one of the only two female language assistants to make tea (much to their indignation), and his driver carried his bag to his car and opened and closed the car door for him. Shamon admonished Thabo, the only UNCA officer who had his desk in the office that the language assistants used, to "keep your distance from the local people. We have standards to keep [up]" (interview with Thabo).

The message in Thezren was that the value of people's contribution was limited to their formal role, and that status mattered, whereas in Banshik, everyone was seen as being capable of contributing something unique, not only the mission but also to society in the shape of the municipality, and whatever that contribution was, it was not inherently better or worse than anyone else's. Given that the mission's purpose included democratic institution building, and that ensuring equal access to education and literacy for everyone is part of that, having the tea lady take literacy classes sent an important message. The municipality's doings were, of course, discussed at length by the local population, and as in all small towns and rural areas, everyone knew what everyone else was doing, so the ripple effect of a small act like that was significant, as Peterson and Fatoohi understood.

Informality is important in organizations where innovation and creativity are prized, where interaction is free-flowing and individually expressive. It is clear that a formal environment that keeps status and position to the forefront and decreases the emotional connection to the organization will inhibit not only the free flow of information but the amount of creative synthesis possible and the degree of identification with the goals of the organization as expressed in a narrative. Joking and informality all tend to foster feedback cycles of emotion, resulting in emotional camaraderie and the establishment of trust more quickly. Innovative, high-technology companies have incorporated higher degrees of emotional attachment to and identification with their work.[11]

So what is formal and what is informal? D. A. Morand suggests there are specific codes for each mode of interaction.[12] When applied to the data from the two municipalities, two distinct organizational cultures are apparent in the UNCA.

Language creates the world we live in, and as the mode of linguistic interaction is usually set by those in formal positions of authority, it can be a tool in the creation of the social order or culture within an organization. If the people in positions of authority do not use informal language, their employees do not do so either; if they are informal, this allows their employees to be so also. Thus language can be both an indicator and a cause either of formality or of informality in an organization, as I argue was the case in Thezren and Banshik respectively. The formal language of Thezren reinforced and helped to create a formal order, whereas the opposite was the case in Banshik.

One strong linguistic indicator of informality is the colloquial and slang expressions that are typically found in more informal, less restricted contexts.[13] Peterson's daily threat aired loudly in the office about somebody who was annoying him was "I'll chop his [or her] legs off and eat them!" In Banshik, everybody called everybody else by their first names, including the MA and DMA. They were Terry and Orash to all, although sometimes the language assistants called Peterson "Boss" or "Chief" in an affectionate manner. When Peterson was being uncharacteristically bossy, Adlije, a language assistant, would say, "Yes, SIR" in a tongue-in-cheek manner. There were also names given by the group; one language assistant's boyfriend was a member of a notoriously corrupt family, and she was dubbed "Mrs. Bin Laden" as a result. The informal interaction was not confined to the UNCA staff; when the local municipal president and a number of senior municipal staff were going to Amsterdam at the invitation of a Dutch municipality, Peterson and Fatoohi joked that the president was really going to Kabul (this was during the U.S. bombing of Afghanistan). The result of all of this was an atmosphere of equality and cohesion.

By contrast, a strong indicator of formality is fully articulated grammatical speech; more formal word choices and proper titles may be selected as a means of signaling the seriousness and overall importance of an organization or occasion.[14] In Thezren, the municipal administrator was known as "MA," not by his name, most of the staff called him "Sir" (when they saw him, which was rare), and one UN worker insisted on calling him—to his face as well as in his absence—His Excellency—in recognition of his status of former diplomat.

The weekly coordination meeting, called the four-pillar meeting in Banshik and the Interagency Meeting in Thezren, was a forum when the opportunity for observing conversational turn taking and topic selection was the most fruitful. Conversation analysts have studied how listeners subtly and nonverbally signal readiness to take the floor, how they use split-second timing to come in at just the right moment with a sentence completion; or how speakers about to end their "turn" indicate this by subtle intonational, grammatical, and nonverbal cues.[15] Such cues are central to the production of formality and informality. At a meeting characterized as more formal, there would be fewer conversational overlaps or interruptions, turn taking would proceed smoothly, the topical relation of one comment to another would be logical; if a change of topic occurred, it would be explicitly acknowledged.[16] Informal discourse is characterized by a greater leeway in terms of interruptions and topical shifts. If people generally feel able to interrupt the speaker, subgroups arise, and the topics of conversation vary and shift rapidly, the atmosphere could be described as informal. Joking or humor, informal behaviors, can often be a mechanism for changing a topic or reorientation of conversation focus.

The interagency meeting in Thezren was very formal. Formalistic interaction is conducted at distances varying from four to twelve feet;[17] the seating design was a series of long tables placed end to end in a square, with the inside of the square a large empty space. Four to six people sat on each outer side of this square. The mediator of the meeting was not the MA in any of the three meetings I attended, but Daniel, one of the UN officers. He conducted the meeting in a formal way, calling the attendees "Ladies and Gentlemen" and apologizing for the absence of "His Excellency." At one of these meetings, he said that His Excellency was away at an important meeting, when I knew he was in fact in his office. Turn tak-

ing was in a strict clockwise manner, and Daniel would formally thank
each contributor and then formally introduce the next person. If someone
tried to interject to make a point, Daniel would admonish the person with
a wave of his hand and a finger to his lips. When a group of Spanish soldiers came in fifteen minutes late, he stopped the meeting, pointed to the
clock, and told them that if they wanted to attend, they must be on time,
an exercise in humiliation and also, inasmuch as they were irregular attendees at the meeting, not behavior likely to induce attendance. There
was no humor used to facilitate conversation turning points.

The four-pillar meeting in Banshik was held at 5 P.M. on Mondays in a
conference room in the UN offices. It was not a large room and usually
twelve to sixteen people would be sitting around the long conference
table in close proximity for lack of space. Nibbles and drinks were always provided, including a bottle of whiskey from the MA's cupboard.
Although conducted according to the rules of a meeting, Peterson, the
MA, always led the gathering, unless he was on leave. Although each person took a turn, it was not in any particular order, and there was a significant amount of humor to facilitate the turn taking. The degree of fa-
miliarity was greatest between the UNCA and OSCE people, because the
other attendees were less regular and had a higher turnover—French
KFOR, typically four months. The conversation remained coherent, and
subgroups would not break off until after the meeting, but people would
interrupt or interject regularly, so that the presentations became more of
a multichannel conversation. Informality is associated with greater lati-
tude of emotional expression. The seriousness of formality is signaled by
an impersonal detached physiognomy, which was the dominant expression at the Thezren interagency meeting, but not at the Banshik one.

Banshik's institutional culture, with its lack of status differentials and
lack of informal rules or codes, facilitated the emotional identification of
staff with one another and the mission and facilitated the production of
trust and information exchange. Thezren, functioning as a hierarchical
organization, enforced status differentials, thereby inhibiting the growth
of a sense of equality and emotional identification with the mission and
inhibiting a free flow of information based on that sense.

In the village of Slavina in the Banshik municipality, when the French
military, Peterson and Giampiero from the UNCA, and local Serbian and
Albanian villagers were walking around a field where water rights were
under dispute (French KFOR had dug a trench for the Serbs against their
and the Albanian villagers' wishes, which would have diverted a critical
water source for both sides of the village to only the Serb one) for four

hours, the solution eventually came from Ilir, a young UN Albanian language assistant. He suggested to the two village leaders that they sit down and agree what was to be done and then put it in writing, saying that KFOR would have to abide by that. Furthermore, if the water pipe were damaged again (one of the reasons why KFOR wanted to dig the Serb-only trench was because the pipe leading to the Serb village had been vandalized), both villages would share the cost of repairing it. Due to the informal nature of the UNCA office, Ilir did not feel that his job was limited to translation, and when he saw a solution that might work, he felt free to suggest it. KFOR was ignoring his suggestion until Peterson came over and immediately agreed that it was the right thing to do and used his authority to get everyone to agree to a time two days later when they would meet and write the agreement.

In Banshik also, Milo, the chief language assistant, would warn the UN officers about who was corrupt in the local community and whom they should not do business with. In Thezren, the language assistants were seen as just that—interpreters—and their rich lode of information and ideas from their knowledge of the place and people was not seen as relevant. The bureaucratic formal interaction prevented the awareness among the internationals of this resource; whereas in the absence of an enforced hierarchy in Banshik, the informal culture meant that no one was seen as just his or her formal position, and people consequently contributed much more significantly to the transfer of information and cooperation.

Social Embeddedness

The third mechanism for producing trust, identification with the mission, information transfer, and collaborative problem-solving capabilities was the degree to which the relationships between individuals and organizations were socially embedded, both among the internationals and in the municipality as a whole.

The term "social embeddedness" has been used in economic sociology and organization theory to indicate the "noneconomic" dimension of exchange relations. Here I adopt that usage to indicate the personal ties that assure loyalty and trust,[18] which in turn facilitate effective communication of information and the assumption of collaborative problem-solving responsibility.

Personal ties promoting loyalty and trust can be established in several ways in environments such as the mission in Kosovo. There can be a conscious fostering of ties and a culture of inclusivity. The degree of formality can be reduced so as to promote emotional identification with other actors and diminish status differentials. Personal ties are recognized as important for the workings of the network organization and are invested with time and energy. An impersonal bureaucracy as described by Max Weber (1947) would not see any role for personal relationships in pursuit of the organization's goals, and this traditional view was evident in the UNCA in Thezren. But with the network organization, where there is a hybrid of hierarchies and networks, formal structures for meeting and cooperation are not enough to bind people together and to create the bond needed for true information exchange. Hence, ties of loyalty and trust are of critical importance.

Marlene Royce, the deputy UN administrator at the Previca regional level, was explicit on the importance of social ties for information transfer and cooperation:

> Personality, the person, is crucial. Organizations don't relate to each other, people do. . . . Contact with the military is absolutely essential. When I arrived, I invited the generals [KFOR] over for dinner along with the regional head of CivPol [the UNMIK civilian police]. They came and we had a great time. Now we do it every two weeks. I think that is part of the reason why things have been calm in Previca for the last few months. We share information and we know about situations before they get bad. For example, they took the tanks away from a position in the north [the majority Serb part of the city of Previca]. It was still being guarded, but it looked different, and there was trouble brewing because of that in the community. So we said it to the general, and he informed the community that the protection was still there, it just looked different. If we didn't have that kind of relationship, it would be very hard to just go and say, "Hey, you need to do this." In addition, we have formal meetings once a week where we all get together. And on Monday, Wednesday, and Friday, I have a security meeting. (interview, October 29, 2001)

In an interview, David Allen, the UNMIK-KFOR liaison officer for the regional level, confirmed the efficacy of this approach: "This afternoon we'll have a formal meeting with CivPol, KFOR, UN, a security meeting, discuss all those issues. If you do informal discussion, you have far better results; the formal meetings are almost confirmatory. It's already been discussed. A question will be posed, which we will then deal with in the informal sessions, and then at the formal meeting, it will be ratified."

In Banshik, the development of social ties was encouraged by the UNCA through the informal culture and through explicitly conducting business in a social context. The MA and DMA visited the home of their chief language assistant regularly, and the MA regularly hosted parties to

which everyone he knew was invited, all the internationals and the Kosovars as well—members of the municipality, language assistants, drivers,
and the tea lady (they all came). The MA also hosted dinner parties to
which he would invite people from opposite sides of the ethnic divide
who were influential in their communities and some key people from the
international community to get some dialogue going. He saw this informal "talking to each other" as crucial if the two communities were ever
to bridge the gap between them.

Besides explicit efforts to bring people together, there were also the informal exchanges occasioned by the fact that there were only two restaurants in the town where internationals ate. It was customary that you
would know most of the civilian internationals in the restaurant, and
sometimes tables would be joined (one night when Peterson and I were
having dinner, the two KFOR liaison officers came in with a colleague of
theirs, so their table was pulled up to join ours and dinner was shared).
The same two KFOR officers began a Thursday night four-pillar dinner,
which was a moderate success. The idea was to facilitate social interaction among the internationals. The first week, there were the two KFOR
officers, two UN officers, four police officers, and one OSCE person,
who arrived late. The conversation ranged from events and issues in the
municipality to sharing of personal information about family in their respective home countries and the challenges of being away from loved
ones.

OSCE threw a reception at every turn in the election campaign, and
the effect was to bring the internationals and nationals working on it together. As the MA frequently visited the Serb enclaves, he frequently had
meals or coffee with the village leaders. When two officers from the U.S.
office in Pristina wanted to know more about Banshik and called Peterson to set up an appointment, their "official" visit began with a Sunday
lunch with the MA, which Milo and I also attended. There were no distinctions made and no formalities; it was a social event, and everyone
contributed information and exchanged opinions. Then one of the officers came with Milo and myself in one vehicle, while Peterson and the
other officer went in another vehicle, to tour the Serbian enclaves and the
municipality, ending up at the house of a village elder in the largest Serbian enclave, where rakia (40 proof home-distilled spirit) was poured
generously and an hour of talk ensued. The amount of tacit information
exchanged was significant, and new social ties based on an enjoyable afternoon were forged. Ebush, the president of the municipality, was a

good friend of both Fatoohi and Peterson. The night before I left the municipality, I accompanied Peterson, Fatoohi, and Ebush to Milo's modest house for dinner. The consequence of such interactions is a dense network of ties that is all-channel; this enormously facilitates communications and cooperation.

In Thezren, relations among the UN staff were cordial, but beyond the group of UN officers, there was an absence of personal ties. Only one UN officer, Thabo, sat in the office where the language assistants were, and this was because he recognized the importance of social relations for information exchange. He said: "I work in the language assistants' office because it gives me a feeling for what is going on. The MA never comes in. I hate working on my own. I like working with the people of this society. I am the exception, yes! I am the only one. The rest would rather only have their own people, the internationals." The police did not live in the municipality, and there was no after-hours contact between the UN personnel and OSCE personnel. Nor for that matter was there much contact during office hours with other organizations' personnel. Henry Ghosh, a young UN officer who had worked for six years in the entertainment industry, lamented the lack of appreciation of the importance of social ties in the UNCA in Thezren. "When I arrived in the mission, I was very gregarious . . . and when the outgoing [KFOR] colonel invited me to his good-bye lunch, and no one else from UN, even though they'd been there a lot longer, it's *clear* that other people here don't cultivate those kinds of relationships."

Maurice England, an OSCE officer, said that the UN administration suffered from not living in Thezren itself. "OSCE, we live where we work, and most of the UNMIK staff doesn't do that. That creates a difference between the local community and the civil administration in this case. OSCE lives here with the people and the same problems—you got the same issues, no water and no electricity. We're all affected. I think maybe if they lived here in the community and notice[d] those problems as part of their everyday life, which they do in Pristina or Previca as well, they [would] also miss water and electricity, but they have other things that they can look forward to, maybe certain things would be able to be helped a little faster, if they faced the same problems. Besides that, it's very good for the local community to see the international presence; that really has an effect, I think. We have very good communication with the local community, at least I do. I'm not sure if that's true on the part of the administration, because they're not here."

Aside from at the interagency meeting, I did not meet the KFOR liaison officers when I was in Thezren, whereas in Banshik I bumped into them in the office at least three times a week. They came into the UNCA office and wandered about, conducting business and exchanging social pleasantries with the UN and local staff.

The more socially embedded the organizational interactions were, the greater likelihood that not only would actors receive the information they needed but that they could and would get it from more than one source. The emotional connections made cooperation easier, because information was passed on before it was needed and people felt comfortable making requests for assistance or cooperation—and, crucially, were more likely to get that assistance. It also had a positive effect on morale, because emotional support was provided as well as professional cooperation. In Thezren, the lack of social ties inhibited the exchange of information between organizations and their ability to call on one another in a crisis.

Accountability

An organization cannot work behind walls in an international intervention. The accountability of the organization, in terms of transparency and honesty to itself, the network organization, and the local population, is extremely important for the creation and maintenance of trust, exchange of information, and collaborative problem solving. Besides the obvious need for effective and accountable use of resources, it is also crucial because identification is difficult if the organization is viewed as having one set of standards for itself and another for others, and if it is seen as unreliable. This is particularly important for institution building—the local municipality is learning from the internationals and jointly implementing governance and administrative structures.

Although both municipalities were fortunate enough to find major donors—the Japanese government in Thezren, the United Arab Emirates in Banshik—their levels of accountability were strikingly different. For instance, two years previously $7 million had been given by the Japanese government to rebuild three factories, including a large and famous brick factory, in Thezren. In fall 2001, none were operational and all looked derelict. Marlene Royce, who had known the former Thezren MA, Jon, at the time of the Japanese donation, was shocked that nothing had been done with the money. Thabo, who had been there all through this period, defended Jon, saying he was hopeless with money. There had been no banking system in Kosovo for the first two years, and "When the money came, it was put in the safe and somebody would need money for this or that and go and take what was needed and the money got used, it just got used. . . . But that time was crazy, you didn't follow formalities. Money came in bags, was put in the safe, and it was very easy to mismanage it."

Henry, a UN officer who had been working in Thezren for twenty months, recalled:

> They put a man in charge of finance, an international, who didn't know how to use a computer. Every week the numbers would be completely different. The negative balances in one department would be positive, the numbers didn't add up. It seems like he didn't even look at the data he was presenting to Jon and all of us. It continued this way, week after week after week, and finance isn't a joking matter, but all Jon would say is "Try to get it right next time." He really really didn't manage things, he would let people get away with a lot. When you let the finances out of control or you don't really know what's going on with the finances, I think that's why a lot of people thought there was a lot of funny business with the money. And I don't think there was, maybe there was, I don't know, but I don't think Jon had control of the finances . . . the UN send in auditors but I don't know if they ever did that. They were supposed to. Whenever you have a project, the auditors come and check all your figures. I don't know if that ever happened in Thezren, but that's supposed to happen. I've never seen an auditor! You've got a situation where there's millions of dollars coming in and there's no control. It's really up to the whim of the people who run the finances.

Thus, if there was not outright dishonesty, inertia and lack of responsibility could have the same effect, both in terms of wasting of resources and damage to morale, not just of the UNCA but also by extension of the local municipality. Given that part of the mandate was to build accountable democratic institutions, the lack of accountability obvious to the local population undermined the credibility of the UN and the international community.

The consequences were manifold: projects did not get done, because the money assigned to them disappeared, this discouraged other donors from funding projects, and, as Thabo put it: "You know, the projects were not being done. Someone would say, the water project, the roads project, where is that project? The proposals were not being accepted as suitable." Daniel, who had served four months as a UNCA officer in Thezren, and had formerly been with the UN Department of Reconstruction in Previca,[19] recalled of that time: "I received one decent proposal from Thezren. I could only think that these people are going to take the money themselves. These plans are not feasible. When I got here, I think, 'What have all these people been doing??' All that money, NOTH-ING had been done." Although statistically, the amount of damage done during the war was comparable in Banshik and Thezren, the war damage was frequently put forward as a reason why things were so bad in Thezren.

> Thabo: All the roads, houses, water, everything was destroyed, it was not possible to mend them all in one year! No way! One year?!
> Me: So what was done in the first year?
> Thabo: The first year was a building relations program. The administrator met a lot of people.

Yet the continuing lack of strong and weak ties evident in the municipality and the lack of progress after that first year did not indicate that any time and effort put into "building relations" had been productive.

Gérard, one of the KFOR liaison officers in Banshik, had done a tour of duty in Thezren when Jon was MA there. His perception of that time confirmed that accountability had been lacking. "I spent six months in Thezren. I was part of a tank command. It was a place a civilian should have a side arm. The MA [Jon] took bribes from the TMK [the demilitarized Kosovo Liberation Army]. The head of OSCE left because of the threats he received."

While I was doing my research, the budgetary affairs of Thezren were still in disarray. Sid, the UN officer assigned to look after the budget, had taken one of the UN cars and gone on unauthorized leave for three weeks. Before that, he had not signed any of the documents needed to release money for key projects and salaries. DMA Cole Thedy, who received endless complaints from the local municipality directors, whose hands were tied by Sid's inaction, reported this to the MA. The MA waved his hands and said, "They must sit down and sort it out among themselves." Thedy was livid because, although the MA did say that he could deputize for Sid, Thedy felt it was not his responsibility. He had his own workload and much of the delay had caused problems that were not solvable. Halit, the local budget officer, was totally frustrated—without Sid's signature he could not release funds. The UN finance officer was a "partner" to the local finance department, offering advice and having ultimate approval on budget spending but yet not in the same chain of command. Four quarterly allocations of money from the UN's Central Fiscal Authority in Pristina were made to the Thezren Department of Education, totaling 323,000 DM (about U.S.$210,000). But only 139,000 (about $90,650) had been allocated. The Central Fiscal Authority in

Pristina took money that was not spent back. Thus, if the municipality fell behind in allocation, it would lose the money that was desperately needed for education in the municipality.

Fuel to heat the schools during the winter could not be bought without Sid's signature. However, the lack of Sid's signature was only one part of the problem. Thabo lamented:

> I told the MA last August that we needed to start thinking about the winter. Now it's November, winter is here, and still nothing has happened. We are here inside a good building, with good clothes and a heater. And we still feel the cold. Many of these children are from poor families. They don't have warm clothes. We only have [about $18,500] from the Center; the rest must come from the municipality, revenues, etc. Last year we needed [about $45,200]. Why is nothing happening? They have to work out how much is needed, it's tied into winterization,[20] so we have to figure out how many families there are in tents who need to be moved into the collective center. So next week there is a meeting about it. Next week! Another meeting! They are too slow.

Anuradha, the UNCA education officer in Thezren, did set up a meeting for the following day at 3 P.M. When I arrived at the designated room, she said it was cancelled and that it had been rescheduled for the following week. At a municipal administrators' meeting I attended later that same week at the regional level, every municipality except for Thezren had purchased heating fuel for its schools.

The same financial structure was in place in all municipalities: operational funds came from the UN Central Fiscal Authority in Pristina, and project and capital investment funds came from donors if they approved projects proposed at the municipal level. In Banshik, Fatoohi said:

> The thing we have done—and I don't think other municipalities have been able to do—is . . . all the savings we make from the operations budget is streamlined to the other projects. For example, from our own funds, the money we save from core municipal activities, we can for instance reallocate to educational institutions, so we spent 300,000 DM [about $195,000] extra, and we created a preschool, a kindergarten, and also renovated the building in front of the municipality. So to be able to do this, you need to have a very firm control over the expenditure . . . my impression with other municipalities is that they try to spend the money without saving. The initiative has to be taken by the municipality. We make sure the projects do not go above the budget line.

The degree of accountability in Banshik was evident when Fatoohi and Peterson had a stern disagreement when Peterson authorized extra money to be taken for utilities; money that had not been formally approved for the utilities project concerned but yet was being put to proper use.

Fatoohi was appalled to hear that Thezren had not bought fuel for its schools. In September he had requested the local Department of Education to put out a tender for the contract to supply fuel to the schools, including distribution. Two weeks later, a bid was accepted and was paid for out of the education budget. However, he discovered that because the supplier had not obtained a customs exemption form for the fuel, he had not supplied it. Fatoohi responded in a direct and immediate manner. He drove to the EU customs office in UNMIK regional building in Previca. I accompanied him and observed as he learned from a EU customs officer that the deputy director general in Pristina had abolished the exemption for the importation of fuel. Fatoohi argued: "My municipality did the budget BEFORE the regulations changed. It should not be applied to this year. We should not apply rules here that we would not apply in our own country [i.e., fiscal rules cannot be changed in the middle of the fiscal year; it happens at the yearly budget]. There is always a delay to accommodate the fiscal year." The officer said he could do nothing, because the rule had come from Pristina. The same day Fatoohi went to Pristina, where he got a stay on the regulation, based on the preceding argument.

The consequences of fiscal rectitude and responsibility were effective allocation of resources and trust in the UNCA and the network organization of which it was a part. As the population, the other organizations, and the local municipality observed fiscal responsibility and a share in its administration (for example, Fatoohi worked with the local Department of Education to purchase fuel for the schools), the value of the lesson in governance and institution building was enormously significant. The consequences of fiscal irresponsibility were a lack of trust in the UN and between the organizations, a reluctance to identify or work with an organization or network that conducted itself unprofessionally and unreliably, and consequently the failure to fulfill the goals of physical reconstruction and of building democratic and accountable institutions in conjunction with the local municipality.

A Network Organization's Institutional Culture

Innovative leadership, informality, strong social embeddedness, and accountability—the degree to which these are present will determine the levels of trust, identification with the mission's goals (and not seeing it as an opportunity for financial exploitation), information transfer, and collaborative problem-solving abilities. These in turn will affect the level of information exchange and cooperation, essential for fulfilling the UN's mandate of maintaining security, interim governance, and the building of the institutions of a peaceful, democratic society. The demands of a network organization are different from those of traditional hierarchical organization, and the organizations in Kosovo are essentially hierarchical organizations struggling to adapt their structure and culture to also participate in a network organization at each level of the mission: local, regional, and center.

The outcomes in Banshik and Thezren demonstrate that the structures of interorganizational cooperation are not enough. There must also be an institutional culture that fosters trust and identification with the other people and organizations as well as the mission; only then will sufficient information exchange and cooperative problem solving occur to fulfill the mission's goals. The appropriate leadership is critical, given the nature of the network organization, and the appropriate leadership in the UNCA is most critical of all. The appropriate leadership fosters a culture within the UNCA, and hence in the wider network organization and system, that fosters identification with the mission and facilitates information transfer and cooperative problem solving. The leadership must be successful in getting the organizations and the local population (both ethnicities) to participate, because they are building institutions that will eventually be taken over by the local people.

Philip Selznick wrote that while organizations are tools, they come to have a life of their own.[21] This is particularly true of organizations created to execute one purpose or a set of closely related purposes, such as the grassroots Tennessee Valley Authority of Selznick's study or UNMIK today. To be successful, such an organization—for instance, UNMIK—must co-opt people and organizations to its cause or purpose. Selznick defines this as "the process of absorbing new elements into the leadership or policy-determining structure of an organization." Banshik municipality's leadership and the institutional culture it fostered were doing this with the other organizations in the network and with the wider population. Thezren was not co-opting anybody to its purpose.

PART III

Information and Communication Technologies

CHAPTER FIVE

The Use and Misuse of Information and Communication Technologies

In the private sector, information technology is an integral part of the shift from vertical lines of authority and discrete market transactions to horizontal mechanisms of coordination with primacy given to communication and cooperation. The question in Kosovo was whether the introduction and use of new technologies helped the organizations to move from a hierarchical structure and culture to a more collaborative one. Did they facilitate the sharing and cooperative use of resources? Did they facilitate the building up of trust, identification with the overall goals of the network, information exchange, and collaborative problem solving, all of which ultimately contribute to the success of the mission?

Hierarchies do not have to be part of a networked organization to be experiencing the organizational changes wrought by new information and communication technologies (ICTs). Just as in the private sector, where firms have had to become more responsive and flexible and to focus only on the part of the supply chain that they do best, subcontracting or joining alliances or networks for the rest, so nonprofit organizations have had to realize that one organization cannot do all the tasks required in increasingly complex situations, such as humanitarian operations. The hierarchies in Kosovo were struggling to make this change. The degree of success with which they were adapting their internal organization had a great impact on their ability to participate in the network organization of UNMIK and KFOR. How hierarchical organizations introduce technologies and how the organization responds to them is not predictable. Little is still known about how technology is actually used in organizations, and as Pablo Bockowski points out, technology only "affords" certain potential uses (intentional and unintentional), and it is the institutional setting that determines whether these "affordances" are recognized.[1]

Information flow and information technology have always influenced the form of an organization, from the pen and paper to the telephone and telex, to the PC and internal network, to e-mail and the Internet. Indeed, formal hierarchies have served the purpose of coordinating and making more efficient the flow of information in organizations.[2] This was accomplished through a division of labor in which functionally specialized units and unity of command constrain communication flows to those defined by the chain of command.[3] By limiting communication so that orders flow down and information flows up, organizations became more orderly and efficient. In hierarchies, managers were warned to constrain informal communication that could undercut managerial control and disrupt smooth organizational functioning.[4] However, norms of not sharing across hierarchical boundaries resulted in a limiting of the amount of expertise that flows upward and laterally inside organizations.

How intrinsic is information technology to the network organization? New information and communication technologies (ICTs) have played a major role in network organizational development.[5] Indeed a number of authors have written of the IT-enabled network organization.[6] Manuel Castells views the organizational shift from hierarchies to networks as predicated on, and impossible without, information technologies.[7]

Yet others have documented the shift to a network organizational design before the Internet started growing exponentially in 1995, observing that uncertain market conditions and the need for high R&D efforts led to a variety of interorganizational relationships, such as alliances, partnerships, joint ventures, and research consortia.[8] Today, all organizations face the imperative of organizational innovation due to rapid technological innovation in an increasingly turbulent world, both for business and nonbusiness organizations. Information technology is a critical enabler of new ways of organizing. Fluid and flexible patterns of working relationships are based on communications networks, yielding innovative contexts for interactions and collaborative work that span traditional organizational boundaries. Point-to-point communication (communication directly between two people, with no intervening person or channels necessary) between groups, often supported by information technology, integrates borders between them. Firms and organizations, including the ones present in Kosovo, are spending substantial sums of money on technology with the aim of facilitating the efficient and effective operation of lateral and diagonal ties.

The Institutional Context of the
Network Organization

Although networked firms are usually thought of as communication-rich environments, with information flows blurring traditional intracompany boundaries,[9] as Nitin Nohria and Robert Eccles point out, "networked organizations are not the same as electronic networks nor can they be built entirely on them."[10] Working relations in the networked organization are embedded in a social context consisting of culture, social norms, practices, and habits;[11] in short, the institution of the network organization is critical, and this institution is itself a hybrid of the network and the hierarchical institutions, because most networks are in reality a hybrid of hierarchies and network.[12]

It is clear from work on the impact of technology on firms that the introduction of new technologies can significantly affect an organization's internal and external relations.[13] Early research in computer-mediated communications was individualistic and technology-deterministic, and assumed that a single person was rationally choosing among media.[14] In recent years, there has been a shift toward considering how social relationship, organizational structures, and local norms affect the use of communication media.[15] A lot of computer-mediated communications research has been conducted in laboratory settings, where the use of the Internet by a group of people gathered together in the laboratory setting was observed. But research also needs to conduct empirical studies of real-life settings, taking into account the social characteristics of participants, their positional resources, the interplay between ongoing on-line and off-line relationships, and their ongoing social relationships.[16] For instance, laboratory studies of the use of the Internet and intranets do not capture the important role played by them in supporting work relationships in sparsely knit, loosely bounded organizations whose members switch frequently and routinely among the people they are working with during the day as they move between projects or need different resources.[17]

The Physical Network

As several analyses of network organizations in the business sector demonstrate, permeable boundaries are intrinsic to a network organization both within the organizations participating in the network organization and between the organizations comprising a network organization.[18]

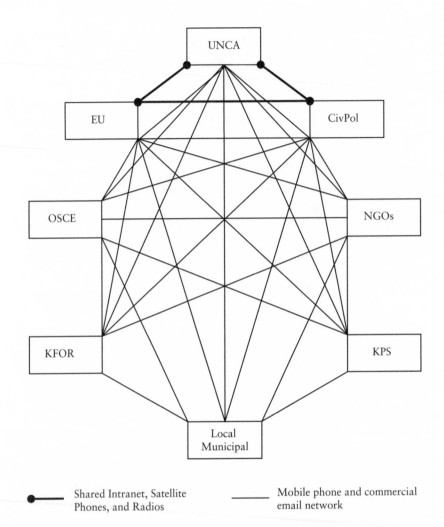

Fig. 3. UNMIK Communication Technology Infrastructure in Kosovo
KEY: CivPol = UNMIK civilian police in Kosovo; EU = European Union;
KFOR = Kosovo Force; KPS = Kosovo Police Service; Local Municipal =
Albanian-Serbian civil administration; NGOs = nongovernmental organizations;
OSCE = Organization for Security and Cooperation in Europe; UNCA = UN
civil administration.

Management is less hierarchical, deriving its authority from expertise rather than rank. This comes from network "output" or achievement of its goals, which demands a high degree of intangible local or specialized knowledge. Communication needs to be direct, while multiple weak ties enable early knowledge of emerging problems. All of this requires a physical information and communications network as point-to-point communication integrates borders between groups. This is necessary within the constituent hierarchies also, because to be part of a network organization, an organization must itself be networked.

The design of information and communication technologies did not closely correspond to the organizational design of the network organization of UNMIK—the four pillars and KFOR. The UNCA, the international police (CivPol), and the EU shared communication resources and thus had a common or shared communication "space." However, OSCE, the NGOs, and KFOR all had their own separate ICT infrastructures, and the local police (KPS) and municipality administration used minimal ICTs: a basic radio network among the police and the (practically nonexistent) local telephone system in the municipal administration.

The UN provided a radio and satellite communications system for the UNCA, the EU, and CivPol. There was a hand-held and car radio network, consisting of "Motorolas," as they are called after the company that manufactures them. More powerful radio links were used to provide some Internet access, including in Banshik, which was possible because there were no geographical barriers between it and the radio signal coming from the UNCA regional office in Previca. The UN also leased space on a satellite to supplement the communication needs of the mission. It put satellite dishes where it was necessary politically and geographically; each regional office, including Previca had a satellite dish, as did some municipalities, such as Thezren, where there was a range of mountains blocking the radio signal. The radio link was used wherever possible, because it was considerably cheaper—each satellite dish cost $250,000. There were a limited number of wire or cable connections used, only over short distances and within UNCA compounds so as to ensure that they would not be damaged. Each UNCA office had at least two and up to four satellite phones (V-SAT phones), but in practice most phone calls were made using mobile phones, because the V-SAT system was restricted to the communications network supported by the UN and was also less convenient—their position was fixed in the public part of the office and the MA's office, so that one could not call from one's desk or in private.

The UN intranet[19] and access to the Internet were limited to the same organizations supported by the radio and satellite phone network. When the mission began in June 1999, the Internet was only available in Pristina and Previca. Staff working in the municipalities were assigned e-mail accounts, but they had to drive to either Previca or Pristina to access the UN intranet on Lotus Notes. The Internet was finally extended to the municipalities in early 2001.

When computer networks link people as well as machines, they become social networks, or, in Barry Wellman's words, a "computer supported social network."[20] Access to the UN's intranet was limited to UNCA international staff, EU international staff, and the UNMIK international police. To access this system, each person had to have an "unmik.org" e-mail address. The messages on the intranet were generally security warnings, travel advisories, and notices about social events and welfare issues.

OSCE had its own ICT infrastructure, which mirrored that of the UN: a Motorola radio system, satellite telephones, and an intranet and e-mail system, with the address "omik.org." The OSCE intranet was more comprehensive than the UN intranet. In the OSCE intranet, a user could access almost all bureaucratic forms in the organization, fill them out online, and submit them to the relevant office. It also included travel, security, and social advisories. The OSCE staff in general did not use e-mail with other organizations on the ground.

KFOR also had its own ICT infrastructure, but it did not include an intranet or e-mail for use in the mission. Within the military, radios were used internally but face-to-face interaction was the primary means of communication between members of the military and other personnel in the mission.

NGOs looked after their own ICT needs: they used Internet service providers (ISPs) in Pristina or Belgrade. They did not use e-mail with other organizations on the ground in the mission but did use it with their home offices and their donors, some of which were based in Pristina, some outside Kosovo.

Thus, the design of the electronic or communications network did not correspond to the organizational design of the mission, and the computer-supported social network was not equivalent to the network of the mission. It incorporated three hierarchies (UNCA, CivPol, and the EU) but did not include the OSCE, KFOR, or NGOs, or the local police or municipal administration. The inclusion of three hierarchies indicates that the mission planners were cognizant of the need to get the communications network and organizational network to correspond as closely as possible, but logistical and political factors intervened with KFOR, OSCE, NGOs, and the local police and municipal administration. OSCE chose not to share the same communications infrastructure, wanting to maintain more control over its internal communications and viewing the UNCA as slower and hence possibly difficult to work with if OSCE were dependent upon it for communications (Hans Gesing, OSCE, interview). KFOR cited security as the reason for wanting to maintain its own internal communication and information structures, and the NGOs were not given the option of becoming part of the UNCA infrastructure.

The Consequences of the Design of the Physical Network

The consequences of the physical network design were significant for the ability of the organizations to be a network both within their own organizations and with the other organizations in the mission. Each of the hierarchical organizations displayed a degree of "organizational imperialism,"[21] because they refused to share costly assets and resources, which in turn inhibited their ability to interact as a network organization. Although each organization wanted and needed it to be a network, they were not willing to share certain assets. Ashutosh, the head of the UNCA communications infrastructure in the Previca region, explained the rationale behind the uneven access to the ICTs and the willingness to share expertise but not equipment. "We control who has access to our communications network. We do not give equipment out to other people or organizations. NGOs and such, if they need technical expertise, we help them out. But not equipment. It is a question of resources. If we give radios to other organizations, they can misuse them, and we have no control. Right now, if someone is using the radio for something he or she should not be doing, we can take the radio away from him or her for two weeks or a month. But with NGOs we could not do that."

Network organizations usually focus functions on a given project simultaneously as opposed to sequentially and so require flattened organizations and more point-to-point communication. The lack of point-to-point communication across all the organizations made it difficult for the organizations to be as responsive as the environment demanded.

Given the possibility of security risks, network membership also requires a high degree of trust or commitment between parties. This in turn enables partners to make riskier investments or transfer unfinished goods (in the private sector), knowing that disputes from unforeseen events will be handled amicably and equitably. Vertical organizations avoid problems with trust and risk by vertically integrating assets they require, as the UNCA and KFOR did in Kosovo. But given that they were also participating in a network organization, this led to problems.

Example of problem The absence of point-to-point communication between key organizations, the vertical integration of key assets within KFOR, and the low level of trust produced a potentially violent situation in the mixed Serb and Albanian village of Slavina in the municipality of Banshik. The KFOR engineering battalion had been instructed to undertake more engineering projects for the Serb population, because they did not want to be perceived by the Serbs as pro-Albanian, in light of their existing projects with the majority population. The engineering battalion, under an officer who was the KFOR liaison with the UNCA in Banshik, proceeded to dig a trench for a water pipe, which the Serb residents had asked them not to do without consulting the Albanians, as we saw in Chapter 4. The liaison major had not consulted with the UNCA, and the local Albanian village leader, in a nice illustration of nontechnical point-to-point communication, immediately brought in Terry Peterson, the Banshik UN municipal administrator, to stop him.

Point-to-point communication is especially important when organizational members at the local level are balancing the conception and execution of tasks within their own organization and fluctuating local knowledge that complicates the carrying out of those tasks. The KFOR major insisted to the MA that he had to follow his orders from the region and proceed with the project, even in the face of the opposition of both communities. Administrative fiat within KFOR ran up against the local network way of solving problems, because Peterson brokered and eventually got a negotiated agreement between all parties. He could have chosen to make it a dispute between the two hierarchies, the UNCA and KFOR, but he realized that any solution would have to be local. Accordingly, he brought all the relevant parties together to seek a solution—KFOR, UNCA, Albanians and Serbs, and a representative of the local utility company.

An IT backbone can help integrate the network organization by providing the means for data sharing and integration.[22] Strong links can potentially flatten an organizational hierarchy by attenuating status distinctions and enabling a redistribution of resources, decision rights, power, and control.[23] The limited nature of the physical network between the organizations in Kosovo severely inhibited this flattening in the network organization. Within the organizations, however, there was more progress in moving toward a flatter organization. With both the UNCA and OSCE, remote locations were in close touch with the region and center as a result of the physical network. However, although the design of each internal network enabled each person to be accessible by e-mail, so that there could be point-to-point communication within the UNCA, OSCE, and KFOR respectively, in practice the flows of communication were vertical, not lateral. Peterson and his DMA, Orash Fatoohi, complained that at the weekly meeting of the six municipal administrators at the regional level, they were the only municipality that talked about concrete issues at the local level; the other municipalities were primarily concerned with administrative issues internal to the UNCA.

As boundaries become more permeable, employees are members of both their own hierarchical organization and the network organization. In the business literature, Charles Handy describes this as members experiencing a "dual citizenship" of affiliation with their project team (here, the municipality) and with their company (here, the organization).[24] They have both in-group and out-group ties yet work to achieve a larger social integration. But they need shared goals, a common background, and a collective vision.[25]

The difficulties of enforcing separation of resources when the organizational boundaries are blurred were apparent in the sharing of equipment by CivPol and the local Kosovo police (KPS). They shared the same building and the same offices and worked together in teams. Yet officially, KPS personnel were not permitted to use the UN radios or Internet. Ashutosh, in the UN office in Previca, said: "You have a situation where an UNMIK international police officer and a KPS officer are sharing the same room and of course, the KPS uses the UNMIK phone and sometimes radio. But if I get a request for another V-SAT phone, I go to the place myself to see who is in the office; if it is a KPS [officer], I cannot give another phone." This had the unfortunate consequence of reducing the shared sense of mission intrinsic to the production of trust, ease of information transfer, and collaborative problem solving.

On a practical local level, having uncoordinated media of communication reduces the degree of responsiveness of the network. I was driving with Peterson to Pristina when we came upon a traffic accident. Peterson did not have a direct link to the KPS, because they do not have the use of UNCA communications equipment. He called on the radio in the UNCA car to CivPol in Banshik, who then told the KPS, who sent a car to the scene. The road was blocked as a result of the crash, and there were no injuries; however, the delay due to the circuitous route to the police could potentially have serious consequences in a security situation, for instance, in a riot or potentially riot-producing situation, neither of which was uncommon.

Employees' identities as expressed in their e-mail addresses were a constant reminder of their "in" or "out" status. Only UNCA international staff, civilian and police, and EU international staff had unmik.org e-mail addresses. Because communications was so central and information flow was so critical to the mission, this distinction was felt keenly. On a practical level, it made it that much more difficult to contact somebody outside of one's own particular physical network. Psychologically, it made it difficult to think of oneself as being part of the same organization, or if that was clear, that one had equal status with other members. Lawrence Gomes, the EU officer in Previca, felt that the UNCA regarded the EU (which shared the building) as a nuisance, evidenced by the long wait and fight the EU had to endure to get access to the UNCA intranet and e-mail system on more than one computer.

Initially, the UNCA refused to give more access, and eventually the issue had to go all the way to New York before it was resolved in favor of the EU getting access to the Internet on another three computers. They got it, Gomes said, "not because we are part of UNMIK and are entitled. . . . we had to beg for it. . . . I tried everything, and eventually we got them to sign a memorandum that they will cooperate with us." Neither Gomes's internationals nor his local staff had UNCA e-mail accounts. He argued for and got two accounts, one of which was used for the twenty-two people who worked with him in Previca, who needed the information relayed on Lotus Notes to do their job. "If we had eumik.org, all my twenty-two staff would have their own e-mail account[s]," he said. "I have two Lotus Notes accounts. . . . If you send mail to me, everyone can open it, can read it. If it's confidential or personal, tough luck. I sometimes use my Hotmail or Yahoo account, but it doesn't look very professional, you know?" He concluded: "Being part of UNMIK means that my international staff is less important than a UN [local] driver."

Hans Gesing, in the OSCE headquarters in Pristina, said that the exclusion of OSCE staff from the social events announced over Lotus Notes had serious consequences for the identification of people with the overall mission and for establishing ties that would be useful in their work. The absence of such opportunities to socialize decreased the amount of trust, information exchange, and collaborative problem-solving capabilities shared by the organizations.

KFOR was particularly set apart, because it had a completely separate communications system from UNMIK. Ashutosh, who was in charge of IT infrastructure for the UNCA in the Previca region, spoke of the logistical difficulties this gave rise to. He said in disgruntlement:

> Our communications system is totally separate from KFOR. They do not even let us into their base camps. We do have some of our equipment in there, but we are not allowed to go in without liaising with the KFOR liaison officer here on the third floor or the UNMIK Military Liaison Officer.[26] But it can take two hours or more to do that, so this can be problematic. KFOR does not want to hook into our communications system. They want to be separate for security reasons.

Besides the occasional difficulty of the maintenance of the equipment stored on the KFOR base, the lack of a link between the KFOR communications system and the UNCA system was a nuisance at the local level. The KFOR liaison officers did not have cell phones or e-mail addresses that could be used for liaison purposes. The only point of contact was a face-to-face encounter. This could be done at the weekly four-pillar, or interagency, meetings, but outside of that, it was more problematic. In addition, the UNCA in Banshik had daily drop-ins by the KFOR liaison officers, Peterson's breakfast meeting with the French military each Monday, his drop-in visits to the UAE's two military camps on a weekly basis, and the encounters most nights in the restaurant frequented by the French military. The UN in Thezren only had the official encounters—the interagency meeting and the weekly security meeting, unless they drove up to the KFOR bases to request security. Many channels of communication produced more complete flows of information; fewer channels inhibited the free flow of information between the organizations.

The Impact of Available ICTs on Interaction

The communication and information physical structure could be used to improve information transfer and to facilitate cooperative problem solving, but by building on rather than replacing traditional forms of networking. Barry Wellman points out that concerns about whether on-line ties can be strong ties is missing the point; although Internet technologies can transcend time and space, not all ties are either totally on-line or totally off-line.[27] Much on-line contact is between people who see each other in person, and people mix e-mail communication with face-to-face communication. Conversations started in one medium continue in another. The amount of time spent in face-to-face meetings could potentially be reduced. "Otherwise there are meetings, meetings, meetings, all the time. They come to the municipality and it's talk, talk, talk for an hour and the afternoon is gone by the time you [i.e., all those who have to leave their place of work for the meeting] go somewhere and come back. Now the situation is calming down a bit, a lot of the meeting discussions could be accomplished by e-mail" (Giampiero, UNCA, Banshik, interview).

Research has linked the technical characteristics of computer-mediated communication to task group outcomes such as increased participation, more egalitarian participation, more ideas offered, and less centralized leadership.[28] From the contrasting experiences of Banshik and Thezren, it would appear that more egalitarian participation and less centralized leadership must be there alongside or prior to the use of information technologies to unlock the IT possibilities for enhancing these qualities.

The Internet can also contribute to the formal or informal nature of the institutional culture. Humorous stories and Internet items circulated constantly in Banshik. "Air force come and they bomb your home" ran a song to the tune of Harry Belafonte's "Day-O (Banana Boat Song)" played at loud volume by the MA, Peterson, in the office the day following the initial U.S. bombing of Afghanistan. A computerized photograph combining President Bush and a Taliban mullah, complete with turban and beard, was circulated by Fatoohi and Peterson and put up on the wall of the office.

UN officers did use e-mail within the UNCA for purposes other than reporting and transfer of information. IT allows decentralization and the removal of status distinctions, so that power and influence no longer derive from rank but from persuading others to accept a particular interpretation of the data.[29] As expertise becomes critical, resources then flow, not to hierarchical posts, but to obvious centers of competence.[30] Henry, the Thezren local community officer (LCO),[31] was particularly adept at maximizing his contacts with his chain of command up to the Community Affairs Office in Pristina. "The fact is that the most consistent way of keeping in touch is my UN web mail. I work with the Department of

Community Affairs in Pristina, and I have to be in touch with them a lot. For example, at the end of this year, we have a lot of money left over. I've been in touch with them regularly about what projects I might be interested in getting funded. I'm in touch with them on e-mail a lot." Henry's counterpart in Banshik was not even aware of the money left over, money that Henry procured by simply sending brief proposals by e-mail to the center. "I mentioned all this money I got, and Charlotte [LCO, Banshik] was completely unaware of it. For greenhouses, agricultural projects . . . I put in my request by e-mail with a brief description of the project and I got it." It was not his rank or status that made the crucial difference but his ability to persuade others to accept a particular interpretation of the data or facts, that such money could be put to good use for certain projects that he was devising in Thezren.

The UNCA leadership in the two municipalities used information technology in different ways, and their use reflected the institutional characteristics of their network organizations. When the MA in Thezren wanted to see somebody, he would summon that person to a meeting in his office; he regarded most of the e-mail he received as "not very useful" and said he preferred to use the fax. He did not use e-mail for networking purposes. Peterson used the Internet as a networking tool and saw its potential as a resource beyond sending information more easily and faster within the organization. He had two electronic address books with approximately 1,000 contacts, one alphabetical by name and the second organized by occupation, including "warlords" and "kings." Peterson said in an interview:

> I'd be interested in finding a web site that I could go to where it could tell me other ideas on how to deal with emerging democracies and the developing world and people who have done that kind of thing before. But who else out there has done this? It'd be like AOL online when you don't understand the system. You can call AOL and say, "Please tell me how to do this." . . . You don't talk to the U.S. Army, because there's nobody in the U.S. Army whose ever done this before. . . . There's a guy based in Washington, D.C., whom I've written a couple of articles with, and when I really don't understand, I go to him [and say], "Tell me about this." He will come back to me and explain the world in one page. I have an extraordinarily good address system and a very good filing system and. . . . I have a computer full of very bright people [and] if I really don't understand something, I'll pop them off a message.

Furthermore, the egalitarian nature of the Internet encouraged the making of requests and the response to them. "It helps solve the problem of inaccessibility. If I want to see or talk to somebody not physically in reach or heavily guarded, then I can send it through," Fatoohi told me in an interview.

The hierarchies' focus on using ICTs within their own organizations but not between them was not readily recognized—reflecting and reinforcing the low level of identification with the mission as a whole compared to identification with one's own hierarchical organization. There was cognizance of the limitations of the physical infrastructure. Such a shared infrastructure was seen as forthcoming and as a potential resource that was not being used. DMA Fatoohi said: "I'm not communicating through IT with other organizations *yet*" (his emphasis). Although almost all UNCA employees extolled the advantages of using e-mail and the Internet within their own organizations, only Fatoohi and Henry spontaneously lamented the failure to use it for communicating with other organizations. "There is no exchange of e-mail between the agencies, and that's a pity," Henry said. "The police, OSCE, KFOR, all these people have e-mail, [and] we could work much more closely."

Limitations on the Use of ICTs

Besides the limitations imposed by the physical design of the network to using ICTs, there were limitations to their optimal use that were peculiar to the environment and applied to all organizations. The lack of a working telecommunications system in Kosovo meant that all equipment had to be shipped in from outside. The capacity of all organizations' Internet link and the speed of it was limited by radio and satellite signals. E-mail attachments beyond a very small size could not be sent over the Internet or intranet, and when there was a power cut (which was typically three or four times a day), the connection would be lost, along with anything the employee was working on at the time. The connection was very slow—it took on average three or four times longer to open an e-mail than it did in America. This was a significant reason why employees kept their time e-mailing to a minimum. Within the UNCA system, Lotus Notes did not allow the user to trash the message until it had been opened, which led to much consternation. Peterson and Fatoohi were so incensed about the time lost as e-mail "grinds away" that they initially pretended that their Lotus Notes were not working and requested that vital e-mail be sent to their free, personal accounts. Each person had a Yahoo or AOL or Hotmail account in addition to the official or professional UNMIK e-mail, and they used their personal accounts as much as possible in their professional work.

A further limitation to the optimal working of the physical ICT infrastructure was the assumption on the part of organizations not only that their employees would be willing to use e-mail but also that they were able to use it. This is important, because often employees do not choose to use e-mail; rather, it is a condition of their employment.[32] Certainly, in Kosovo, in the UNCA, OSCE, NGOs, EU, and police, there was an assumption that everyone knew how to use the Internet and e-mail. In the UNCA, initiation for new employees included a brief meeting with the IT department at the regional level, where they were assigned computers. Getting an e-mail address tended to take longer. Although there was training available, it was not offered; the assumption was that if someone needed training, he or she would ask for it. This is potentially problematic for older personnel who are less familiar with the technology and might be reluctant to admit that they don't know how to use it or might not see it as important, and hence might not avail themselves of what training there is. In an interview, Khalid Shamon, the MA in Thezren, expressed his belief in the importance of technology and said he had been using e-mail and the Internet for some years. However, Hideyaki, the most junior member of the UNCA staff in Thezren, told me that each morning, he had to print out the main news headlines from the Internet for the MA, who would choose the articles he wanted Hideyaki to print out, because "the MA doesn't know how to use the Internet."

John of the OSCE in Banshik said that some of the older people in the OSCE regional office in Previca had asked him not to send material by e-mail, explaining, "Some of the older people in Previca are not so adept at computers. People fifty years old or up who are not at ease in the digital world, don't really use attachments and the like. I'm a junkie, everything you send me is great, it keeps things off my desk."

This was less of an issue for the OSCE, because it has a different employee profile—its staff are younger, with more diverse backgrounds, and not part of a permanent structure, with its tendency to IT obsolescence. Training was also given a higher priority in the OSCE, because so much of the organization's internal workings were dependent on using the intranet. The NGOs and militaries also had a younger age profile and more technical knowledge and training. The NGOs saw IT as critical. "We couldn't do our jobs without it," said Tim, a 27-year-old architect working with the NGO K-LED.

The views or attitudes of the personnel of the different organizations as to what could be achieved using e-mail, the intranet, and the Internet were a final limitation on the optimal use of the physical network design. In Thezren, the person who most appreciated the Internet and who saw its potential in networking was Henry, aged thirty-four, whose previous career had been that of an entertainment agent, a role in which he had spent 95 percent of his workday on the phone or Internet. "Workwise, it's critical—even though I'm in a little town called Thezren, the fact that I have e-mail . . . makes an enormous difference."

For most employees of the UNCA, besides the time and effort saved in transmitting and receiving information from the regional and central levels of the UN, the primary benefit of having access to e-mail and the Internet was personal. Most UNCA employees said that the ability to stay in touch with loved ones at home was the most beneficial aspect of e-mail. E-mail and the Internet were seen as critical for morale, because staff were members of a global network of family and friends that provided companionship, information, and social support. The ability to stay in touch with loved ones and social networks outside of Kosovo was the most frequent response of those asked what the biggest advantage of having e-mail was. Ashutosh, the UNCA officer in Previca, said that he got two lines of e-mail every morning from his family in India and that this enabled him to work free of worry for the rest of the day. People also said that they used it to "stay in touch with the outside world." Ricky, the IT officer for the region, monitors the UNCA's use of the Web and says that the most frequently visited sites are financial ones; UN staff can manage their bank accounts, bills, and financial affairs over the Internet. The second largest use is for news; the most frequented sites are Yahoo and MSNBC, followed by individual language sites.

The Mobile Phone Network

Unexpectedly, the one medium able to overcome the physical and institutional limitations of the network organization was the mobile phone network, which was what did most to link people within all the organizations in the network. It was independent of the organizational network, in terms of provision, control, and maintenance. Bernard Kouchner, the first special representative of the UN secretary-general in Kosovo, opened a global competition for companies to bid to establish a mobile network in Kosovo. Alcatel, a French mobile phone service provider, won the pub-

lic competition and now provides the mobile phone network in Kosovo.
It was available to anyone willing to pay for it. Thus, it was the one network that the KPS and the local municipal administration could share
with all the organizations. There was no real competition to this company except from Mobtel, a Belgrade-based mobile phone company that
the majority of Albanians would not use for political reasons.

Out of more than a hundred nonmilitary internationals I met, only one
did not have a mobile phone. Although not part of the official infrastructure provided by the organizations, it was the medium most frequently used, and all the organizations pay for phone charges incurred by
employees in the course of their official duties. UNMIK or OSCE or the
EU did not pay for their personal calls or for the purchase of the phone
itself, the average price of which was the equivalent of about $185. The
mobile phone network was not present in the initial days of the mission
and most of the UNCA staff saw its introduction as more critical than the
Internet. Especially for those who spent a significant amount of time in
the field, the mobile phone was described as "indispensable." Henry
(UNCA, Thezren) said that it liberated him from fixed locations; people
called *him*, not his office. The use of mobile phones allowed workers to
make the best use of traveling time, and of time between meetings, if
those meetings were not in their base office. The use of mobile phones
had considerably reduced reliance on the radio network. "I'm so used to
my phone—I don't use the radio really any more," Henry said.

The closest thing to a "virtual organization"[33] in Kosovo was the one
based on the mobile phone network and, to a lesser extent, commercial
e-mail. Every international had a free, commercial e-mail account in addition to an organizational one. Most locals working with the UNCA
also had free, commercial e-mail accounts that they checked on UNCA or
OSCE or NGO or CivPol computers—whichever organization they were
working with. Because the UNMIK intranet (Lotus Notes) was so slow,
many of the UN staff chose to use their commercial account for professional purposes if they already knew the people they were communicating
with. The CivPol commander in Banshik announced at the weekly four-
pillar meeting in the UNCA office in Banshik that he was going home to
the United States for three weeks, and added: "I'll be away on vacation
but will be running the office through e-mail. You can e-mail [my Hotmail account] if you want, anyone." The hierarchies' official physical infrastructure was less successful in promoting networking on the ground
than the uncontrolled mobile phone network and commercial e-mail.

The Role of ICT Within Organizations

The more networked the organizations were internally, the easier it was for them to be part of the external network organization. A requirement of a networked organization is the free flow of information, and information technology was heavily impacting the flow of information and the management of information and knowledge within the organizations. Acquisition and distribution or the obtaining and sharing of information were enormously improved within the hierarchies by information technology. The professional advantage cited most frequently was speed and ease of transmittal of information. Before e-mail, the UN and OSCE officers in the municipalities would have to deliver their paperwork, including daily and weekly reports, to Previca by car, an hour's round trip from Thezren, and a forty-minute round trip from Banshik.[34] Maura McSweeney, the UNCA regional officer who compiled the weekly report for the region, would have to wait for this hand delivery before combining it into a report for the mission's head office, and then she would have to get the paper delivered by car to that HQ in Pristina. The whole process could take two or three days. The central and regional compiled reports were then recirculated to the municipalities, which again took two or three days. Now each municipality e-mails her an electronic report, and she compiles them and e-mails her combined report to Pristina. OSCE followed a similar hierarchical reporting procedure and also said that e-mail saved a significant amount in terms of human resources and physical resources (use of cars and time). The amount of time saved is of enormous importance to employees in both Banshik and Thezren. John (OSCE, Banshik) said: "It saves a lot of time, that's the biggest change, because much of my time was spent simply driving documents, administration, procedural things, bringing forms to Previca. That might take an hour and a half of my day . . . now I have a lot of time to spend working in the field instead of spending it driving around. It's a phenomenal tool."

The importance of information assets to network organizations raises important questions about managing information resources.[35] Theories of organizational learning provide a framework by breaking information management down into acquisition, distribution, interpretation, and memory.[36] Organizational memory describes the storage of information for ready access and future use. Information technologies play a vital role in this. Hence, information technology was improving the efficiency of information flow within the hierarchical organizations tremendously.

But as technologies provide "affordances" and not determinants, the use of technologies has to fit the institutional environment of the organizations. The hierarchical organization in an environment like Kosovo faces two problems with management of information. One is the problem of diffusing existing information and interpretation to joining members. The other is the problem of maintaining organizational history and experience in-house when members leave.[37] With the high turnover of personnel in Kosovo and the potential loss of learning, a technology-based organizational memory may lessen the effect and greatly improve the management of intellectual capital.[38] The organizations in Kosovo handled this differently. Although the UNCA had the infrastructure for managing information, it did not have an efficient institutional mechanism for ensuring storage and transmission of institutional history. Each municipality was asked to produce a daily and weekly report, but there was no sanction if they did not do so, and there was no online database of municipal reports, except that maintained at his initiative for the municipality of Banshik by the MA, Peterson. Banshik had produced a detailed report every working day since the start of the mission, providing a detailed picture of the process of institution building and the relations between the organizations and the population. In Thezren, when I asked to see the equivalent institutional history, I was told it did not exist. The previous MA, Jon, had not kept a daily record, and the current MA did so only sporadically. There was no written record of activities in Thezren for the first two years of the mission and only an infrequent and sketchy one for the six months prior to my study. Thus, there is no information to manage or to be used elsewhere.

Maura McSweeney, the assistant to the UN regional administrator in Previca, said that there was no system for passing on knowledge to your successor in your position. It was entirely dependent on individual care and initiative, which led to great waste of time and resources. Maura said: "Institutional history? The UN has none. KFOR has. When I leave will I spend a month putting together a dossier for my successor? No. Nothing is done. Not so much as a presentation. So the wheel keeps getting reinvented, and people are just getting the hang of their jobs when they have to leave. Neil Cameron, for example [head of infrastructure for the UNCA in Previca region], when that man goes, he takes all the knowledge about the infrastructure with him." The French were passing on information more efficiently she observed. This, she said, is partly because of the higher turnover in KFOR, but also reflects the French military's institutional mechanisms for transmittal of institutional history. "The French are in and out every four months, so institutional memory is crucial [for them]." Again, within the UNCA, realizing the "affordances" of technology is to a great extent dependent on personal initiative. David Allen, the blue beret who is the military liaison for UNMIK and KFOR (he is with the UNCA, not KFOR) said: "E-mail is a wonderful thing. I'm already e-mailing my replacement every two or three days. I e-mail him every report I write, I e-mail him little notes on what kit to bring, what kit not to bring, what he should be studying, learning, what things are available here, what's not."

The production of too much information without management is one potential pitfall for organizations using new technologies. The OSCE had better knowledge management, in that more tasks were done on-line, but still faced the problem of information overload. Gesing, a cabinet member of the OSCE organization in Kosovo, said that there was a danger of information overload with the deluge of reports being produced within OSCE. OSCE produced reports on everything it did, and everyone constantly had to record what they were doing. Unfortunately, as Gesing pointed out, these reports were mostly descriptive, when what would be most useful would be analysis. "What we're faced with is an abundance of reporting on seminars, workshops, which are of no use to the outside world at all. They're not interested in why OSCE is organizing a women's workshop in a particular municipality. They want an analysis, to know how these activities tie into and impact on the life of the municipality, rather than reporting on the details of the activities themselves. For example, we would like to know whether the main obstruction for us in the municipality proves to be the PDK [Democratic Party of Kosovo] or not, what's going on, and how does that tie into regional trends." Like Fatoohi, the DMA in Banshik, who says the Internet is like a knife—"It can kill or it can feed"—Gesing sees IT as a double-edged sword. "In earlier times, people would send in a fax and make sure the information in there was succinct, because it would create another physical thing to read. And it takes time to fax, to send the admin assistant down to the fax room. It really creates a hassle. You'd better put things on one page rather than three pages. You better make up your mind beforehand what you want to report. Nowadays, you would have everything on it, useless stuff. You really have to cut the crap, to see where this little piece of information fits."

As McSweeney in the UNCA and several other internationals confirmed, KFOR had a very good system for transmitting information and knowledge to each new contingent. A large part of its mission was to gather intelligence, so KFOR in theory had a high level of knowledge of who was who and what was going on. However, there was a substantial amount of information, tacit knowledge of the field and of workers in other organizations, that could not be transmitted so easily, and misinterpreting it could give rise to security risks both for the forces themselves and the internationals and local communities. KFOR therefore focused on face-to-face interaction, which facilitated understanding across cultural and organizational boundaries.

An inadequate system of institutional memory can be devastating for institutional learning, and the system in the UNCA was a waste of the potential of IT to broadly distribute information and promote organizational learning by rapidly diffusing ideas.[39] Increased sharing might form the basis of better decisions and learning-curve effects; it might also amplify knowledge generation by focusing additional sources of expertise on important issues within the network.[40]

The Future

ICTs are playing an increasingly key role in the network organization of UNMIK in the postconflict environment of Kosovo and will play a key role in similar interventions. In Kosovo, they contributed to the sharing and cooperative use of resources, as well as to the building up of trust and identification with the network organization's overall goals (the mission). The use of ICTs increased the exchange of information and contributed to collaborative problem solving, all of which ultimately contribute to the degree of cooperation, which determines the extent to which the mission's goals can be realized. The direction of change is clear—more extensive deployment and use of ICTs. The organizations involved are in a process of transformation, and the lessons learned in Kosovo will facilitate this process. Lessons from Kosovo include an emerging realization that the limitations imposed by the design of the overall physical network and the persistent tendency to organizational imperialism of all the organizations made networking with other organizations very difficult.

The most comprehensive electronic networks were those that the organizations had no control over—the mobile phone and commercial e-mail. All the organizations, all levels of personnel, and, crucially, the local police and municipality used them. A comprehensive UNMIK intranet would have had the potential to connect the international organizations, but the limited version that was established excluded some people and created "in" and "out" groups, because there was no interactive space shared by all, such as a missionwide intranet. A shared intranet would arguably provide the sense of "dual citizenship,"[41] or identification with the mission as well as one's own organization, that would yield a sufficient social base for e-mail to be used interorganizationally. In Kosovo, in 2001, e-mail was primarily used within organizations. It was not used between organizations, partly because at the embryonic stage of UNMIK as a network organization, there was a need to have at least initial face-to-face interaction or voice-to-voice interaction with people from other organizations, and partly because it was only slowly occurring to the organizations that it could be used interorganizationally. The technology provides "affordances," but ultimately it is the organizational structure and institutional environment (within and between organizations) that determines whether technologies will be used and what technologies will be used for different tasks.

Within the hierarchies, each organization was grappling with the organizational consequences of introducing ICTs—wanting the flexibility and knowledge management such technologies made possible but unsure of how to alter its organizational structure and institutional culture to realize this potential. The flow of information had definitely increased with the introduction of ICTs, but knowledge management had yet to catch up—the biggest danger was being drowned in a deluge of detail while suffering a dearth of useful and non-time-consuming analysis. In addition, the importance of institutional memory in a situation with such diverse organizations and high turnover of personnel was also slowly being realized, as was the potential of ICTs to transform intraorganizational coordination. In sum, ICTs were slowly transforming organizational practice to encompass what was required by participation in a network organization such as UNMIK, but that change was as yet unevenly distributed and unevenly advanced.

CHAPTER SIX

Transactive Memory

The environment in Kosovo demanded flexibility and responsiveness. All the organizations needed one another, and it was not enough to have an efficient flow of information within each organization. There not only needed to be structures and a facilitating institutional culture for sharing information across organizational boundaries but also structures and a culture that were equipped to deal with a very turbulent environment. It was turbulent not only because of the security situation but also because the organizations were engaged in institution building in an environment that had been totally destroyed. Both internally and externally, too, the organizations had to deal with a high turnover of personnel.

The complexity of the environment meant that the high turnover of personnel hampered the process by which shared information acquires meaning and is translated into shared maps, frames, or schemas, or interpretation.[1] The appreciation of this was not always present within the organizations. Despite Terry Peterson's strenuous efforts to keep each new batch of French military "on the same sheet of music," the battalion that arrived during my time in Kosovo forgot to leave word at the gate to allow Peterson to enter one Monday morning and were lackluster in their response to his communication of information when the meetings did happen. Peterson distributed his weekly reports precisely because they contained not only description but also analysis of events. As a consequence, the recipients of the reports could contribute to a shared interpretation of what they were doing.

In the UNCA in Thezren, some facts were shared, but not in written form. There was sharing of facts at the interagency and security meetings, but from what I observed, these facts were not put in shared maps or frames or schemas. According to G. P. Huber, more learning occurs when information is shared more broadly, when more numerous and varied interpretations are developed, when different organizational members comprehend each other's interpretations—even if their own interpretations differ, and when latent information is recognized as potentially useful.[2] So how did the use of various ICTs affect this sharing of information and common learning? How did it fit in with face-to-face interaction?

Different Degrees of Social Presence in Different Communications Media

Information and communication technologies in contemporary organizations make it feasible for a broad range of work groups to be formed with members who do not necessarily work in close proximity or within the same organization. The people in the international organizations used a range of ICTs—face-to-face meetings, cell phones, land telephones, radio, e-mail, Internet, and intranet. However, they did not use these media interchangeably. The choice of media was determined by the "fit" of the medium for the environment, both internally, within the hierarchies, and externally, in the field with the other organizations. The choices made by the different organizations yield insights into the role of such technologies in turbulent environments like Kosovo.

The amount of information and the variety of different perspectives make the interpretation of frames of understanding critically important. The more interpretations there are available, the greater the likelihood of finding common ground for working with other organizations. But this can only be achieved at the local municipal level—interpretation is based not only on information but also on the knowledge created by interaction and communications on the ground. A variety of ICTs are needed, and just as important, an appreciation of which is most appropriate for which type of interaction or situation.

The principle of "requisite variety" aids our understanding of the importance of having a diverse range of ICTs for use by a diverse group of organizations. Drawing from general systems theory, the principle of requisite variety contends that an organization's internal regulatory mechanisms must be as diverse as the environmental complexity with which it must contend.[3] Networks can be seen as a response to the principle of requisite variety. "It has become increasingly clear that the organizational

[handwritten margin note: The role of ICTs in turbulent environments]

form associated with flexible specialization is the network," M. J. Piore argues.[4] Contingency theory helps explain why there is no one best organizational form and organizations must map structural elements to structural variables in the environment.[5] Thus, in the turbulent environment in Kosovo, with different organizations using different media and information technologies, members of organizations had constantly to shift to match the technology they used with the communication needs of the project or task they were working on with another organization.

The communications medium or information technology chosen for use depends on the type of communication involved and the environment in which the communication takes place. "Rich" channels of communication, or channels of communication with a high degree of social presence, are needed for equivocal and uncertain communication where the meanings are ambiguous and values and schemas for interpreting may be different, or where data may be missing.[6] For instance, when UNCA personnel were communicating with KFOR, their schemas and values were different, and they did not always understand the process of operations in the other organization, so "rich" communication was required to prevent misunderstandings and miscommunication. "Richness" can be measured in two ways, in terms of bandwidth and synchrony. Bandwidth refers to the ability to exchange information from all human senses: sight, hearing, and smell.[7] Face-to-face communication has more bandwidth than telephone communication, telephone communication has more than voice mail, and voice mail has more than e-mail.[8] Synchrony refers to whether people can communicate at the same time. Face-to-face interaction and telephone communication are synchronous (except when one leaves a message). E-mail and voicemail are not synchronous.

The importance of bandwidth and synchrony depends on the environment. In Kosovo, as indeed in any network organization, the goals of the mission could not be attained without trust; the social information provided by high bandwidth was extremely important.[9] Telephone communication, voice mail, and e-mail differ in bandwidth, and hence in how much social information they provide.[10] Telephone communication allows people to exchange more social information than voice mail. Voice mail allows people to exchange more social information than e-mail.

In Kosovo, face-to-face interaction was the preferred mode between organizations at the local level, because the environment and differences in organizational cultures required a high degree of trust, the production of which needed a high degree of bandwidth. When face-to-face interaction was not possible between organizations, the mobile phone was used. When that was not possible, voice mail was used. Only then would e-mail be used, if it were available. Within organizations, face-to-face interaction was used first if the person was in the same office. If not, e-mail was used before the mobile phone for work matters. If it was a social matter or a complex issue, the mobile phone was more likely to be used. This was the pattern in both UNCA offices and in both OSCE offices.

Interpersonal, face-to-face contact is important. From an organizational perspective, dispersed work teams require social as well as technical support.[11] Studies of collaboration among scientific communities suggest that an initial period of physical proximity is necessary to build trust and to come to a consensus on the focus of proposed projects.[12] In turbulent environments where nonroutine complex problems have to be solved, face-to-face interaction as the basis of cooperation and information exchange is crucial. Even if the relationship continues virtually, an initial face-to-face meeting is generally seen as critical for communication. Fatoohi, the DMA in Banshik, said: "The most important things can only be done through human contact. You cannot send an e-mail saying, 'Send us a couple of million dollars' [laughs]. Later, when they know you, then you can do a lot [by e-mail], but in early contact, the human contact is essential, in my experience, especially in the area of finance." Jacques, the UNCA agricultural officer in Banshik, agreed: "For me the first face-to-face contact is absolutely necessary. But after[ward]—why not?" Once the human contact has been made, working by e-mail can save time and resources.

Communication outside of the chain of command and outside one's department is more likely to connect people having weak ties than those with strong ties.[13] Social information exchange is required to establish trust and maintain weak ties,[14] hence interorganizationally, after face-to-face interaction, the preferred and most frequently used mode of communication was the mobile phone. The synchrony of telephones allows a lot of information to be exchanged in a given unit of time, as well as providing ongoing feedback: people can adjust what they say to one another, correct misunderstandings, and fill in details. People perceive rapid exchange to be important for lateral communication,[15] as well as for collaborative planning and problem solving under uncertainty.[16] Because the telephone is synchronous, it allows people to get faster responses in a given unit of time than asynchronous technologies.[17]

"When I need an answer NOW I get on the phone," Peterson said. "I get ten e-mails a day, and eight of those would be business," John, the OSCE logistics officer in Banshik, said. "I just ask a question and wait for a response. It's usually a logistics question. If I have to go on and on about something, I wait till I see the person or I use the telephone." But sometimes, when people had their phones switched off or were out of range of a signal, asynchronous communication was used, usually voice mail between organizations. Within organizations, where the culture was familiar and understood, e-mail was used to ask questions. "I'd fire off an e-mail with a question and get back an answer, " John said. This was also true within the UNCA. Lateral communication is more likely to be collaborative and to require more discussion than vertical communication,[18] so employees engaged in lateral communication will tend to use the telephone. In Kosovo, they also strove to meet face-to-face as much as possible, using the telephone to check the availability of the person they needed to talk to. The OSCE people would always go to the UNCA, not the other way around, reflecting the UNCA's position as the hub of a municipality. KFOR would not use technology communicating with non-military organizations in the mission. The militaries were aware that theirs was an often misunderstood culture, especially by people with no knowledge or experience of the military, and they couldn't afford misunderstandings that might give rise to security risks. So KFOR only used the richest information medium—person-to-person contact.

The on-line storage of e-mail messages allows participants to be in different places and on different schedules, thus giving them more control over when they read and respond to messages. The rapid transmission of large files between individuals and among groups increases the speed of communication, supports collaborative work, and sustains both strong and weak ties.[19]

The Four-Pillar Interagency Meetings at the Municipal Level

At the local level, the variety of ICTs support and supplement interpersonal or face-to-face knowledge transfer and offer a means for optimizing knowledge transfer. Such point-to-point communication at the local level is essential, because decentralized conception and execution of issues and decisions is critical to the effective working of a network organization.

The effectiveness of the most direct point-to-point communication, the face-to-face interaction, was greatly influenced by the institutional rules and the environment, as the contrasting experiences of Banshik and Thezren demonstrate. The UNMIK network organization did establish an explicit, formal process for sharing of expertise and knowledge locally in the weekly interagency meetings. These were required meetings, intended to ensure compliance with the cooperative necessity of the mission. But as reactance theory suggests, forcing people to do something may produce exactly the opposite result, because people rebel against the constraints imposed on them.[20]

In Thezren, the feeling was one of compulsion, whereas in Banshik, the interagency meetings were felt to be extremely useful, and there was a sense of cooperation. As the Banshik UNCA recognized, knowledge sharing requires the transfer of knowledge across boundaries, along with the development of a shared understanding of the material, which less rigid organizational control facilitates. In Banshik, there was a lot of contact in addition to the weekly meeting, to the point where the organizations could be described as "groups of people who are informally bound together by shared expertise and passion for a joint enterprise."[21] These groups tended to interact regularly by meeting face-to-face and relying on technology to facilitate discussion. People belonged to such "communities of practice" because of a desire to exchange knowledge, but the network organization had to create an environment in which these communities of practice can thrive.

But as the interagency meeting was the only formal mechanism for bringing the organizations together on a weekly basis, the exchange of information at this meeting was critical. In order to ensure that all the knowledge that needed to be shared in order to maximize problem-solving effectiveness was available, the meetings brought together people representing different organizational functions, perspectives, and expertise. However, getting individuals to exchange information is not easy. Turning tacit and explicit knowledge into group-level knowledge is believed to be associated with the development of transactive memory.[22] This is a shared system for encoding, storing, and retrieving knowledge available to the group. Specifically, it involves directory updating, the process whereby the members of the group come to learn where knowledge is likely to be stored among group members (who knows what); information allocation, the process of distributing knowledge to the member(s) whose expertise is best suited for its storage; and information retrieval, the process of retrieving knowledge most effectively, given knowledge of expertise distribution in the group.

For instance, in Banshik, at one of the four-pillar meetings I attended, there were two instances of matching up "who knows what" and of distributing knowledge to the member(s) whose expertise was best suited to its storage. The process was quick and easy, because the participants knew whom to ask and clearly had a history of working together at these meetings. The police were matched up with OSCE over organizing security for the elections, and they agreed to meet later independently of the four-pillar meeting. Giampiero, the UNCA utilities officer, was matched up with the police to keep them informed about roadworks, and the police informed Giampiero of situations that public utilities could fix—for instance, where there was a large pothole. The UNHCR representative requested that KFOR coordinate with NGOs to distribute clothing, because there had been a lot of overlap.

The conversation was built on prior knowledge of who was in charge of what—each person asked the relevant party directly for what he or she needed, without having to ask whom to ask. Each participant also provided information that would be of relevance to others in the meeting and directed this knowledge to the person most concerned. There was no need to explain in detail; everyone was clearly familiar with the issues. The UNHCR representative was leaving and had brought along her replacement, who was introduced and followed the meeting closely. The meetings began with Peterson, the MA, bringing everyone up to date on pieces of news relevant to them, such as plans to move Serbs back to the villages they had fled from after the NATO campaign ended and the Albanians returned, and he also managed to comment on everything everyone said and to provide additional information. For example, Carolina from OSCE asked about a complaint by Serbs that their Albanian neighbors had cut the electricity—she had requested a police investigation. Peterson had looked into it and discovered that it was a blown fuse. Carolina (who is Spanish, and whose English is not fluent) thought "a blown fuse" was a person's name and asked: "Who is that?" to much laughter. She laughed too. Rather than there being a sense of having to maintain a serious, formal demeanor, there was a sense of sharing a "thick" amount of information, both explicit and tacit.[23]

Not least, this sharing showed that not all problems were necessarily related to ethnic hostility. There were also at least two or three meetings set up during the meeting, and the parties involved got together in small groups immediately afterward to work out the details. For example, Captain Delon, a relatively new KFOR liaison officer, arranged the security schedule for that week with the OSCE . At the end of my first four-pillar meeting in Banshik, I had been given an idea of what the different organizations did and which ones linked up with one another on what issues.

In Thezren, at the end of the first interagency meeting, my impression was of people who did not know what the others were doing, and there was very little discussion of cooperative projects. The typical response was to say, "Nothing to report" or to give a list of items an organization had worked on in the previous week; it was a reporting exercise, not a transactive one. When a party did ask for direct information, there was difficulty getting a direct answer. The gendarmes and KFOR did not usually have anything to report, and there seemed to be little prior knowledge of who knew what and who should be given the information. The police simply listed what they were doing, rather than asking for cooperation or seeking to brief interested participants. When an issue arose concerning "directory updating," "information allocation," or "retrieval coordination," there was clearly very little transactive memory.

Spanish KFOR requested information about an issue concerning electricity transformers. In two of the Serbian enclaves, the transformers were being changed. The larger enclave was getting a new one, and the second enclave was getting the one from the larger enclave, a secondhand transformer but more powerful than the one they were using. Spanish KFOR, who shared security with the French for the enclaves, wanted to know why the second village was getting a secondhand transformer. Daniel, the chair, did not know the answer to this and did not know whom to refer them to. In fact, the responsible person was Henry Ghosh, the UNCA local community officer, but Daniel did not know that, and Henry was not at the meeting. When the Spanish asked where the smaller village's used transformer would go, Daniel said in a sarcastic tone of voice, "You know that some of the villages here don't have any transformer. They were burned. So they will get it." Yet he knew nothing about the issue and did not ask when he didn't know.

Giampiero, the UN utilities officer in Banshik, who had formerly worked at the regional level, recalled a meeting from that time in Thezren that exhibited a startling lack of transactive memory or synergistic knowledge:

> Thedy [the Thezren DMA] is a normal person, but he was doing nothing. He has no kind of managerial capabilities; he was lost. One day at 5 P.M. in Thezren, there was a meeting. I was in charge of supervising a polling station and had to attend. This meeting was chaired by Thedy. He didn't say anything useful. We had a task force up there. . . . I was with a person from this task

force, and we were looking at these people. . . . the worst people in Thezren, few people, not motivated. People were doing nothing. An older Japanese person was there, with feet on table, six or seven people around, there to monitor the brick factory, money's been spent, nothing been done. Ozman was there, good person but totally lost. All these people just there, floating, waiting for instructions from Thedy, but Thedy was unable [to provide them].

Synergistic knowledge also needs to be created; this is the creation of tacit knowledge within an individual and explicit knowledge at the group level. For instance, two members of the group may have different ways of solving a problem, but together they come up with a new, third solution.[24] Synergistic knowledge is knowledge developed through the group's interaction. The synergistic solution might not emerge at the interagency meeting but at other meetings during the week. Most of the meetings and general interaction among the internationals in Banshik exhibited a higher degree of transactive memory and synergy than in Thezren. For instance, over lunch with Peterson and myself, the civil-military liaison officer in Banshik, a French Foreign Legion officer named deBurgh, suggested a solution to a problem faced by K-LED, an NGO that was distributing cows, which were being stolen from Serb recipients and then claimed as Albanian. He suggested that two different-colored breeds of cow be used—one for Serbs and one for Albanians, so that it would be clear when either ethnic group stole from the other.

ICTs and the Institutional Environment

The factor that determined the different outcomes in Banshik and Thezren, where the same organizations and the same ICTS were present, seems to have been the institutional mechanisms developed for the network organization in the municipality. The technology provides affordances, but ultimately it is the institutional environment that determines what technologies will be used for different tasks. The turbulence of the internal and external environment demands a variety of ICTs that can carry content of varying degrees of social presence. The effectiveness of information flow and exchange, and the effective use of ICTs in the networked organization, will depend on the availability of a wide range of technologies that can be used for appropriate tasks.

The face-to-face level of interaction in a networked organization is critical, because trust can only be developed between people from diverse organizations on the basis of at least one face-to-face meeting, and members of some organizations, like KFOR, feel that this is the safest mode of communication when dealing with organizations that might not understand their organization's culture. This is particularly the case when security—people's lives—is at stake. But as the contrast between interagency meetings and interaction in Banshik and Thezren shows, face-to-face interaction is no guarantee of effective communication. To build transactive memory, the institutional culture of a network organization must be in place. Such an appropriate network institutional culture would be necessary if e-mail were to be used between all the organizations. Equally, the very existence of an interactive space shared by all—for instance, a missionwide intranet—would arguably provide a sufficient social base for e-mail to be used interorganizationally. In the meantime, e-mail is primarily used within organizations, and face-to-face interaction and a range of ICTs are used between organizations with varying degrees of effectiveness.

The use of ICTs is a new and key variable in the workings of international interventions. ICTs are becoming an essential part of any interorganizational effort and have an important role to play in contributing to greater cooperation and more successful democratization, institution building, and reconstruction.

PART IV

Members of the Network

CHAPTER SEVEN

The UN Civil Administration and KFOR

All of the organizations in UNMIK and KFOR were in the process of internally transforming themselves into organizations that were capable of working effectively as part of a network organization. The UN mission in Kosovo was the first real attempt by the UN at governance, and it has offered an opportunity to see how these diverse organizations cooperating within one overarching project or mission, all playing an essential role in the establishment of peaceful, democratic governance, actually approached this task. The organizations involved have to maintain the integrity of their own organization and simultaneously identify with, and work with, the overall mission and network organization. The problem or challenge of providing security and of facilitating a democratic transition and of reconstructing the society after war is too big for any one hierarchical organization.

The range of expertise and resources required cannot be provided only by the United Nations or only by NATO or only by an NGO. Working cooperatively, however, they can achieve a significant amount. The aim is to create synergy: a whole that multiplies the value of its parts and generates increasing returns. As the word "returns" indicates, this concept is usually used in business contexts.[1] However, it is equally valid for multi-organizational humanitarian interventions. Among cooperative problem solvers, distributing portions of complex tasks allows the group to solve larger and more complex problems in less time than might be possible for individuals. Single agents face bounded rationality and finite resource constraints that are relaxed through cooperation.[2]

From a sociological perspective, coming together in a goal-directed ac-

tivity involves the creation of identity, norms, and processes for intera-
gent association and control, incorporating whatever organizational
processes and resources agents bring with them. In short, the major purpose in network organizations is to direct collective action toward common goals. In Kosovo, the major purpose of the UN-led mission was to
direct the action of all the organizations toward rehabilitating Kosovo,
maintaining peace, and building democratic institutions.

Each of the organizations involved was undergoing a transformation,
because almost all of them were increasingly functioning as network organizations, rather than being wholly hierarchical. The architecture and
culture of hierarchical organizations—vertical integration, functional
work groups, narrow job descriptions, and centralization of key decisions—can militate against successful construction and execution of network organization structures and processes that depend on decentralized
decisions, project teams, broader job descriptions, and trust. In the literature that concentrates on business firms, the attributes of a networked
organization are integration across functions, more emphasis on market
forces, less emphasis on organizational hierarchy, and flexibility—any
member can easily link to any other person, or information, horizontally
or vertically.[3] An individual's contribution to the ad hoc teams that arise
is based on knowledge, not formal position or title. The organization is
information-rich, and by connecting information, people, and skill (tal-
ent) together more effectively within the firm or organization, the organization in aggregate is made more effective.

The United Nations

There is no one in charge. Polite anarchy.
—Giampiero, a UNCA officer in Banshik,
on the UNCA in Kosovo

On the face of it, the UNCA was poorly equipped to function in an environment like Kosovo. The UN is run by a combination of career international civil servants and short-term contract hires. Procedures are heavily
bureaucratic and centralized. Officers in the field have little leeway to
take initiative, and decision making is very slow. Many of the operations
of UN agencies are hostage to special interest international politics and
are ransomed to whims of the member states that provide financial support.

The UN itself is aware that it needs to adapt to fit the challenges of the times. The changing environment internationally, the increase in recruits from the private sector,[4] and the enormous increases in organizational efficacy made possible by new information and communication technologies have generated an internal pressure to change. The slow, bureaucratic organization that was filled with careerists and managers hobbled by political considerations is feeling the strain, and there are attempts to change it. The very lack of planning and guidance has served to make visible what works and what does not in the UN when it is working with other organizations on the ground.

Based on what I observed and interviews with UN personnel, there are an "old" UN culture and a "new" UN culture that is struggling to emerge. The "old" and "new" are respectively reflected in the elements of the UN that are traditional and bureaucratic and those that are more comfortable with the ideas inherent in a network organization. For the "new" UN, it is expertise not rank, egalitarian cooperation not status, and decentralization not centralization that yields effective execution of duties.

Expertise Not Rank

Recruitment for UNMIK was neither systematic nor thought out in advance. In 1999, CVs or resumes were sent out from the United Nations in New York and screened by Sid in Pristina (who later turned up in Thezren as the UN finance officer). Terry Peterson had applied for ten years to work for the UN, and it was only when somebody he knew was in a position of influence and spotted his name among the pile of resumes that he got called for service.

Peterson and his deputy Orash Fatoohi turned out to have complementary skills very appropriate to the needs of the UN on the ground, but that was a fortunate coincidence. Michael Smith, the human resources director for the UN in the Previca region, was very critical of the way the UN recruited and managed people. "People recruitment is the big issue," he said. "They get hired, (1) because of privileged information, and (2) because somebody pulls them in who shouldn't." David Allen, the UN military liaison officer in Previca, described it as being like "an insider trading system. Who knows who, who's got the information." Once in the organization, if a UN staff member is seriously underperforming, or is corrupt, he or she gets transferred to a new job within the UN to avoid any conflict with the country of origin.[5] For example, I was told that UN Previca had wanted to remove Jon, the first MA in Thezren, from his position, but did not because his country of origin was donating large amounts of money to the mission.

The diversity of nationalities is what many staff members see as what gives the UN its strength, drawing on a wide variety of perspectives and cultures. However, political representation without *actual* (officially, it exists) meritocratic recruitment and application of universal standards of skill and performance raises serious problems for the effectiveness and accountability of the UN. David Allen said:

> The necessity they have for national balance is a real problem. People come to the mission not based on their individual skill and ability but based on the fact that they're from a certain country. It very much pervades my part, the military part, people with varying, I'm trying to be polite, varying skill levels, varying professionalism, varying ethics. And that does not help in a working environment. We would be far better served if there were some links between skill and the job, not because some country has to put in more people.

The obvious solution would be to send people who did not have the skills or work ethic back to the country that should not have sent them in the first place if they did not meet the criteria for the mission, but this was rarely done, as Bob Farmer, operations officer for Thezren police, discovered when sent police officers who could not drive a car or fire a weapon. Allen observed:

> Within the UN system, it's very, very difficult to discipline or remove someone. In my previous mission [in Kosovo], I had fired two military officers, kicked them out of the mission. One . . . guy, he was OK, he just didn't speak English, [and] he was transferred. . . . The other guy . . . refused to do anything. I'd say to him, "OK, tomorrow I want you to be at work at 8, we're going on a reconnaissance." He'd walk into work about 10 o'clock. I said, "You were supposed to be here at 8 o'clock." And he'd say [in lazy drawl], "Ah yeah." And this was from a military officer! If you try to remove somebody, it's very easy to get accused of things like racism or being unfair. So even though somebody is lazy, to get them removed for laziness is a very difficult thing.

John Green, the regional commander of CivPol in the Previca region, told Allen that only 30 percent of his staff were effective. Allen agreed and said that his strategy was to find that 30 percent and focus on them to get the work done.

The lack of emphasis on performance was a problem in the UNCA too. Sophie argued frequently, for example, that Peterson was not her boss and that no one could tell her what to do. If they did, she would complain to her country's representative. Thus, when her colleague, Giampiero, asked her to make a short list from the social welfare rolls of families eligible for winterization assistance, although given a week to do so, she eventually handed over a printed-out list of all the people on the social welfare rolls. When Giampiero challenged her about this, pointing out that it was useless, she responded first by saying that she had not had the time (yet she spent at least half of each workday writing e-mail and browsing the Internet), then by saying that Giampiero was not her boss and could not tell her what to do. Another day, when Dunne, who worked downstairs signing registration documents, was away, and Sophie was assigned to deputize for him, she went down for two hours in the morning. After lunch, a worker came up from downstairs to say there were people waiting for travel documents. She waved them away, declaring that she had already spent two hours down there and she wasn't going down again, "What do they think I am? Running up and down stairs all day?"

There was an unwillingness to let expertise go to where it worked best. Henry from the UN in Thezren recalled:

> When I first started, when they asked me what I wanted to do, I also said I was interested in doing liaison, because I'm extroverted, I can deal with KFOR, police, different agencies. Technically, [DMA Cole] Thedy is responsible for security, so he is responsible for liaising with KFOR, etc. But I found I was doing it more in practice. But when I said this, they said, "Well, that's Thedy's responsibility." Jon [the MA] didn't accept people's strengths and weaknesses to the benefit of the municipality.

The UN has acknowledged the problems with its management of human resources,[6] and more recruitment from the private sector, the changing organizational imperatives resulting from technological innovation, and the nature of a multiorganizational mission like Kosovo are raising new issues. The traditional careerist approach, where countries send people who get well paid and are often rehired regardless of their performance, is still the dominant one, but there is a feeling that the mission is demanding a type of ability that is not met by staff who will follow orders but have no initiative or self-management skills. "In an environment where there are clear roles, they are good," Giampiero said of staff who have been in the UN for most of their careers. "If they have a boss giving instructions, they are good, but in the end, here, everybody must take action to do their work."

Unfortunately for the speed of change, it is the careerists who are in the positions of authority who have to make the changes. Estelle, the UN welfare officer for the Previca region, said: "I think it's time for rock and roll! One way or another, it'll change, but it's going to take time to trickle down to have an impact. If you criticize things, you're seen as a trouble-maker, not a troublemaker, you're bold. You've got a whole network of . . . they're responsible for changing the organization but they want to do it with what they're familiar with. Does that change anything? No."

Often, the most effective employees were noncareer UN volunteers (UNVs), who were paid an allowance, not a salary, people who had worked in the private sector and former military officers from specialized branches of the forces. Peterson, the MA in Banshik, said that if he could, he would only hire UNVs; he described them as "young, bright, ener-getic." The UNV in Banshik was given tremendous responsibility—she was the local community officer (LCO) for the 5,000 Serbs in the munic-ipality. In Thezren, the language assistants told me that they thought Hideyaki, the UNV, was treated as "slave labor" and often scapegoated. He had a lot of technical knowledge and experience, but he was forced to do routine "UNV-type," "grunt-type" work, rather than focus on maxi-mizing the benefit of his knowledge for the municipality.[7]

The staff with private sector experience were not people who had long set their sights on a career with the UN and who, once in, were deter-mined not to move. Rather, they were people impatient with the bureau-cracy and the complacent attitudes among staff members; they were both more effective and more frustrated. Marlene Royce, the deputy regional administrator in Previca, formerly MA in Kamanica, and incidentally one of the few women in senior positions in the mission, said: "I can tell straight away whether someone is a long-term UN person. It's the bu-reaucratic attitude, the 'don't rock the boat' approach. Don't stay too long in the UN or you will become one of them, my friend said to me." Royce had worked with Kodak in the private sector, with a large NGO in Albania, and had done a master's degree in international relations. She said the most useful part of her background for her position as MA was "three months' sales training at Eastman Kodak almost twenty years ago. That has stood me in good stead ever since. When I was negotiating out in Kamanica, that's what I was doing, sales, convincing people to do things a certain way. I thought, 'I'm using what they taught me in Ko-dak.'"

Henry Ghosh, a UNCA officer in Thezren, commented on the differ-ence he felt between those with private sector experience and those from the public sector. "Most of these people come from public administra-tion, and often my impression is that people with a background in PA

Age, Background, and Positions and Responsibilities of UN Staff
in Banshik and Thezren, Showing the Heavier Preponderance of
Career UN Personnel in Thezren

	Age	Years with the UN	Previous experience	Position or responsibilities
		BANSHIK		
Terry Peterson	57	2.5 years	military	MA
Orash Fatoohi	56	5 years	banking/academic	DMA/finance
Giampiero	40	2 years	business, NGO	utilities and infrastructure
Jacques	53	4 months	NGOs	agriculture
Pierre	40	10 years	Career UN	housing
Sophie	30	6 months	student	NGOs and administration
Charlotte	32	2 years	student	local community officer (Serb enclaves)
		THEZREN		
Khalid Shamon	Late 60s	6 months	diplomat	MA
Cole Thedy	50+	20 years	career UN	DMA
Thabo	41	15 years	career UN	utilities
Priya	50	20 years	career UN	administration
Anuradha	51	15 years	career UN	education
Sid	40s	10 years	career UN	finance
Henry	34	1.5 years	private sector	LCO (Serb enclaves)
Hideyaki	27	1 year	NGO	UNV
Daniel	42	2 years	private sector	infrastructure and housing

NOTE: The official position titles and the division of duties varied between municipalities. For instance, Fatoohi looked after finance in Banshik as well as DMA. The DMA in Thezren, Thedy, looked after security, which Peterson took care of in Banshik.

[public administration], they don't really think HOW you do something matters, that things will kind of just get done anyway. And I think how you do something matters the most."

A French businessman who was working for the EU in the UNMIK HQ in Previca, who had previously worked for Proctor and Gamble and Thomas Cook, said the culture of the mission as a whole, which he saw as a UN culture, needed to learn some lessons from the business world. His parents had left Kosovo as young adults and settled in Paris, where he had grown up, and he had joined the mission to learn more about where they had come from, but he was growing more frustrated by the day. He said that one of the biggest problems was that the organizations that formed UNMIK did not know how to market themselves and what they did. The second biggest problem was the lack of creativity and initiative when it came to setting up structures, the lack of thought that went into it. The high turnover of staff was also problematic. "Six months, even one year is not enough. People just come for the money; they have no incentive to work hard. To have an investment in the mission, to be able to achieve goals and to be able to measure the achievement of those goals can only be done if people are there for a minimum of two years. Have fewer people, longer contracts, and pay them more."

Decentralization Versus Centralization

The UNCA had a hierarchical structure, with the Pristina headquarters at the top, then a regional office, and then the municipalities. The reporting structure was centralized, and the chain of command went up and down the hierarchy. The leadership that the UNCA needed was not coming from the top, where priorities and practices were often far removed in every sense from the realities on the ground. In practice, cooperation was good on the ground but not so good at the regional level and even less good at the center. In practice, decision making was best when decentralized, I was told at a dinner party in Previca where each organization (UN, OSCE, EU, an NGO, KFOR) was represented by people who had been in the mission for at least several months and some of whom had moved from the region (Previca) to the center (Pristina) but still retained professional and social ties in the region. Maura, the hostess, worked as the assistant to the UN regional administrator and so had a very good knowledge of the workings of the municipalities, because all the MA reports came to her and she always attended a weekly meeting of the regional MAs.

In a vigorous discussion on the topic of cooperation between the UN and KFOR, the group's consensus was that decision making and cooperation on the ground (i.e., at the municipal level) was generally very good, but that it was problematic at the regional and central levels. However, they agreed that Marlene Royce, the deputy regional administrator, had improved UN-KFOR relations significantly during her tenure. The group concurred that the ability of the decentralized units (working at the municipal level) varied considerably, because there was little guidance and no experience within the UN of this kind of mission. Thus, the mission had begun as a network form without a network organization institutional culture.

UNMIK Culture

UNMIK logistics were slow. A printer ink cartridge had not arrived two months after it was ordered in Banshik. A local driver in Banshik who had been promoted to interpreter had to wait a year for the UNCA in Pristina to process his paperwork and alter his pay. The IT team in Previca had still not issued an e-mail address to Jacques a month after he started work for the UNCA in Banshik. He eventually went to the regional administrator, who had a word with the IT team, and the e-mail address was dispatched within two days. Jacques was especially frustrated with the speed of things in the UNCA, because he had come from an NGO where the pace of work was an "operational speed."

Focusing on Economic Development

Until 9/11, economics was seen by many as having overtaken the role of politics in international relations.[8] Even now, many argue that economic development and the reduction of poverty are the best weapons against the spawning of terrorism. Although the UN has been involved in economic development through other agencies, the focus in institution building and civic administration in Kosovo has been political not economic. As a young Serb man in Palaj, a Serbian enclave in Banshik, said with great bitterness: "UNMIK gives everything to the old people. But they are the ones who got us into this mess. They are too political. First, they are Tito's people, then [former President Slobodan] Milosevic's, now [Serbian Prime Minister Vojislav] Koštunica's. And the young people, we have nothing. I cannot get a job. I don't want to marry and bring children into this situation."

Several of the most thoughtful internationals I encountered echoed this statement. Bob Farmer, the operations chief of police in Thezren, looking out on a street thronged with teenagers,[9] said that the first thing the internationals should have done was get the factories working again. Fatoohi, the DMA in Banshik, said that the goals of the mission were being undermined by the neglect of this vital aspect. "We did it backwards. The first priority should have been economic development, never mind politics, integration, pshaw, if you give people jobs, they will live and talk together. Now it is too late. All the money that came pouring in here should have been used for economic development. All the money given to older people, if some of that had been diverted into economic development . . . we have beautiful schools, good roads, better than we had before. But for what? There is still no freedom of movement or security, and the young are leaving." All the young Albanians and Serbs I met said they'd leave Kosovo the next day if they could get visas for a western European country or the United States or Canada.

Cooperation with Other Parties

Getting local leaders used to operating in a tough, violent world to work together and with the international contingent is a delicate process, and "there is a limit to how much the boat can be rocked by the international presence," as the *Economist* noted in 2000.[10] From the Kosovar perspective, for the previous twelve years, civil society in Kosovo had been struggling to make its voice heard: first, under Serbian rule, then during war and exile, and most recently under the UNCA. Kosovars' complaint is that instead of drawing on the "parallel society" built up by Kosovo Albanians since 1989, Western governments used their own NGOs for the implementation of humanitarian programs. Foreign relief workers poured into Kosovo; the Kosovar NGOs were marginalized, and when educated Kosovars were used in the relief operation, it was as drivers, guards, and interpreters. The UN dismantled what remained of the parallel administrative structure on the grounds that it was "politicized."

The "old" UN attitude of superiority to locals was still evident when I was in Kosovo and militated against the cooperation needed to achieve the mission's goals. The attitude of UN personnel to the local population and municipal administration was critical, given that it was intrinsic to the success of the mission, although not officially part of the network design or network organization. The goal of the mission was, after all, to cooperate with the local administration in setting up functioning democratic institutions.

In Thezren, the "old," almost colonial, attitude of the UN was in evidence. The MA warned his international staff to "keep their distance" from the locals, saying, "we have standards to keep." The internationals spoke of and treated members of the local administration as if they were children. Priya, a UN officer in Thezren, explained:

> We are trying to push them [the Albanians] into democracy, into running their own affairs, but they have been put down for so long that they don't know how. They are very intelligent—the CEO [chief executive officer] managed the meeting this morning excellently—but the self-esteem is low. I tell them, "You are GOOD!" We don't want to be [makes motion like an ogre over somebody, pushing down with her hands] over them, telling them what to do, we want to gently prod [them] in the right direction. You see them living in the villages, their lack of sanitation; this is not an issue for them, they are living in the Stone Age.

The attitude of the UN was evident in meetings with the local administration, including the board of directors in Thezren, the weekly cabinet meeting at the local level, which the UNCA co-chaired. The meeting was taken up with discussion of minor items that should be handled by the in- • dividual local departments, not at the municipal board of directors level. For instance, there was a dispute between the local bus company and the local taxis over the rights to use a stopping place in town, an issue properly dealt with by the local Department of Urbanism. DMA Thedy said that the locals did not trust one another; but they did not trust the UNCA either. And the UNCA did not trust them. Thabo, the UNCA utilities officer, said: "Albanians don't know what to do, and they don't accept they have to learn." But their perception of the UNCA and the UNCA's perception of them undermined any cooperative potential. This was unsurprising given that the UNCA held the local administration to standards that it did not apply to itself. Anuradha, a UNCA officer, told of how she had reprimanded a member of the local municipal administration for taking unauthorized leave:

> One director . . . took time off, and he wasn't supposed to. They would be offended when you check[ed on] them and [said], "Why have you disappeared for three weeks without telling anyone?" I found out after about ten days when I was looking for him and he wasn't available. When he came back, I said, "Come in here please. You are not reporting for work." I talked to the CEO, and he said he [had given him] punishment. I said, "How did you give [him] punishment?" He then changed his mind and said he had given him annual leave. I said, "How can you do that when [he hasn't] earned enough leave?" He said he [had] advanced it to [him]. I said, "How much can you advance? Three weeks?!" I requested that he put a hold on [his] salary for a month. The director was under his control. I said to the person who went, "You cannot go like this. We have a procedure." Finally, they said they would deduct his leave. So he had no more vacation time available. A month after that, he took another leave. I said, "Where is he?" They said, "He's on vacation." I said, "What vacation? He's used up his leave." You can only go as far as they want to go. There is nothing you can do.

But the local administration was aware that UNCA staff also broke the rules. Sid, the UN finance officer, went away for three weeks without having obtained permission, but when I mentioned this to Anuradha, she got very angry, denied that he had taken unauthorized leave, and then said that he did not have to report to anyone.

The local administration was not in the same network organization as the internationals, even though they worked alongside one another. The local administration had no authority over the UNCA, and if there was mistreatment of local staff by the internationals, there was no formal means of redress. In Thezren, I witnessed an encounter that was highly unprofessional and demeaning to a member of the local staff. Sid came into the office, walked over to the desk adjacent to me, where Halit, the local budgetary officer, was seated and proceeded to shout at him: "When are you leaving? Huh? When?" Halit looked intimidated and upset but replied firmly, "I am not leaving. You are not my supervisor." Sid walked out, and five minutes later, the local director of finance, who was Halit's boss, entered the office. He spoke to Halit in Albanian, and Halit turned and said to me that Sid had told his boss that Halit was distracting me and not allowing me to do my work! I had witnessed Halit working for several days and knew that his boss and the rest of the staff considered him to be a meticulous employee and decent person. He was very frustrated, because Sid's irresponsibility and unauthorized leaves made it difficult for him to do his job. When he spoke to Sid about this, Sid had gotten very angry, and ever since, he had been demanding that Halit leave the job he had held for the previous two years. I was appalled at what I had witnessed and at Sid's attempt to use me to get Halit into trouble. I breached the objective researcher role to ghostwrite, with Halit, a letter in English from Halit to Michael Smith, the regional UNCA human resources officer, outlining the situation. Even though Smith had no power to intervene on the local side, at least Sid's behavior would be on record. When I spoke to Smith later, he acknowledged the inability of the UNCA organization to deal with somebody like Sid or indeed to do anything at all when there is office bullying of the locals by internationals.

Although the two administrations were supposed to be working together, there was not very much hands on cooperation. The MA held an occasional meeting with the mayor and the CEO, the two most senior local people, but for the most part, there was no guidance but plenty of remonstrance.

In Banshik, there was a very different relationship between the UNCA and the local administration. The UNCA team there did not assume superiority over the locals. The Banshik MA, Terry Peterson, asked himself:

> Has my team ever done anything like this before? The UN in Cambodia made a hash of it. . . . I remember . . . [asking at a meeting of the municipality shortly after the mission began], "Everybody who's done this before, worked in a municipality, please raise your hand." I was expecting two or three, and 80 percent of the people put their hands up! They'd all been working here before 1989, when the Serbs fired them all. They'd done this before. Nobody on my team [the UNCA team] has done this before.

There was close contact between the mayor and CEO and Peterson and his deputy, Fatoohi. The CEO was acknowledged to be "difficult," in that he was constantly trying nepotistically to get jobs, money, and favors for Albanians, in particular, the so-called "families of martyrs," relatives of people killed fighting the Serbs. However, the UNCA closely monitored the local administration's work, and he was constantly countered by Peterson and, in particular, Fatoohi. Fatoohi attended some of the board of directors' meetings, but not all of them, because he felt the best way for the municipality to learn was to do. I attended one board of directors' meeting with him, which focused on finalizing the municipal statute. It was an invigorating and serious business, very unlike such meetings in Thezren, where one had the sense of an exasperated parent pulling a bunch of errant children along. Fatoohi did not run the meeting; it was run by the CEO. The matters dealt with were directly relevant to the task at hand, such as referenda and quotas, and there was no discussion of minutiae. On the whole, it resembled a political science seminar.

KFOR

The goals of KFOR are to establish and maintain a secure environment in Kosovo, assist UNMIK, and monitor the Military Technical Agreement (MTA) constituting the legal framework for the cessation of hostilities between NATO and the Federal Republic of Yugoslavia (FRY) and the ensuing occupation by KFOR of part of the FRY.[11] KFOR has multiple patrols, checkpoints, escorts, and intelligence sources that allow ongoing contact with the population, enabling it to anticipate and respond to any security threat. KFOR also acts in close cooperation with international organizations and NGOs through its civilian-military cooperation unit. This unit provides medical assistance to the population and transports food and goods to isolated villages. It also takes part in the rebuilding of infrastructures by providing supplies and expertise.

KFOR was a "network" organization in Kosovo at two distinct levels. Although it was distinct from the UNMIK four-pillar structure, in practice, it formed a fifth pillar working in close cooperation with the other pillars and was thus part of the intervention network organization. At the same time, however, it was a network organization in and of itself, because it was staffed by troops from NATO and several non-NATO countries, who were required to cooperate with one another. The ability of these militaries to perform well in both of these networks varied considerably.

The locus of my study was Previca North, where one of the five brigades in Kosovo was based. In Previca North, France had seven army battalions (around 4,500 soldiers) and a unit of the French Gendarmerie nationale (around 130 gendarmes) on the ground.[12] The seven battalions were the command and support battalion, the motorized rifle battalion, the mechanized infantry battalion, the army helicopter battalion, the armored battalion, the engineering battalion (which, as we have seen, caused considerable consternation by unilaterally deciding to dig a water trench diverting most of the water to the Serbs in the mixed Serbian-Albanian village of Slavina in Banshik), and the logistics battalion. The French were supported in Banshik by 1,000 UAE troops, and in Thezren by 500 Russian troops. However, since the Russians refused to be under NATO command, they were not technically part of KFOR. In addition, members of a Spanish battalion worked in one of the Serb enclaves in Thezren, part of a brigade from a neighboring area, not Previca North. This caused logistical problems in providing security during elections, because all the organizations in UNMIK were organized along regional and municipal lines.

Just as the UN is struggling to cope with a new type of mission that includes governance and cooperation with other organizations besides the traditional administrative role, so the military is shifting to adjust to missions that involve working closely with civilians and other organizations, as well as security. The militaries are struggling to balance a traditional military culture and the structural and management imperatives of that culture with the need to change to be effective in a situation where they are cooperating with civilian organizations and civilians in a military operation other than war.[13]

The flexibility needed for working cooperatively with other organizations is difficult for the military; because military operations require officers to distill order out of chaos, the military has developed an institutional culture that abhors disorder and uncertainty. The military is structured by rank and protocol and works under the direction of the campaign plan. Decision making is sequential, orderly, and based on fact and the consistency of the outcome with preconceived precepts. Military personnel work routinely on the directives emanating from the operational level, although strategic guidance comes from their respective national governments. It is politicians who control the military budget, appoint and confirm military leaders to the highest positions, and give strategic orders. So the new type of mission, requiring responsiveness and flexibility, and predicated on communications and information flow, in essence the capabilities of a network organization, is shifting priorities within militaries. The militaries are realizing the importance of innovation and flexibility, which requires a shift from a rigid, hierarchical culture where there was little or no room for individual thinking to a more responsive, flexible organization capable of adapting to unique situations and to working with other militaries and other organizations.

Different militaries had different rules for tours of duty, but there did not seem, as of 2001, to be much coordination in terms of what operational rules worked optimally for security and the military personnel. A French civil-military liaison officer felt the tour of duty for French soldiers was too long at four months, with only ten days off in that time and the soldiers doing twelve-hour shifts at checkpoints. He said: "It is very stressful out here. People think standing at a checkpoint is not stressful. But it is. They see everything that is going on behind the people walking on the streets and in the cars. And they are ready for potential incidents all the time. For twelve hours a day, that is really tough. The soldiers on the checkpoints, they get depression, it is very hard on them." Other militaries were more cognizant of the strains. He continued: "The Swedish soldiers are here for three months only and they get two weeks off in that time." Balancing the need for less turnover of military personnel and the needs of the soldiers could be achieved by establishing a better system for transmitting institutional memory and common operational criteria. For instance, the optimal turnover consistent with soldiers' mental health could be determined by observing the practices of different militaries.

Expertise Not Rank

Recruitment and training for international interventions were being given more serious thought in the French military. There were considerable differences between the French civil-military cooperation (CIMIC) personnel and regular military personnel. CIMIC is an area of expansion within the French military, which is monitoring it to facilitate growth and development. According to a visiting French military inspector of the CIMIC personnel, the number of French CIMIC personnel in Kosovo had gone from six in the early days of the mission in 1999 to a hundred in the autumn of 2001. The preparation for regular military personnel was a day of orientation to give them a sense of mission and provide very basic guidelines, such as what to do if their military vehicle was surrounded by a mob of children. Preparation for CIMIC was much more extensive and a separate career path within the military. There were exams and day-long interviews with and assessments of recruits to ensure that the right type of person is working for CIMIC.

The French military inspector of the CIMIC personnel explained: "They must not be too aggressive, [and] they must be interested in international affairs and working with people. Then we train them, and they have a specialty, for instance, they are in a mountain regiment." However, he felt that missions such as that in Kosovo required special training for all military personnel—training that they were not given. The inspector had been one of the first CIMIC officers in northern Kosovo, and he recalled one of the first challenges:

> I was up in a municipality on the north side of Previca, and the children were so traumatized, they couldn't speak. My wife is a teacher, so I called her and asked her what I should do. She said to get them to sing, but a very simple song, just one line over and over. So for days I did that, I went in with my guitar and sang this one-line lullaby and eventually they started to sing. I went back there this visit, and it's two years later, but they recognized me. They said, "It's Microphone!" I always had a piece of wood in the car . . . shaped like a microphone, [and] they'd take it and pretend to sing into it. I was also Father Christmas, the clown, you name it. . . . As the saying goes, peacekeeping is not a soldier's job, but only soldiers can do it!

CIMIC brought out experts or specialists as needed. For instance, one of their epidemiologists went out regularly for a short period of time, two weeks, did his work, and then returned to France. The French military planners are also part of a learning exchange scheme for military planners with the United States, Germany, and several other countries involved in this kind of mission. They are working to develop a joint expertise in this area and to share and learn from one another's perspectives and planning.

Decentralization and Centralization

KFOR decided that it did not want to be part of UNMIK but to work alongside it, which caused difficulties in command, because KFOR was inextricably tied in with the other organizations on the ground and a de facto part of the intervention network organization. A prime hazard with team organizations is that individual team members tend to overvalue their own contributions relative to those of other members.[14] Many refuse to subordinate their interests to the interests of the community (or, in this case, network), and the distribution of authority in networks permits them to act on their own behalf, giving rise to the problem of organizational imperialism. Recurring conflict is inevitable in networks,[15] and to avoid the network being destroyed, one solution is collocating decision authority with knowledge of local conditions or giving authority to actors on the ground to deal with situations. If issues have to be referred back up to the center, it can create difficulties or even ruin relations on the ground.

KFOR was acknowledged to be reluctant to fit into the network, and even sometimes to refuse a request from UNMIK if it was felt that doing so might damage KFOR's reputation or interfere in how it wanted to conduct its work. This caused severe difficulties for UNMIK, made worse by the hierarchical nature of information flow and command within KFOR and the organizations. Hans Gesing of the OSCE described one such clash over KFOR's handling of the issue of Serb returns. Part of the mission's goal is to get Serbs who fled Kosovo after the war to return to their homes. However, very few Serbs have taken up this opportunity, and the whole process is fraught with tension. Besides averting intercommunal hostility and the endangerment of returning Serbs by Albanian neighbors, the organizations have to coordinate to make sure that accommodation is available for the returnees (usually families). As Gesing described it:

> KFOR had adopted a new policy of checking up on individual records of attempted returnees, who would come from southern or central Serbia under UNHCR guidance, checking out the place, probably with the intention of returning. KFOR adopted a weird policy because they were under threat or under pressure from the Albanian politicians, who would say, "We would not want any Serbs to return who have . . . criminal record[s]." Whatever that might be, either during the war, before the war, or after the war. KFOR on the very local level adopted the policy of checking on individual criminal records before allowing a returnee to even check out his or her house. Which was in breach of many, many human rights. Freedom of movement, privacy of information . . . they would pay no regard to that. OSCE on the field office level were very critical of this new policy, but KFOR still wouldn't change their policy. So OSCE sent this report up the chain to the human rights officer, who forwarded it to our department, our director.
>
> What apparently happened here is that the entire issue was . . . put into a nice letter from the ambassador [head of the OSCE mission] to Com [the commander of] KFOR. . . . As a result, the policy doesn't exist any longer. But as a second consequence, at the local level, it has destroyed their working relationship with KFOR. You're sitting with KFOR, right? We're all the international community here, we differ on certain subjects, but now we've been rep-

rimanded severely for this. In the future, you might as well not request information. This is where the structural problems really emerge. That you have to
deal with your international partners at the field level but cannot address issues with them authoritatively. If you could, you wouldn't have to go up the
chain. KFOR is not part of the UNMIK structure, this is another perverse situation where you would have the police as part of the four-pillar structure,
part of the UN mandate, but not KFOR. . . . The thing is . . . [that] in order to
gain information and to gain access to these people, you have to develop a relationship of trust. . . . So what [a] few people are encouraging is to forget
about the chain of reporting and . . . address these things in a localized manner. . . . you can really only do that with the force of the argument. If that
doesn't work, it doesn't work. . . . when a problem reaches a certain stage,
then you should report it, but not in the beginning stages. It's really difficult!

Thus, to avoid conflict that can threaten the working of the network organization on the ground, decision-making authority needs to be collo-
cated with knowledge of local conditions, which means giving authority
to actors on the ground to deal with situations.

KFOR people were regarded as being very reliable, always keeping
their word. However, they were not always flexible enough on the
ground, having to check all actions with their chain of command. This
took time and was problematic in situations that required a speedy response. There were some problems that could have been averted or more
speedily solved if the military had been more willing to listen and take on
board genuine frustrations and suggestions from the local populations
and the other organizations.

One such problem was the type of security they provided in the Serbian enclaves, which consisted of villages surrounded by farmland. The
military secured the center and based themselves there and at the roads at
the point of entry to the enclaves. However, they did not regularly patrol
the farmland or provide security for farmers working in the fields. There
were several attacks on Serbian farmers in the fields by Albanians, who
then escaped into the surrounding countryside. The military found it
hard to reorganize their "secure the center and perimeter" approach and
were also unwilling to provide escorts without twenty-four hours' notice.
Since many escorts of civilians were of a relatively urgent nature—for example, medical emergencies—such a system was justifiably seen as inadequate by the Serbs and unnecessary by the UN, OSCE, and NGOs who
worked with the Serbian population.

As has been noted, the turnaround time for the military in the enclaves
was four months, so as soon as one contingent had learned these lessons

and revised its operations, it was gone, and the incoming unit made the same mistakes all over again. The problem was a combination of always having to go through a chain of command external to the immediate situation and the high turnover of military personnel. The turnover was not only within national militaries but could also involve the rotation of militaries of different nationalities (e.g., French, UAE, and Greek). The situation required either a decentralization of authority to the military units in the enclaves or the setting up of a system to communicate these difficulties to the next units coming in, so that local frustrations would not be built up again with the arrival of every new military contingent. There was insufficient institutional memory within the French military and within KFOR, and this led to high levels of frustration, with negative repercussions on the attainment of the security goals of the mission.

Cooperation

Cooperation extended on three fronts for the militaries: with other militaries, with international civilian organizations, and with the local civilian population. Military liaison officers dealt with the first and second of these. The liaison officers ensured that the international organizations had security when they needed it. The arrangements for such security were usually made at the four-pillar interagency meeting or at a security meeting at KFOR. UN, OSCE, and NGO personnel also made individual requests to KFOR liaison officers, either dropping by their offices or driving to the KFOR base to meet with them. In Banshik, the two liaison officers were based in the UAE camp and spent their days gathering intelligence and arranging the military support the international organizations needed. Most of their work was face-to-face. However, just before I left Banshik, the two CIMIC officers, Loïc and Gérard, on their own initiative, had gotten hold of a mobile phone and were jointly using it to facilitate contact with personnel from other organizations. These two liaison officers had a very strong awareness of being part of something bigger than their own French military. In the UNMIK office on his first day, a UN staff person asked Gérard, "Are you French?" He replied stoutly, "No, I am KFOR. I am not French here." When I asked him to explain, he replied, "What I say is that everybody is here, all nationalities, so it is important that we are seen as the sum, not the parts."

This was particularly critical for the militaries, because they were perceived by the local population as having secret affinities with one or other side. The vast majority of both French and UAE personnel I met were thoroughly professional in their expressed views and observable behavior. However, a major problem for the French military has been a perception by the Albanians that they are pro-Serb (largely as a result of France's alliance with Serbia during World War I). It was also partly fueled by the French perception of the common Western and Judeo-Christian culture of the two nations. I witnessed some grounds for the Albanians' misgivings. Two French military personnel in Previca told me that they thought the Albanians tended to be "dirty" and that the Serbs were "more like us." They were unswayed by the fact that garbage collection had stopped and infrastructure maintenance halted in Albanian areas during the 1990s, so that it was much more difficult for Albanian districts to maintain public sanitation. The Russian military in Thezren also experienced this suspicion, and one Russian soldier had been shot dead by a teenage Albanian while on security duty outside a UNCA meeting for no reason other than that he was a Russian and hence viewed as sympathetic to the Serbs.

The Serbs in turn viewed the UAE military with suspicion because they were Moslems like the Albanians. This was despite the fact that Albanian Kosovars are determinedly secular. However, the UAE did fund the building of many mosques in the area and paid for local municipal personnel to travel to Mecca, although the majority of those who took advantage of this benevolence to go on the hajj viewed it with some bemusement. UAE funding was welcome, but the religious connotations in general were not. Prejudices on all sides could complicate issues. Both militaries needed to combat these attitudes actively and assuage such fears among local populations. The best way was to see themselves as part of the intervention, not as French or Russian, and to focus on their task of providing optimal security. It was a good idea to demonstrate impartiality through choice of projects to work on and consistently impartial interactions with local populations.

Cross-cultural understanding was also a challenge between the militaries. The French viewed working with the UAE as challenging. French officers said that the UAE personnel were not disciplined and did not behave like a proper military. It was true that the UAE military did have different ways of operating than the French; they did not have minimum levels of physical fitness and they argued, for example, that the rules of their military forbade them to leave their warm vehicles in the winter. However, there were also considerable efforts to establish a good working relationship. At the going-away ceremony hosted by the UAE troops before they left Banshik, there were awards given out to honor people in both the French and UAE contingents who had contributed to a cooperative relationship. The evening was memorable for its bonhomie: the French and German generals present got up and participated unskillfully but enthusiastically in a traditional Emirates dance being performed in full uniform by the UAE soldiers.

The dominant view in both the French and UAE contingents and among the organizations in UNMIK was that the different militaries contributed to the synergy of the wider mission network. The mantra in Banshik was "The French are good for security, the UAE for money." The UAE contingent might not have been a typical military force in many ways, but the Emirates poured millions of dollars into the municipality.

One of the thorniest challenges for cooperation between KFOR and UNMIK was the demolition of illegally constructed buildings. On this issue, there was a reluctance on the part of the militaries to spend their own resources, including social capital, even if in the interests of the mission overall. This "organizational imperialism" had serious implications for UNMIK's authority at the local level. The French military in Banshik and Thezren refused to carry out demolitions of buildings that had been built illegally and that the builders refused to pull down. In the postwar situation and given the links to organized crime of many illegal builders, no Albanians would allow their equipment to be used for pulling down such buildings. Nor was it politically expedient to use Serbian-owned machinery to pull down Albanian constructions. The only organization with the equipment and expertise capable of and legally able to pull down the buildings was KFOR. But the French did not want to be perceived by the local populations as "destroyers," even if this meant that the authority of the UNCA and its regulations on construction were undermined. The cooperation needed by the UNCA was not forthcoming. A UNCA officer in Thezren described the situation: "Some Albanians linked to the local mafia built buildings where they shouldn't, they've been cordoned off by the municipality, and now UNMIK cannot find anyone to demolish them. KFOR said they weren't going to do it. The general said 'We are in Kosovo for reconstruction, not to destroy buildings.'"

The Future

As Kosovo has shown, the UN Secretariat is out of shape and struggling to hold its own in a world of fitter, faster organizations. There are certainly seeds for change within it, but those seeds tend to be the most undervalued members of the organization and have relatively short tenures. The demands of the changing international situation and the changing organizational imperatives, driven by information and communication technologies, have overwhelmed an organization that is only beginning to grasp the internal changes that will be necessary for it to be really effective in an interorganizational milieu. NATO militaries are showing signs of greater emphasis on intermilitary cooperation, indicating that thought is being given to the organizational changes wrought by ICTs and the turbulent international environment. However, militaries by their very nature are top-down, hierarchical, bureaucratic entities. Without leadership fitting the new environment, as in the UN Secretariat, the militaries are in danger of seeing international interventions primarily through the prism of security, without enough appreciation of the intense interorganizational cooperation necessary to attain the long-term goals of an international intervention.

CHAPTER EIGHT

The OSCE, the International Police, and NGOs

The OSCE

How was the Organization for Security and Cooperation in Europe (OSCE) faring as part of the network organization of UNMIK and KFOR? Did it add to the synergy of the mission? Yes, but not in the obvious ways that KFOR and the UNCA did.

The OSCE was in a peculiar position, and it was adjusting to its status as partner with some disgruntlement. It had been the first international organization in Kosovo, as the Kosovo Verification Mission in 1998, and it had also been a central actor in Bosnia in the late 1990s, although the mission there was not one of governance like UNMIK. Many people thought of the OSCE as an NGO, but it was technically meant to be part of the international governance in Kosovo. There was also not very much knowledge of its culture or role.

When I asked Terry Peterson what the OSCE did, he said, half in jest, "Damned if I know!" but in practice he found the head of the Banshik OSCE, Klaus, and Klaus's team, very useful when working together on issues in the Serbian enclaves. The local population equally had a difficult time understanding the role of the OSCE. Even the OSCE was uncertain about its role in the mission. It was in "partnership" with the UN but often did not feel as though it was. Its role was less visible and more abstract than the nitty-gritty work of the UNCA and consequently was not always appreciated or its potential value recognized. Its "monitoring" role sat uneasily with OSCE personnel. As Hans Gesing, the political affairs officer in the OSCE cabinet in Pristina, said: "We don't want to be monitoring the UN in terms of human rights; we want to be inside making policy on human rights." The OSCE had the resources to do this and the UN did not (or so the leadership in Pristina told the OSCE cabinet), but thus far, the level of interconnection had not made such meshing possible. In the meantime, in terms of governance, the OSCE was left outside looking in.

The OSCE originated in the idea of a pan-European Security Conference in the 1950s, which was eventually realized as the Conference of Security and Cooperation in Europe in the 1970s. This process then became institutionalized as OSCE in 1995—after the end of the Cold War—as permanent structures became necessary to support a growing number and range of tasks, many of which needed daily support. The OSCE's fifty-five participating states, all of which have equal status, span the globe.[1] It is an instrument for early warning, conflict prevention, crisis management, and postconflict rehabilitation. It deals with a wide range of security issues, including arms control, preventive diplomacy, confidence- and security-building measures, human rights, election monitoring, and economic and environmental security.

It is a hierarchical organization in that it has a permanent headquarters and institutions, permanent staff, standing decision-making bodies, regular financial resources, and field offices. Most of its instruments, decisions, and commitments are framed in legal language. However, it has many of the characteristics of a networked organization. The OSCE describes its approach as comprehensive and cooperative. Decisions are made on the basis of consensus,[2] and although they have no legal status under international law, they are, the organization claims, politically binding. The basis of the participating states' approach to security is comprehensive and cooperative; comprehensive in that the protection and promotion of human rights and fundamental freedoms, along with economic and environmental cooperation, are considered to be just as important for the maintenance of peace and stability as politico-military issues, and as such are an integral component of the OSCE's activities. In fact, the protection of human rights and the coordination of elections were the principal activities of the OSCE in Banshik. As with a network organization, the assumption is that cooperation [between states] can bring benefits to all participating states, while insecurity in one state or region can affect the well-being of all. The OSCE's aim is "to work together, achieving security together with others, not against them."[3]

How well that networking consciousness translates into networking on the ground is open to debate. In principle, the OSCE says unequivocally:

> In many of its activities, the OSCE comes into contact with other international and non-governmental organizations. Increased priority is therefore being given to inter-institutional cooperation and co-ordination. The OSCE's work in countries like Kosovo has demonstrated that the Organization can complement, and in some cases, provide the co-coordinating framework for, the efforts of other European and international institutions and organizations. Cooperation has been very close in Kosovo, where the previous OSCE Kosovo Verification Mission (which was withdrawn in March 1999) operated in synergy with NATO aerial verification. Since the deployment of the OSCE Mission in Kosovo, in July 1999, the Office in Pristina has developed links with the Kosovo Stabilization Force (KFOR) which provides a secure environment for OSCE activities in Kosovo.[4]

Expertise Not Rank

Effective cooperation in a network organization relies on primacy being given to expertise rather than rank. Expertise and rank seemed to go together in the OSCE, however. Olga, the elections officer in Banshik, who had also worked with the UNCA in East Timor, said that by comparison,

> OSCE is more organized, yet more flexible, does not tie you [down] so much. It has roles that help you. The structure is cleaner, more transparent [as to] who is responsible. There are no overlaps, no people in the middle, where one doesn't know where they fit. There is a quicker response to your requests. I guess this is achieved by better communications, people are more responsive, and there is more eagerness to respond. In my job, I can get the fix to a problem very fast. In the UN, I spend some time finding out . . . here they are passing on the message, are cooperative. People here are much more responsive and somehow more expert on what they are doing, there is more a feeling of confidence in the team. If they are not sure, they will try to find the answer. With the UN, that was not always the case.

The OSCE was known as a very responsive organization. A young Serb in Palaj who had been employed by both said: "The UN runs to catch up with the OSCE."

Although the OSCE is seen as a faster, more responsive organization, it is also more structured, with less scope for individual initiative or action on the ground than the UNCA. Several people likened it to a military organization in the way it was run—very disciplined and structured. It was also seen as an intellectual organization, full of lawyers. However, it was not good at explaining what its role was and consequently was considerably underutilized.

Centralization Versus Decentralization

The OSCE has more control than the UN over the local level of the organization. There is a constant production of reports from every person working in the organization, or, if they are not part of a subsidiary chain of command (for instance, the human rights officer reports to the regional human rights officer, and the latter to the Human Rights Department in Pristina), they contribute to the local office report. For instance, John, the logistics officer in OSCE, Banshik, contributes to the reports that go out from the Banshik OSCE office as a whole. Everything is documented, according to Gesing, and because the information system works so well and is so organized, the center and regions are more aware of what is happening on the ground than the UN is for its local offices (however, this level of documentation results in overload when it is more description than analysis, as is the case with this mission). As with all the international organizations in Kosovo, however, the OSCE has been instructed to cooperate with the other organizations on the ground. The instruction carried very little detail beyond the structural organization of weekly meetings, and so in practice cooperation was somewhat decentralized. Unfortunately, when it came to conflict with other organizations, the local level did not have the authority to deal definitively with the situation.

Cooperation

On the local level, although part of its mission is capacity building, OSCE had no contact with the local municipal administration on a day-to-day basis. In both Banshik and Thezren, its staff were housed in a separate building, a fifteen-minute walk from the municipality buildings. The UNCA was in practice doing the guidance and mentoring of the local administration. OSCE's role seems more malleable than those of the rest of the mission. Klaus, the head of OSCE in Banshik, said of what had become a large focus for the organization in Banshik: "I think at the beginning nobody had the idea that we would be an advocate for the minorities to get better service from KFOR and [the] UN police."

In Banshik, thanks to the leadership of Peterson and Klaus, the relationship was collaborative, although still not clearly defined. Klaus was very good at coming up with ways the OSCE could help or support the

UN. He described in an interview how the OSCE had come up with a solution to a problem that confronted UNMIK:

> Another project where we are cooperating is, for instance, recruitment of staff for [the local] municipal administration. The staff in the past were from 1999, when the municipality was still dominated by the PDK, the political wing of the UCK, or the former KLA. The people were not selected based on qualification, a vacancy arose, strings were pulled, and people were hired on [the basis of] their relationship and political affiliation. And in spring this year, the UN administration decided that all the contracts had to be terminated, or rather not continued, since nobody had a working contract. To simply recruit new people, to screen the existing ones. This created a lot of tension among the people as well as the political parties, because the PDK was afraid that after the election, the LDK [Democratic League of Kosovo][5] had the majority in the municipality and they would use the strings in rehiring of people by getting the PDK affiliates out and getting their people in.
>
> . . . [When] the PDK threatened to block the whole municipality's work, to obstruct everything and to walk out of the municipal assembly, we offered that OSCE would monitor the selection of personnel and would be a monitoring presence: on the one hand, would provide some influence that this decision would be based on qualification only, and, on the other hand. . . . [report whether] it was free and fair or it was biased and certain political parties were disadvantaged. . . . And the parties would have to accept our findings. And they did, so we monitored about 300 interviews, the background of these people, based on that, we produced a report, and it helped to overcome the tension between the political parties. . . . the PDK accepted and agreed that the selection was objective. This was part of our role as mediator and neutral party.

In addition, when there was any trouble in the enclaves, the UNCA and OSCE were on the spot, usually with Peterson and Klaus leading the way. In Thezren, there was almost no contact, let alone cooperation between the two organizations. They did not come together to respond to a crisis as they did in Banshik. While I was in Thezren, two Albanians cutting wood illegally were murdered in a wood next to a Serbian enclave. The Serb villagers claimed that the wood was theirs (no documentation existed to prove or disprove this), and two days before the murders, I had attended a meeting in the village that KFOR had convened with Henry Ghosh, the UNCA local community officer (LCO), to respond to the anger of the Serbian villagers. The UNCA MA was unaware of the situation, and neither the OSCE nor the police were brought in on the matter. Two days later, I was in the police station when the news of the homicides came in, but neither that day nor over the next several days was there any response at all (for instance, in the form of a meeting or working group to address the grievances of both Albanians and the Serbs on the matter of illegal woodcutting) from either the UNCA or the OSCE.

The MA and Ghosh often did not attend the weekly interagency meeting, and the OSCE sent different people (whereas in Banshik, Klaus and Peterson always attended the four-pillar meeting), so as Hans Gesing from the Pristina head office of the OSCE pointed out, "It's really a question whether . . . the field office[r] or the human rights officer is very actively interested in working together with the UN counterparts. There is NOTHING to really require him or her to do this." Ghosh echoed this. There was almost no contact, let alone cooperation between the OSCE and the UNCA in Thezren. The OSCE human rights officer was also supposed to be focused on the enclaves, but Ghosh said the only time it really worked was when there was an HR officer with whom he had gotten along very well and they had gotten together on various issues. But their working relationship was based on their personal one, and when the OSCE officer left, Ghosh's contact with the OSCE ceased. He said that they should be helping each other more, but that he did not know how to get the two organizations working together in a better way.

CivPol

Did the UNMIK civilian police force in Kosovo (CivPol) contribute to the synergy of the mission? Yes, but it was the "weakest link" in it, according to the UNCA deputy regional administrator in Previca in 2001, and also according to most internationals and locals.

The problems of CivPol were an intensified mirror of the problems of the UN organization in Kosovo in general. They were making excellent progress in vehicular traffic control and in the issuing of drivers licenses, but not in the solving of crime. There had not been one successful prosecution of an interethnic theft or assault in Banshik or Thezren. This was one of the biggest sources of tension in all municipalities. CivPol was training the Kosovo Police Service (KPS), the new local police force, but this training was basic and did not include how to do investigative work.

Expertise or Rank

CivPol has its own hierarchy, and it is weak and riven by lack of authority, because the police do not come as units from their countries, as KFOR contingents do.[6] As a result, there might be police officers from thirty different countries in one police station, all with different training and cultures. This made it difficult to develop a cohesive force with a common understanding and work style. The contrast with KFOR, where there are no such difficulties with cohesion, is stark. When a group of police officers from one country work together, the improvement in efficiency and efficacy is obvious. "I know one of my counterparts in the Central Region, and he is Irish and he has five Irish officers, and they are so much more effective," David Allen observed. Different skills and training render cohesive and consistent policing impossible. In addition, many of the international police are near or over forty, because most countries require considerable experience before they let personnel go on a UN mission. They are usually officers with families, whose priority is to earn some extra money and do nothing physically risky. Although they bring anti-riot gear, they are not usually trained as an anti-riot unit. As has been noted in connection with the UNCA, there are criteria laid down for skills and training, but in practice, these are not uniformly imposed, because of the political considerations of including particular countries and particular numbers from various countries.

In Previca, when there was a riot, most of the police officers went in the opposite direction. The ones who did not run away were the U.S. police, the German police, and the (former) Royal Ulster Constabulary, the officers of the latter having been professionalized in an environment very similar to Previca, namely, in the sectarian violence of Belfast and Northern Ireland. In Banshik, two international police officers were in the Serbian enclave of Gracie when the villagers pointed to two Albanians stealing a cow from their field. The police officers looked at their watches, said, "Sorry, our shift is over," jumped in their car, and sped away. This sort of thing was not an uncommon occurrence. The residents in the Serbian enclave of Pro Buluyo were outraged because even though they phoned the police when a cow or tractor was stolen, the police did not come.

Peterson's "strong links" in the police station, a pair of police officers, one from Bangladesh, the other from the Czech Republic, who had become firm friends, maintained that the Albanian approach was that of "one big family." No Albanian was going to testify against another Albanian. The international police had an unpleasant job in this situation, but they were intimidated and threatened, and since most of them were, in their own words, "here for the money," they chose not to act. In Thezren, the police did not live in the town, and investigations were conducted from Previca, which further reduced the police's authority and reputation.

Decentralization or Centralization

The chain of command is a structural problem. The police share responsibility for security with KFOR, yet they are not part of the same authority structure. KFOR is not even within UNMIK. The UNCA, even though it is the local government and administration, has no authority over CivPol. In Thezren, that authority would not have helped much, because there was little communication between the organizations, but in Banshik it might have helped resolve situations where the local populations expressed their dissatisfaction with policing to UNCA. Peterson was very aware of the problem.

Ineffective policing prompted a riot in Palaj in October 2001 after a Serbian farmer had his tractor stolen and was severely beaten. This followed a period in both Palaj and in Pro Buluyo when cows and tractors were being stolen under the eyes of KFOR and CivPol. The Serb farmers could point to one of their tractors being driven by an Albanian neighbor, but the police would not investigate further. The beating of the farmer was the last straw for the Serbian community, and they took to the streets to express their frustration.

Cooperation

The structure and (in)action of the police were very frustrating for the other organizations in the municipality. This was less true of Thezren, where there was little common knowledge and cooperation, but in Banshik, dealing with the anger in the local communities toward the police was a major focus of attention for the UNCA, OSCE, and KFOR. Once again, we see that the mission has to be looked at beyond the network organization to the wider society, because the local population played a key role in the way the police did their job. Most police investigation work relies on the community, and in the case of interethnic crimes (which were the most contentious and relatively frequent), the Serbs were not going to report another Serb to the police, just as the Albanians were not going to report an Albanian to the police.

NGOs

NGOs are seen as nonhierarchical, responsive, and flexible, with optimal use of information technologies, and hence as close to the network organization ideal. Thus, in Kosovo, one would expect them to be among the most networked organizations and able to participate in the mission network organization with ease. Their technology is as sophisticated as the technical limitations of the environment allow, and they are informal in culture. I draw my points here from observations of several NGOs in the two municipalities and also at the regional and central level. I did a more in-depth study of two divisions of one NGO in Banshik, where the factors I have just cited were a significant barrier to effective cooperation on the ground. Although part of the mission network organization, the NGOs I observed were impatient with the slowness of the bureaucracies, their organizations were not hierarchical but were centralized to a significant degree, and one of their primary occupations was survival and beating out other NGOs to get grants from donors—none of which contributed to effective cooperation.

In 1999, hundreds of NGOs arrived in Kosovo to implement programs funded by the flood of money from international donors, in particular the European Community Humanitarian Office (ECHO).[7] However, by fall 2001, the mission had moved beyond the initial emergency phase and the work of NGOs was winding down. For instance, the number of NGOs in Banshik had dwindled from twenty-four in 2000 to eleven in 2001, and more were winding up their operations at the start of 2002. In the initial emergency stage, they were largely responsible for the logistical arrangements in providing emergency housing and food to the returning refugees.

The principal focus of my discussion here, the French NGO K-LED, had been in Banshik since the start of the mission. The majority of the population of Kosovo (65 percent) work in agriculture, and when they came back after the war, their houses were destroyed, their animals were gone, and their machinery was gone or damaged or burned. It was close to the planting season, and K-LED managed to repair 600 tractors and buy enough equipment, seeds, and fertilizer to ensure that the planting season was not missed. It and the other NGOs have undoubtedly contributed to the synergy of the mission at every stage so far. They are the face of the European Union pillar at the local level—the implementing partners of the funding agencies centralized in this pillar for reconstruction.

Many people see NGOs as *the* face of humanitarian missions and as uniquely apolitical and independent. They have gained new prominence in the past decade. The phenomenal rise in the number and type of NGOs in the 1980s and 1990s has coincided with the rise in the number of failed states and in the level of instability crossing borders.[8] It has coincided with the phenomenal rise in new information technologies and a network organizational dynamic.[9]

Jonathan Bach and David Stark[10] argue that there has been a coevolution of NGOs and interactive technology. The operations of an NGO—fundraising, coordinating relief, communications—have made optimal use of many of the new ICTs. Certainly, for many NGOs, the concept of the network is intertwined with their operational logic. However, as Bach and Stark point out, "It would be an error . . . to see NGOs as having an elective affinity with interaction technology, and . . . to claim that NGOs plus IT equals new organizational forms capable of transforming global space."[11] NGOs do indeed have many characteristics of a network organization; in particular, their use of information technology is advanced and is seen as intrinsic to operating as an organization in the twenty-first century. However, they are not as close to the ideal of a networked organization as popular and popular academic perceptions would have us think.

Expertise Not Rank

Expertise is certainly given priority, because young professionals abound in the NGOs in Kosovo. They are given enormous responsibility and are seen as having the necessary combination of skill, initiative, and energy for this type of mission. However, if age can be seen as a form of ranking, there is a reverse discrimination, because older people are perceived as less amenable and more capable of inconvenient critique of the NGOs policies. Jacques, an agronomist who was the UNCA agricultural officer in Banshik, and who had formerly worked for K-LED there, said: "The secretary-general of K-LED back in France did not welcome constructive criticism from older experienced people—she did not act on our advice. So now there are many more younger workers, who are cheaper but who do not have the experience and sometimes do not learn from the indigenous people, which is very important."

Jacques believed that age also influenced the NGO's necessary relationship with KFOR:

> I am fifty years old, [and] I have credit [i.e., legitimacy] with the soldiers; if I make a mistake, they do not think badly, they think of me with credit. As a consequence, they help me. For example, they are helping me make sure that people do not cut wood illegally. They don't have to, that is not their job, but they know me, and they want something to do. But with the much younger [K-LED] workers, many of them party a lot, are after the girls, they do not have credit with KFOR. If they need help, KFOR thinks they are only here to

party; they would rather help someone else. And it is important, they need security for escorts [of Serbs going outside the enclaves], for example.

Thus, although expertise is given key importance, so is youth, not because of youth per se, but because the younger professionals are willing to work for less money and also will not question the NGO's policies.

Centralization or Decentralization

As Jacques indicated, the NGOs, contrary to the popular perception, are often tied into a hierarchical structure with a head office and ultimate authority in the NGO's country of origin. In K-LED's case, this was France. The contracts NGOs negotiated with the funding agencies also exercised a centralizing influence. They were often fiercely negotiated, because their priorities were not always shared and the donors would not always understand the limitations on the ground and would expect things that were not feasible. Once a contract was signed, it was difficult for an NGO to be flexible in the face of changing circumstances or new knowledge. For instance, K-LED's agricultural division agreed with the World Bank to implement village elections for the representative who would be the liaison with the organizations in the municipality. Jacques, a veteran of K-LED, warned the new workers not to agree to this, because it would cause political fighting on the ground, but they ignored his advice and then were stuck with a very difficult policy to implement. In fact, as I shall go on to discuss, it was the UNCA in Kosovo that was instrumental in trying to ensure that NGOs did follow a democratic, inclusive procedure in their collaborative work in the municipality.

As expected, NGO workers were suspicious of the established organizations, seeing KFOR as a necessary evil and the UNCA as a bureaucratic nightmare. William, the project officer with K-LED reconstruction, had a very cynical view of the UN's motivation for being in Kosovo. "They're not humanitarian, not in my opinion. Including UNMIK. They do their jobs instead of letting the municipality do it. They don't want Kosovo to have independence." Yet he went on to say that the NGOs' need to stay in operation often conflicts with the need to finish a project and leave. "You as an NGO have to try and find new projects to keep going. So it's a fine line between needing to stay and wanting to."

Première Urgence, an NGO that had done a lot of work in the emergency phase of the mission, was struggling to survive in fall 2001. I sat in on a meeting between the NGO and Giampiero, the UNCA utilities officer in Banshik, who was also the UN regional winterization coordinator.

The NGO representatives outlined imminent catastrophe for thousands of families if Première Urgence were not given money immediately to start buying wood and coal to distribute. Giampiero commented after the meeting that what the representative was saying about needy beneficiaries was really not true right now. But, he said, the NGOs needed to survive too. Although they are usually seen as highly principled, which they are for the most part, this need to survive sometimes led them to be economical with the truth or to tell the donors what they wanted to hear. An American working for the NGO Crisis Web, which wrote independent reports on the situation in Kosovo, said:

> We're becoming top-heavy, the usual thing that happens to an NGO. We wrote a report on Macedonia saying what was going to happen, and they [in the head office] said, "No, change it." Then it happened just like we said! Now they want us to change what we write to fit with the prevailing political wisdom. They're worried about money. All the money is pulling out, and we work on a project-by-project basis, so we're constantly looking for money and are very vulnerable to shifts in donor moods.

Cooperation

NGOs found it difficult to cooperate with the other actors on the ground, and their impatience with other organizations and desire to carry out their centralized agreements ended up being a significant impediment to cooperation in the municipality.

There was little cooperation between the NGOs. Within the municipalities, other NGOs were seen as competition, and although there was some initiative to prevent overlap, by and large, they worked on their own, guarding their own information. William said:

> It's very difficult, actually. Everybody guards information about beneficiaries and families. Nobody likes to give out that information . . . a large portion of the work done is that. You've invested in doing something. But it is clear that cooperation does not exist enough. There's only us and ACT in Banshik at the moment, so we have to discuss things so we don't overlap. There's a local NGO, or is it German NGO, they have a project, which is they have a doors and windows factory, and we work quite a lot with them. We met them through the NHC [National Housing Committee]. We worked with them last year. From time to time, we get random bits of information from NGOs saying, "Can you help this case?" . . . but . . . [cooperation] is quite uncommon.

The NGOs also found it challenging to work with the bureaucratic UNCA and with the network, including their donors within the reconstruction pillar. The basic barrier to cooperation was the clash between what Antonio Donini has called the "free spirits" of the NGOs and the bureaucrats.[12] The NGOs were reluctant to work with the institutions of the large international organizations, and this was hindering effective operation within a network organization. They were impatient with the speed at which they operated and had a "go it alone" mentality. In the 1960s and 1970s, NGOs were seen as "the most appropriate catalytic agent for fostering development from below, because their organizational priorities and procedures are diametrically opposed to those of the institutions at the top."[13]

So the early NGOs were purposeful "outsiders" to the establishment; they refused to cooperate with the state, perceiving this as leading down the path to co-optation or collaboration, and they refused to work with the market because it might lead to the corrupting of community solidarity. Instead, they held to the principles of self-sufficiency, independence, and social entrepreneurship as they built up alternative models of development and self-governance. But the largest sources of funds were from the private sector or government, and in the 1980s, the need to become self-sustaining drove NGOs into the arms of international institutions of finance, governments, and other NGOs.

However, the NGOs' unease with their new "insider" status was still evident in Kosovo and was a major barrier to cooperation. K-LED was obliged to participate in the network organization because it received its money from the European Union and had to work with the UNCA, the local municipality, and the leadership of villages to draw up lists of beneficiaries. The funding of the project came with guidelines for selecting beneficiaries, and the EU and UN had decided those guidelines in Pristina.

In an interview, William spoke glowingly of working for K-LED in Afghanistan, where there was no government to have to deal with and they could do as they saw fit:

> When you work, say, in Afghanistan, you work without UNMIK; you have the UN, but they don't do the same kind of task as here. So you have a local government you can't work with, so you work directly with major donors like the World Bank. Here you have UNMIK and the European Agency for Reconstruction [EAR], and major donors like the World Bank work through them in Pristina, and then these organizations will mete out the work to NGOs. So your influence over the funders, the actual people with the money, is very small, because you don't really get to see them. In Afghanistan, because you can't trust the government, the World Bank will come and see K-LED and say, "We want to fund this." So you have a lot more influence over things.

This impatience with bureaucracy and lack of a larger view of the mission, the lack of a network consciousness, inhibited K-LED's willingness to listen to and work with the other agencies.

Hence, there was a high awareness of the need to cooperate but less so of the system being a network structured so that all were equal partners. William acknowledged that collaboration with other actors was crucial. "You couldn't do it [selection of beneficiaries, i.e., which families get a new house built for them by K-LED] without them. You just couldn't run a project without UNMIK and also without the municipality." But he believed that lack of ultimate authority has led to problems:

> That's one of the things that's a bit difficult, it's not really clearly defined who IS in charge. The municipal housing committee is made up of councilors, and essentially all the other NGOs working on reconstruction in this municipality, plus some local organizations, like the Mother Teresa Society and [the handicapped association] Handikos. Plus a European Union representative from Previca. The head of reconstruction from UNMIK and usually representatives, usually the director, from the Department of Urbanism in the municipality, and somebody from Social Welfare.

Selection of beneficiaries was a very collaborative process and one that yielded tremendous problems in Kosovo. In Thezren, it was an open secret that the families who got their houses built first were the ones best connected to the local politicians. In Banshik, it was not quite as blatant, but there were still problems. Several of the organizations in the network system were involved: K-LED, the UNCA, the local municipality, village leaders, and the department of Social Welfare in the municipality (under direct authority of central Department of Social Welfare in Pristina). William described the process in an interview:

> There were four workers, two expats, two local, the social staff, who did the assessment. Then we have a technical staff who did all the technical stuff, they're deliberately kept quite separate. So technical problems don't influence your choice of beneficiary. We would visit a number of families from the village, complete the assessment based on the list provided by the village representatives that were elected. We would then divide the beneficiaries into the categories A, B, [and] C. A are supposed to be the most urgent cases. As far as I can tell, Pierre's job [UNCA reconstruction officer] is to manage the other components in the municipality in the exact same selection process. They are local people, and they have a lot of influence over the process, because, for instance, the Social Welfare, they know a lot of people who are receiving social benefits, so they are a very useful source of information if they are working well. But if they're not working well, they're not any use at all. They drive the process into the ground. The problem was we had a very short period between

when we give the list of the central beneficiaries to UN and the day we should sign the contract that the beneficiaries will receive assistance. In that period, we have to get approval from the village representatives, approval from the NHC [National Housing Committee], and the list of beneficiaries, which we publish publicly and there is an appeals period.

That whole process is done by us, not by UNMIK. The village representative is our responsibility, but UNMIK could have been much more part of the process. We did elections in twenty villages, and UNMIK turned up twice in that process. So they [the village representatives]became sort of K-LED employees, but they're not paid, they were under the responsibility of K-LED. But they're supposed to be really under the responsibility of the municipal council. I think the difficulty is . . . this project, houses are very expensive items, so there's a lot of pressure, everyone's trying very hard to get a house, so nobody actually wants the responsibility of choosing who gets a house and who doesn't. No one [in the NGOs, UNCA, and local administration] wanted to be seen as responsible for turning down people [cf. KFOR's reluctance to be associated with the destruction of anything, even illegally constructed houses]. . . . The final decision rests with the municipal housing committee. We link with them through the weekly meeting with the reconstruction committee, which is chaired by the person responsible for reconstruction in UN-MIK. It's all the NGOs working, the local NGOs and the Center for Social Work. And it's at that meeting that the lists of beneficiaries are approved or not approved.

Thus, the process of determining beneficiaries was a complicated process that involved a lot of people, with diverse priorities, but one that K-LED managed, albeit with a degree of frustration and impatience. K-LED was divided into two, the reconstruction and agricultural sections. Overall, the reconstruction side had worked quite well. This was not the case with its agricultural division, which was distributing cows and tractors to both Albanian and Serb villages. The villagers were very unhappy with how K-LED had selected the recipients. Jacques, who had worked with K-LED in Banshik as an agronomist, supported the villagers' complaints. He attributed the unfair selection to the centralized decision making in the NGO and to the recruitment of young people who did not listen to the local people. They had signed up with the World Bank and Food and Agricultural Organization, even though Jacques and the local Albanians had advised them to renegotiate the contract requirement for village meetings. The two young French NGO workers refused to do so, and sure enough, the village meetings to select the beneficiaries were rife with conflict and nepotism.

The situation reached a crisis point in November, when the UNCA in Banshik got the message that the villagers in Gracie (a Serbian village) were furious. K-LED had delivered cows to the village the previous Saturday, but there was disagreement about how they should be distributed, so K-LED had simply taken the cows, driven away, and given them to Albanian "families of martyrs." Peterson organized a meeting at 2 P.M. with the director of the K-LED Banshik field office, the mayor (Ebush), and the director of agriculture in the local municipality. Peterson telephoned Pristina K-LED, its Kosovo head office, outlining the source of the problem: "We have lists of needy families, an LCO, a municipal council, but we were left out of the process. Now it looks like unless we get thirteen cows to Gracie, we're going to have a major pissing contest. I don't know how it happened or why, but we've got to sort it out. I'm putting a hold on the distribution of tractors also until we know what's going on." He then said to me: "If they don't stop distributing them, I'll get them arrested for causing a riot."

When I interviewed him, Jacques shook his head in frustration at the inflexibility and unresponsiveness of the NGO:

> We—UNMIK—are trying to establish working procedures and democracy, but acting like the politicians did before—pulling personal influence, bypassing procedures—is not on. But then William, from K-LED, is the other extreme. He is totally inflexible, no one gets any leeway. If I have an upset farmer who didn't make the criteria and he asks me to put him on the reserve list, I do it. He is happy, I am happy, he doesn't get it in the end, because there is no reserve list, but this is the human way to do it. But William, he will say there is no reserve list and everyone is angry and upset.

Thus, the principled inflexibility of K-LED's young employees not only angered the villagers but caused a potentially volatile security situation. They became more concerned as the date for their departure drew near to finish the project, even if finishing it meant upsetting a lot of people, including their network organization partners.

Participating in a network organization with established hierarchies is difficult for NGOs, because it is contrary to their institutional history. They had the lowest level of network consciousness of all the organizations in the municipalities and region I studied in Kosovo. When it came to the survival and well-being of their own organizations and the local populations, their own organizations came first, whether from an unwillingness to deal with disdained organizations or from trying to wind up on a schedule or on contracts from above in their own hierarchy.

Each organization's ability to contribute to the synergy of the mission was dependent on how networked it was as an organization internally. If it had managed to incorporate changes that made it closer to a network organization, it was able to function more easily within the network organization externally. The key features were less emphasis on hierarchy and more on flexibility and responsiveness, the ability to let an individual's contribution be based on relevant knowledge or expertise, not rank or title, and the ability to connect with information, people, and skill as needed both within the organization and outside within the network organization. All the organizations were becoming more networked, but at different speeds. Their ability to change affected not only their own effectiveness but also the effectiveness of the network organization and the ability of the mission to induce cooperation and participation by the local population.

Conclusion

Implications for International Interventions in Kosovo, Afghanistan, Iraq, and Beyond . . .

Lessons Learned That Are Relevant for Other International Interventions

The following lessons from Kosovo's experience so far, if given due consideration by organizations going into other interventions, will save considerable time and resources. They will also immeasurably contribute to the institution building and reconstruction processes.

1. There must be an understanding of the difference between a hierarchical organization and a network organization and what it means to work in both. There must be a network consciousness, particularly on the part of the leadership. There must be awareness that participation is best induced through an organizational culture that is informal, socially embedded, and accountable. Trust is the key organizational quality and must be continually and actively produced. Trust in turn contributes to the amount of information exchanged, the feeling of identification with the mission and its goals, and collaborative problem-solving capabilities. Each of these, in turn, increases the level of trust among the organizations and their personnel.

2. The network organization must be fluid and flexible enough to include local organizations and populations. The local municipal administration and local populations should be treated with much greater inclusiveness and respect—as full partners—because they are truly the key to the long-term success of an intervention. Without their participation and cooperation, the efforts of the international organizations will come to nothing.

3. The value of the institutional culture of the network organization can be significantly enhanced if the information and communications technology (ICT) infrastructure—the electronic network—is inclusive. It must include all the international organizations and the locals working alongside or with the international mission. This inclusiveness increases trust, encourages a sense of identification with the mission, facilitates information transfer, and gives everyone the ability to communicate with anyone else on the intervention. In the process, it considerably increases collaborative problem-solving capabilities. Mobile phones could be used by everyone in the intervention, obviating the need for more expensive and proprietary radio systems and satellite phones.

4. Information technologies can be utilized to improve the transmission of institutional history both in terms of quantity and quality of information. Institutional history can include explicit and tacit knowledge. Reports should be available electronically and exchanged weekly between organizations and have succinct analysis rather than detailed description. For information to be effective interorganizationally, it must be "fit for use," that is, in a familiar language and syntax. There must be a commonly established interpretative space where succinctly written documents can be accessed by all organizations. For this to work, there must be synchronized understandings and interpretations. If this is the case, there can be reciprocal learning about the other organization's stock of knowledge, its historical line of acquisition of that knowledge, and especially the actual self-interpretation by the owner or writer of the knowledge. Finally, facilitating face-to-face interaction is important in an attempt to synchronize associations and to establish common interpretative space.

5. The international civilian police (CivPol) should be organized in small national groups, like KFOR. This would enormously increase the authority and effectiveness of CivPol.

6. Organizations should have the authority to resolve crises at the local level and not have to resort to letters being exchanged at the top of their respective hierarchies.

7. Economic development in any postwar situation should be given priority. All the senior UN people in Kosovo who were effective, and the many young people who expressed a desire to emigrate at the first opportunity, agreed that if the money pumped into the province in the two years from 1999 to 2001 had been put at least partly into job creation, the intervention would be much further along the road to the fulfillment of its goals.

8. There should also be an effective auditing system by each organization and by the mission overall. It existed in Kosovo in theory but not in reality.

9. Recruitment of internationals by the international organizations should receive more attention—more people with eclectic backgrounds should be recruited, and merit cannot be sacrificed to political representation. People with experience in the private sector often bring the flexibility, pragmatism, and can-do approach necessary for a dynamic and rapidly changing environment. Similarly, people from certain parts of the military, for instance, those with civil-military liaison training, have skills and experience suitable to the environment of an intervention.

The success of any intervention is dependent on the ability of the organizations involved to cooperate in a temporary network organization and to draw the local populations into it. In Kosovo, as in Afghanistan and Iraq, there are individuals and organizations vested in trying to hinder, control, or hijack the process of democratization, institution building, and reconstruction. Cooperation between the international organizations and the local populations is the only effective way to know who these vested interests are, come up with responses to their threats, and in so doing provide the security necessary for the various nonmilitary international organizations to do their tasks.

In Afghanistan, the deputy governor of Zabol province has observed that the lack of communication between local communities and coalition soldiers means that the latter "would not recognize Mullah Omar [the fugitive Taliban leader] if he stood in front of them. All the Taliban have to do is put down their gun and say hello. No one would know them. Until the Americans are on the ground and negotiating with the local community leaders and disarming them, they will not win."[1] Not only does the intervention find it hard to know who is who on the ground, the population knows this and is fearful that it is only a question of time before the international contingent gives up and the Taliban and warlords hold full sway again. With a significant security presence confined to Kabul and Kandahar, it is easy for the Taliban and warlords to intimidate the population; they attack international workers and local people who are working with international organizations. This is deeply problematic for the intervention, because getting the local populations to trust the intervention and international organizations is vital if they are to participate in the institution-building process. The deputy governor of Zabol explains, "People are too much afraid of the Taliban. But they are not optimistic about the government's future, so they support them. If they fight against the Taliban, they will have nothing."[2]

In the UN mission in Kosovo, the UNCA, OSCE, EU, NGOs, CivPol, and KFOR all recognized that they needed one another. No one hierarchical organization could do all that was required in such a complex intervention—each organization had unique resources and skills but also needed what the other organizations had to offer. Each organization had to resist the temptation to be organizationally imperialistic—to want to extend its influence over other organizations' area of expertise for its own benefit and not that of the larger mission. Organizations also had to overcome a reluctance to share resources with other constituent organizations in UNMIK and to recognize that this sharing would contribute to the intervention.

The mandate of the mission was not only to establish a peacekeeping presence but also to work with the Kosovars to build functioning, sustainable democratic institutions, so the success of the intervention depended on the ability of the international actors to cooperate and coordinate with the local municipal government and local police and populations. The open, communication-rich, inclusive, and egalitarian culture of a network organization significantly contributed to this, as the experience in Banshik demonstrated. If the institutional culture of the internationals is one of a cluster of hierarchies concerned primarily with following their own rules and procedures and not seeing the task and results as dependent on participation and cooperation, there is little chance that local populations and organizations will be successfully assimilated into the new structures. They are left outside and in opposition to each other, as was the situation in Thezren.

The organizations involved—the UN, militaries, OSCE, police—are traditional hierarchical, bureaucratic organizations, used to operating behind their respective walls. The ability to work effectively in UNMIK required each organization to retain its organizational integrity while simultaneously adapting itself to function as a networked organization in a network organization such as UNMIK. The organizational design of UNMIK was a hybrid: a combination of each organization having a hierarchical chain of command, from the local through the regional to the center, and simultaneously working together as a network organization at each level. An awareness of the organizational changes required for an intervention designed in this way was not widespread among the international organizations in Kosovo. Even the planners seemed to be groping toward setting up what was needed without being able to explicitly articulate what was happening. Consequently, aside from a minimal network structure at the local, municipal, and central levels, there was little guidance on how to establish a working relationship with one another.

At the UN HQ in New York and in NATO, there was also some, but not enough, thought given to the role of communication and information technologies. The electronic network only encompassed part of the network organization and was fraught with issues of ownership, lack of training, and suitability of technology. A coherent strategy for its role in integrating the organizations was lacking. Information technology enables the sharing of resources and information. Yet the UN information and communications network (the intranet, Internet, radio, satellite phones) only included the UNCA, the EU, and CivPol.

KFOR, the OSCE, and the NGOs had their own ICT systems. The local municipality and local police had what was available locally—that is, very little. The only electronic communications medium available to all was the mobile phone system. People with access to the Internet could use free web-based email services such as Yahoo and Hotmail. Information and the communications infrastructure are the blood and skeleton of a network organization; the lack of a shared physical ICT infrastructure and the resulting lack of a common interactive virtual space severely inhibit the generation and maintenance of trust, a sense of identification with the mission, open communications, and collective problem-solving capabilities.

But not all organizations or people will use ICTs in the same way. Depending on the degree of trust and knowledge of the other organizations or the degree of social presence required, a variety of media are used. E-mail is used when there is reciprocal understanding and no need for visual or vocal cues, the telephone when a visual presence is not required, and face-to-face meetings when there is need for all the information possible to ensure effective communication. In crisis intervention, face-to-face interaction is essential at least once before people feel comfortable using e-mail with people from other organizations, and sometimes even with people who belong to their own organization. Communication is dependent on more than technology. The level of trust, identification, and collective problem-solving capabilities and experience will greatly influence the level of "transactive memory" among the group. As the transactive memory enables the participants in the group to learn who knows what, whom to give different information to, and whom to get information from, the efficacy of the weekly interagency meetings increases exponentially. Within the organizations, the use of ICTs enormously increased the speed of transmission of material, and helped establish an institutional history that incoming personnel could access and learn from, making it easier for the organizations to function as part of a networked organization.

The institutional culture of a network organization is the glue that holds it together, and like glue, it can vary greatly in strength. As in many other areas of human activity, an awareness of what it takes to work in a networked environment is slowly percolating through the organizations, but it is distinctly uneven. This is particularly difficult when most of the personnel in a mission come from lifelong careers in hierarchical, bureaucratic organizations where rewards are given based on stability, longevity, discretion, and loyalty to that particular organization. In Kosovo, several individuals in all organizations, but crucially in the UNCA, because it was the hub of the network, did have qualities and skills appropriate to the network organizational form and culture. In the absence of coherent guidelines for implementing the mandate through the structure of the organization, this situation allows individuals to be organizational pioneers in their willingness to experiment and be innovative.

Banshik and Thezren had the same organizational network, and the same ICTS were available, yet they had different outcomes. Each organization had the potential to act as a network organization, but if the hub did not have that capacity, as in Thezren, that potential was stymied to a great extent in the other organizations. It was also stymied in the local community, because the local populations were kept firmly outside the walls of the UNCA in Thezren, and related to in a superior-subordinate manner. The institutional culture in Thezren's UNCA was that of a traditional, bureaucratic, hierarchical organization with little apparent awareness of what being part of a networked mission involving democratization and participation involved.

In Banshik, the institutional culture of the UNCA included the ability to function as part of the UN hierarchy, but the emphasis was on the UNCA as part of the local network organization. The leadership was appropriate for this: Terry Peterson and Orash Fatoohi had the awareness and the skill to bring people together cooperatively, and each of the organizations drew on its own network attributes to collectively build an institutional culture appropriate for this type of temporary network mission. It was a question of cultivating a particular institutional culture that became independent of the people within it even as they perpetuated it. Every type of organization has its own institutional culture, and the institutional culture of a bureaucracy has certain personnel requirements—everyone recognizes that. A network institutional culture requires somewhat different personnel characteristics, or personnel characteristics that would be less important in a hierarchical context. These characteristics of leading from behind, persuasion, telling a broad inclusive story, establishing links with people inside and outside the organization, fostering an organizational culture that is informal, socially embedded, and transparent, and hence responsive and flexible, can be inculcated and learned, just as bureaucratic culture can be. Only then can enough trust be generated to ensure identification with the network organization as well as one's own, effective information transfer, and collaborative problem-solving capabilities. The firms in the new globalized hi-tech network economy think like this.

Interconnectedness

Where are these challenges and changes coming from? Why are they so important? The enormous changes in organizations in the late twentieth and early twenty-first centuries have been prompted by several factors: the decline of sovereignty and the rise of human rights as an issue in international relations, the demands of democratizing societies previously under a communist regime or a dictatorship, the increase in turbulence in both the business and nonbusiness sectors, the imperatives of rapid developments in ICTs, and the rise of the network organization both in terms of organizations changing internally to become more responsive, with information as the key resource, and in terms of organizations coming together temporarily to form an alliance or network to achieve something that one hierarchy could not do alone.

This new organizational form began in the private sector, because firms competing in the global marketplace discovered that ICTs enable them to reorganize so as to be much more flexible, responsive, and efficient in what is an increasingly competitive environment. Networking is a third way of organizing: not relying on discrete market exchanges, not relying on economies of scale in enormous organizations that do everything in-house, but involving several organizations all working on different parts of the supply chain, combining and recombining as market opportunities arise. In effect, competition between hierarchies has been replaced by a combination of competition and cooperation—the desire now is to be competitive but to recognize that your organization's competitiveness is critically dependent on other firms in the supply chain. You want those organizations to be efficient, for today's competitors could be tomorrow's collaborators on a different project.

The regional economy in Silicon Valley epitomizes this approach. The organizational culture of this "co-opetition" is quite different from that of the organizational culture of hierarchical firms—organizations that are collaborating need the speed, flexibility, and responsiveness that greater trust, the sharing of information and knowledge, the flattening of hierarchy, the ability to identify, not only with your own organization, but also with whatever network organization you are temporarily part of, and a culture focused on expertise, not status, provide. A hierarchical culture would significantly impede an organization's ability to perform well in this environment.

The turbulence of the world economy since 1990 requires flexibility and responsiveness. There has been an exponential increase in the scale and form of interconnectedness in economic behavior and economic institutions, encapsulated in what we understand as globalization. Participants in the global economy are adapting to the global, that is, transborder, nature of business and the impossibility of being economically successful and maintaining rigid barriers against the rest of the world.[3] Globalization has been predominantly an economic phenomenon, because the world sees the momentum toward bringing down trade barriers and the development of a free market in capital, with movement toward a freer market in labor and goods. The ICT revolution has enabled and is reinforcing globalization, particularly, thus far, in global business. It has transformed existing organizations and their behavior, allowing the supply chain to be stretched across borders and time zones, and ramping up productivity in the process.

This economic interconnectedness has received a huge amount of attention in the past decade, but little attention has been paid to how these ICT-driven organizational changes are affecting politics and the process of democratization, apart from the rise of transnational NGOs.

Most fundamentally, at the global level, such economic interconnectedness is not balanced by democratic interconnectedness. The necessity and the political will for interventions are evidence of the same forces working at the political level. However, the organizational changes that were necessary for economic interconnectedness to reap productivity rewards are in an earlier state in the process of democratization both globally and in interventions. The organizations involved in interventions must be able to work as part of a network organization and to see themselves as part of a dynamic environment that will call for them to combine and recombine in different ways as the need or demand arises. Both transnational and local NGOs transcend borders and are much more networked,[4] but NGOs are only one type of organizational actor in the international arena.

The UN, NATO, OSCE, and other political and military bodies and alliances all have to adapt to a truly interdependent world where borders are no longer sacrosanct and the tasks are not rigidly divided into military, civil, and political. The best insurance for long-term stability—democratization—won't work without the participation of local populations, whether in Kosovo, East Timor, Afghanistan, or Iraq. Again, looking to the business sector, the ability of the organizations to combine and recombine effectively is critically interlinked with the flexibility and responsiveness facilitated by the drawing in of the local institutions and culture conducive to the network type of organization.[5] In Silicon Valley, the local institutions and culture were a key factor in enabling this flexibility and responsiveness. Northern California's lack of pretension and lack of established social hierarchy, the cooperation between universities and colleges, and the resultant willingness to be innovative and to do business whenever and wherever you could exchange information—such as in informal socializing with people in other firms—and to get together to build local institutions for sharing critical information, all contributed to the region's ability to function in a networked way. Equally, the local institutions and culture in Kosovo could contribute in a much more significant way to the mission, as could the local institutions of Iraq and Afghanistan. In Kosovo, in 1999, there was a functioning parallel system of governance and administration committed to democracy and liberty that had worked underground after Albanians were excluded from government and administration in 1989. To condemn this as politicized and to dismantle it wholesale was going too far—it was a waste of resources, goodwill, and commitment. Clearly, it could not have been accepted as the de facto government and administrative structure, because Serbs were not part of it. But the Serbs had the dismantled official structure. Elements of both in terms of expertise and structure could have been salvaged and reincorporated into new structures in a way that did not negate the resources of expertise and goodwill.

The interconnectedness of the world is not going to disappear but will increase. Sovereignty is no longer sacrosanct, and democratization in postconflict zones is too large a project to be done by any one or handful of hierarchical organizations. To deny and ignore these realities, as the United States did in Iraq after the war there in 2004, is only to make the task that much more difficult, because it will eventually be seen that there is no other way forward except through cooperation and coordination. New ICTs make it possible for different organizations to cooperate in a network organization to achieve goals impossible for any one organization. In troubled parts of the world, the UN and the international organizations will increasingly be designing missions to include each other and making full use of information technology. They will need to understand the differences between a hierarchical and a network organization, the role of a network organization's institutional culture, and how to foster this culture to facilitate working together and alongside local organizations and actors in building institutions that will protect against war and conflict in the future, both in the territories in question and in the wider international community.

Afghanistan, Iraq, and Beyond . . .

Kosovo was the first intervention with a high level of international cooperation on behalf of stability and human rights both during the military campaign and in the postconflict democratization and reconstruction efforts. It has had tremendous resources put into it by the international community. Money has not been poured into Afghanistan the way it was into Kosovo, despite promises from the Bush administration, among others. Money is a more important factor in Afghanistan, because it has a high level of illiteracy and a totally destroyed infrastructure. This is not the case in Kosovo and Iraq, both of which have high levels of literacy, secularized institutions, a degree of industrialization, and an infrastructure that, although heavily damaged and eroded by war and years of neglect, provides a base to build on. In Afghanistan, there is limited international cooperation but no money. So far in Iraq, there is money but little international cooperation.

Some of the same actors—international police, the U.S., British, and other NATO militaries, UN agencies (although significantly not the UN Secretariat, which staffs UN civil administrations), and NGOs—are on the ground in Afghanistan. However, coordination and cooperation between all partners in the process has been lacking. Contrary to reports that the money is lacking but the model is successful in Afghanistan, both lack of money AND the "model" are major problems there. President Bush's "new Marshall Plan" for Afghanistan never materialized. International assistance has declined and a lack of political will confines the peacekeeping mission to Kabul, even as the central government loses control over the Afghan countryside. This security vacuum outside Kabul makes it impossible for civil organizations to work together or with the local people, who are targeted by the still armed and active Taliban if they work with the internationals. Security alone is not enough, but without it, there is no trust among the local people that the internationals are going to stick around until a real recovery is made, and consequently nothing else can happen. The consequences of the lack of cooperation by the local populations are serious. Until the local populations are on board, democratization and reconstruction are stalled.

Equally, the lack of access for most Iraqis to the civilian administration in Iraq, the destruction of institutions, and the lack of significant attention being given to anything other than the military front by the U.S.-led coalition created a situation that begged for cooperation between all parties, including the local organizations and their burgeoning leadership. In Kosovo, there was leadership, but it had been driven underground. The international intervention could have used it more effectively, but where it was worked with in partnership, the results were promising. In Afghanistan, leadership has been based on tribal and warlord loyalties.[6] The challenge for the intervention is to get those warlords and tribal leaders into the process of institution and nation building, to impart a genuine sense of sharing common interests and goals.

In Iraq, the long tyranny of Saddam Hussein stymied the development of alternative leadership. The international intervention can facilitate the emergence of genuine leaders from each community—Sunni, Shiite, and Kurds—but must generate a vision of leadership and the future that is not based on ethnic and religious differences. There is plenty of scope in each of these communities for leadership to use past sufferings to promote affiliation on the basis of religion and ethnicity, but the very experience of shared pain and discrimination could, with the right innovative interorganizational leadership, provide an alternative basis for trust, identification, and future plans.[7] And, most practically, the international intervention should ensure that each community is fairly represented in posts at all levels. In this way, decision-making power that had atrophied under

Hussein's regime can be slowly reconstituted, as can the institutions of civil society.

But for this to happen and to be effective, Iraq needs a parallel civilian administration similar to, if not as significant as, that in Kosovo. Both Iraq and Afghanistan would benefit from a model of cooperation and co-ordination closer to the Kosovar one. But cooperation necessitates having the relevant actors on the ground in the first place and is based on the perception that no one organization can do everything and that even if it could, political considerations would make it inadvisable. The dangers and consequences of one organization trying to do it all is evident in the persistent hostility and insurgencies against the United States in Iraq and the unwillingness of international partners and organizations to get involved. Effective cooperation requires a ceding of control. The United States must cede authority to international partners and to Iraqi organizations and populations. The coalition must move from a hierarchical mindset to one that can also encompass a network orientation. It is only then that all the resources, including but not just security, can be mobilized for effective democratization. It is only then that Iraqis will have a sense of owning their future and take responsibility for stopping those who want to destroy it, and this is also true of the Afghans.

Looking at and thinking of democracy only in the narrow electoral sense limits our ability to guide processes of democratization and economic development.[8] Rapid democratization through international interventions requires a multiplicity of organizations to work together and with a web of local institutions. The task of building the liberal institutions of democracy is too complex for any single or even two or three organizations—a peacekeeping force and the organization of elections are just not sufficient. Every level of society needs to be developed, and this has to be done in conjunction with the local populations. Without full psychological participation, without people being persuaded to participate in the building as well as the operation of institutions, democratization will stall. How to do this? There is no easy answer. But adapting some of the ideas emerging from economic globalization and interconnectedness to the political realm can contribute significantly to our understanding of how best to harness disparate organizations' strengths and mitigate their weaknesses. They can contribute to our understanding of how to get organizations to cooperate in attaining a set of goals; to see themselves as part of a larger project and to behave accordingly.

REFERENCE MATTER

APPENDIX

Background and Methods

Between my first visit to Kosovo in 2000 and my second in 2002, September 11 exploded on the world. I flew to Pristina, the capital of Kosovo, days after 9/11, and the U.S.-led bombing of Afghanistan began while I was in Kosovo. Developments in Afghanistan were keenly watched by the internationals in Kosovo for what they might mean for them and their organizations. Indeed, they were watched in countries around the world for what they might mean for the international community. Despite initial rallying around the need to tackle what it was becoming apparent was a global terrorist threat, and despite coordination among nations in the war in Afghanistan, it soon became clear that the Bush administration was moving away from a cooperative multilateral response to the fundamentalist Islamic terrorist threat and toward one reliant on traditional notions of military superiority and sovereignty. This was despite the growing evidence that the network of terrorists was not going to be defeated by conventional military means and that their existence was dependent on the tacit support produced by a lack of democracy and economic progress in large sections of the world. Afghanistan and Iraq have shown that conventional military prowess will still bring victory in conventional military situations. But conventional military victory is but one battle in a much longer war when the task is to build democratic institutions and to facilitate cooperation among the organizations and states contributing to the intervention, and to facilitate cooperation among the different populations in the postconflict area.

In Kosovo in 2001, my choice of cases, the municipalities Banshik and Thezren, was based on a preconceived theoretical framework as distinct from a preconceived theory. I knew that I would be investigating the qualities that facilitated cooperation and networking among organizations, so I had as an orienting theoretical framework the qualities that have been studied in various studies of mainly for-profit organizations in a temporary network organization, namely, trust, information flow, ability to jointly solve problems, and identification with the mission. I was interested in how these factors were produced and how they facilitated or by their absence obstructed the participation of the organizations in a network organization. This study gives a unique insight into how a network organization comprising several different international organizations managed to cooperate in the humanitarian mission in Kosovo, the first UN "governance" mission.

In the field, I used an "interactionist" or social constructionist approach that emphasizes how organizations are socially constructed out of recurrent micro behaviors that transpire at the face-to-face level of analysis.[1] Organizations are generated and sustained out of patterns of common behavior and language use. If social and organizational realities undergo such a continuous process of enactment and reaffirmation at the face-to-face level, it is important that we develop models consistent with this. The ethnomethodologist Harold Garfinkel argued that we must pay "to the most commonplace activities of daily life the attention usually accorded extraordinary events"; that by so doing, we may be able to understand these mundane activities as substantive social phenomena in their own right.[2] An interactionist perspective also enhances our understanding of the relations between the realms of action and structure in everyday routines. At the same time, the continuous unfolding of everyday behavior routines is integral to the reproduction and replication, even the modification, of macro structural features.[3] The implications are important, not only for understanding, but also for designing organizations and building institutions. For instance, we can now see why and how the degree of informality can build distinctive cultures in network organizations. The ideas in the discussion of formality and informality provide schemas for describing and recognizing cultural/normative aspects of network organizations that have heretofore been underdefined.

In wanting to study the workings of a nonprofit network organization in a humanitarian intervention, I was faced with the problem of how to gain access to a socially and geographically insulated and still relatively physically risky setting. In the end, access was facilitated through the strength of weak ties.[4] My research trip to investigate how the U.S. military was adapting to its peacekeeping role in Kosovo the previous year, 2000, culminated in a half hour chat at Pristina airport with an acquaintance of the professor I was accompanying. The professor introduced him as a municipal administrator with the UN and we joked about my coming back to research his team's work. He responded positively to this idea—in the half hour of talk, it emerged that he had an academic orientation, with a PhD in political science as well as a military background. We exchanged cards and parted ways. I put this offer of access at the back of my mind as I got on with getting through the PhD program in sociology at UCLA. The ideas circulating in my head came together to take the shape of a study exploring the developments in networking theory in economic sociology, including the role of new ICTs, in a region where international organizations were working together in an unprecedented way. I contacted Terry Peterson by e-mail to see if his offer of cooperation was still open. He responded enthusiastically to the idea, and we continued to exchange e-mails as I received the funding for my project, passed my dissertation proposal defense, and finally pinned down a date for my arrival in Kosovo.

On the day I arrived in Kosovo, I experienced the worst moment of my entire research trip when I emerged on a warm September Sunday afternoon into the crowds of Kosovars milling about outside Pristina airport and I realized that I had not arranged any backup plan if Peterson was not at the airport to meet me as we had agreed. I knew no one else in Kosovo except for a woman I had chatted to on the plane. We had exchanged e-mail addresses, so in the worst-case scenario, I could ask her for assistance. I searched around trying to remember what this man looked like. Then I saw a trilby hat, a beard, and a pipe and thought, "I think that's him." Not 100 percent sure of this, I approached the man and said, "'Excuse me, are you Terry Peterson?'" "Indeed I am," he responded, shook my hand warmly, and said, "Follow me." We wended our way through the crowd to his UN car and left the airport.

There was no setup time required for my research. I arrived at 3 P.M. on a Sunday afternoon and was gathering data from the moment I met Peterson. As we drove to Banshik the back way through the Serbian enclaves, he immediately began talking about his work, and I began straightaway to get a picture of the setup of the municipality. That evening, over dinner in a very basic local café, we met his chief language assistant and a local man seeking the MA's (Peterson's) and UNMIK's support for a cross-ethnic business venture. After dropping off my luggage and before dinner, we went to the UN office, where I was shown the layout of the building and met Orash Fatoohi, the deputy MA, who usually, as I was to discover, worked several hours on Saturday and Sunday as well as his regular workdays. The next morning, I arrived at the office in Banshik at 7.30 A.M., and I didn't stop collecting data every waking moment until I left six weeks later. The first day was spent meeting everyone in the office in the UN in Banshik, sitting in on meetings, setting up interviews, conducting interviews, accompanying officers out into the field, having lunch with the UN staff, the four-pillar meeting at 5 P.M. that spilled on after its official end at 6 P.M., getting business cards, and arranging meetings and interviews later in the week, an hour and a half to write up notes from the day, then dinner with Peterson and Fatoohi as they filled me in further on who was who and what was what in the municipality. Each day was like that, with variations depending on where I was (Banshik or the second municipality, Thezren), whom I was meeting, and where I was eating, but always observing and collecting data. Given that I was interested in building up a complete picture of the international organizations and the locals in both municipalities I studied, every conversation, every throwaway remark contributed to my understanding and data. On weekends, there was always somebody working or a town hall meeting going on, or people who had been busy during the week were available to be interviewed, or there were delegations/visitors to the municipalities to be shown around, or social occasions.

After spending an initial period in Banshik, it was time to see about gaining access to another municipality, necessarily one that was similar in many respects to but that had gone in a different direction than Banshik. Several people suggested Thezren, because it was adjacent to Banshik and was very similar in key ways yet had had a different experience since the start of the UN mission after the war. Peterson phoned the MA there, who agreed to the proposal. For the rest of my research period, I interspersed days in Banshik and Thezren, depending on research needs and logistics, mainly the availability of transport. I was usually able to hitch a ride with a UN officer to get between the municipalities, the region, and the center, Pristina. When I couldn't, I took a local taxi. I spent several days interviewing UN, EU, OSCE, and NGO personnel both at the regional level and in Pristina. However, the focus of my research was the two municipalities, Banshik and Thezren.

The Selection of Interviewees

All my requests for interviews were face-to-face or, if not, then by e-mail or phone after an initial face-to-face meeting. Only two people out of sixty-six were unwilling to be interviewed. Besides working my way through the key personnel I was meeting in all organizations in each municipality, I used a "snowball strategy" to ask for contact details of people interviewees mentioned. In all, I conducted sixty-four in-depth interviews, attended fifteen key meetings, and followed personnel around, going with them into the field, visiting the police stations, military bases, and OSCE and NGO offices. Luckily, the UN offices, the police station, OSCE, the military bases, and the NGOs offices were either within easy reach of each other in both municipalities or were accessible by accompanying a UN officer (true always of the military bases). In addition, there were numerous social occasions that were illuminating. These included over a hundred dinners and lunches, because there were always some internationals eating out, and I would go at every opportunity. There were typically people from a range of organizations in the handful of restaurants frequented by the internationals in the two municipalities and the region. French military rubbed shoulders with UN personnel, OSCE officers, NGO internationals, international police from within the municipality, and representatives of the same organizations from another municipality or the regional headquarters. Business was often conducted over or supplemented by dinner.

Many interviewees found it cathartic to talk about their experiences with somebody who was not part of the mission and who was only there for a short time. After any meeting or interactional situation, I would take the opportunity to ask each person who had been there what they thought of what had just happened, including representatives of the local municipality and local villagers (facilitated by UN interpreters). The questions varied depending on the situation, and I was quickly able to construct a multifaceted, multidimensional picture of the issues. This also led to invitations to dinners, formal and informal gatherings, and anything people thought would help me with my project.

I conducted half of the in-depth interviews in offices, half in restaurants or over coffee. Formal interviews, nearly all with single informants, varied in length from forty-five minutes to three hours. I conducted informal interviews where and when I could. Sometimes these consisted of nothing more than a few conversational turns, but sometimes a hallway conversation might stretch for an hour as an informant and I "shot the breeze."

To direct my questions, I used a loosely structured format based on an interview "guide" consisting of a repertoire of question clusters, which I tried to ask in every formal interview and, when I could, in informal interviews. Because of time constraints, not every question was asked across all informants, although I attempted to maintain as much consistency as possible in terms of topics and key questions within each cluster. Some of the questions, particularly those concerning current issues or controversies, evolved over the first few interviews. These became an important part of the interviews.

Serendipity helped again in my third week, while I was working from Thezren. Another Irish woman, from my own hometown and near my age, who worked in the UN's regional office and whom I had met briefly on one of my transit stops there, invited me to her birthday dinner. When I got there, I found myself with a group of key people from the different organizations at the regional level, plus one person from the UN in Thezren. I subsequently interviewed most of the people and in fact, after dinner, the entire table was discussing my topic of research with vigor and passion, bringing up great ideas, confirming a lot of what I was theorizing. Each of these people subsequently gave me considerable help. It was an invaluable evening in terms of future contacts and as an unguarded and uncensored focus group on what I was investigating.

Recording Field Data

I taped all formal interviews except four, where the interviewees requested that I not do so. Two of these also requested that I not take notes, so I rushed to type up what they had told me immediately after the interview. One of the unrecorded interviews was over dinner, so it was not feasible to take notes, which would have inhibited the interviewee. On some occasions when I thought the environment would be too noisy to pick up the person's voice clearly, I would type their answers directly into my laptop. Another unrecorded interviewee was happy for me to take notes. In the informal contexts, I either took notes or, if talking while on the road, tape-recorded the interview. Conversations while driving often revealed nuggets of information and unexpected insights. During meetings, I would take notes by hand. If it was a meeting with a local present, it was possible to get everything verbatim, because the translation time slowed the proceedings down. Every couple of hours, I would sit in a quiet corner, take my laptop computer out, and write up observations. My laptop was wrapped in plastic bubble wrap for protection in my omnipresent backpack, and I never let it out of my sight for fear of losing it and my research notes for that day. Each night I backed up my notes for that day onto a floppy disk. I would expand any jottings I had taken, trying to remember as many things as possible that I hadn't written down. I wrote from the perspective of the broad question repertoire I had and did some preliminary analysis if possible—initial thoughts and theoretical leads. In this way, I immediately began organizing my data as I harvested it every day.

Participant and focused observation was extremely fruitful, because being a fly on the wall accepted by everyone as a temporary part of the mission allowed me to see the issues in action. I usually had conducted interviews with some of the people present in any particular situation and always did follow-up short interviews afterward, which enabled me to get diverse perspectives and a full picture of what had happened. Interviewing many of the internationals working together was invaluable, because the world of UNMIK and KFOR in the two municipalities was a relatively small and quite enclosed one. My position as an objective outside researcher, not working for any organization in the field, and the pent-up frustrations as well as satisfactions of doing this kind of work, meant that most people were more than willing to speak frankly about their experiences. My immersion in the everyday lives of the participants was necessary for understanding the meaning of their actions, the situation itself, and the process by which the people involved construct the situation through their interaction. As has been noted, to preserve confidentiality, I have used pseudonyms for people and, for the most part, for places.

Notes

Introduction

1. Charles Moskos dubbed these post–Cold War noncombatant missions Military Operations Other Than War (Moskos 2000).

2. The mandate of the UN Support Mission in Haiti (UNSMIH), authorized by Security Council Resolutions 1063 (1996) of June 28, 1996, 1085 (1996) of Nov. 29, 1996, and 1086 (1996) of Dec. 5, 1996, was "to assist the Government in the professionalization of the police, maintenance of a secure and stable environment conducive to the success of efforts to establish and train an effective national police force, and to coordinate activities of the United Nations system in promoting institution-building, national reconciliation and economic rehabilitation" (www.un.org/Depts/dpko/dpko/co_mission/unsmih.htm [accessed Sept. 8, 2004]).

1. Democratizing Through Networks

1. See Brian Uzzi's elucidation of components of an embedded relationship in Uzzi 1997. In a study of embeddedness and organizational networks among firms in the New York City apparel industry, he delineates the qualities of trust, information transfer, and collaborative problem-solving.

2. Regulation No. 2001, Section 2, Use of Flags, Symbols and Emblems. "Only the flags, symbols and emblems of the United Nations and those that are duly authorized by UNMIK may be displayed or used in public places in Kosovo or on public buildings used by the Interim Administration, including the Provisional Institutions of Self-Government and municipalities, as well as in official documents and correspondence."

Section 4, Municipal Flag "A municipality may adopt its own municipal flag, provided that such flag does not contain elements that may be perceived as provocative or offensive to particular communities and that such flag is authorized by UNMIK."

3. See Zucker 1986.

4. See, e.g., Berger and Luckmann 1966.

5. Garfinkel 1967, 1.

6. Symbolic interaction traces its roots to pragmatist philosophers such as Charles Sanders Peirce, John Dewey, Charles Cooley, and George Herbert Mead. The sociologists who developed and have continued this perspective include Herbert Blumer, Howard Becker, Erving Goffman, Norman Denzin and Arlie Hochschild. Blumer 1969, 180, observes: "The term 'symbolic interaction' refers, of course, to the peculiar and distinctive character of interaction as it takes place between human beings. The peculiarity consists in the fact that human beings interpret or 'define' each other's actions instead of merely reacting to each other's actions. Their 'response' is not made directly to the actions of one another but instead is based on the meaning, which they attach to such actions. Thus, human interaction is mediated by the use of symbols, by interpretation, or by ascertaining the meaning of one's actions. This mediation is equivalent to inserting a process of interpretation between stimulus and response in the case of human behavior."

7. As boundaries become more permeable, employees are members of both their own hierarchical organization *and* the network organization. In the business literature, Handy 1995 describes this as members experiencing a "dual citizenship" of affiliation with their project team (municipality) and with their company (organization).

8. See Evaristo and van Fenema 1999.

9. See DeSanctis and Fulk 1999.

10. See Saxenian 1994. Saxenian attributes the continued success of Silicon Valley to regional specialization. She contrasts that area's experience with that of declining Route 128 in Massachusetts and suggests that industrial systems built on regional networks are more flexible and technologically dynamic than those in which experimentation and learning are confined to individual firms. In the case of Route 128, adaptation was hindered by the separate, isolated, and self-sufficient organizational structures. Geographic proximity enables the building up of trust through collaboration and facilitates the continued recombination of technology and skill. Although it refers to business organizations in a conventional setting, this argument can be usefully applied to nonprofit organizations in a humanitarian intervention setting as well.

11. See Meyerson, Weick, and Kramer 1996, and also Preiss, Goldman, and Nagel 1997. These authors address how each organization contributes interactively to a coherent, aggregated performance that individual organizations could not achieve. The intricate connectivity among contributing firms implies exchange of valuable resources like knowledge and information and an increased formation of quasi organizations made up of individual organizations that have overlapping interests. However, this doesn't preclude them from having interests that are partially divergent.

12. The term "co-opetition" was coined by Brandenberger and Nalebuff 1996.

13. Seminal writings developing the concept of the network organization include Powell 1990; Nohria and Eccles 1992; and Arquilla and Ronfeldt 2001.

14. For more information on UN peacekeeping, see "United Nations Peace-keeping: Meeting New Challenges," www.un.org/Depts/dpko/dpko/ques.htm (accessed Feb. 25 2004).

15. Natsios 1995a, 79.

16. For example, an individual and a transnational NGO, Jodi Williams and the International Campaign to Ban Landmines (ICBL), received the Nobel Peace Prize in 1999 for their work to attain an international ban on landmines.

17. There is debate about the degree to which the NATO campaign accelerated the Serb campaign to drive Kosovar Albanians out of Kosovo. See Chomsky 1999. The U.S. Department of Defense argued that the increase in Serb activity in Kosovo began the day after the Rambouillet talks were suspended, four days before the NATO bombardment began. See Kozaryn 1999.

18. Kosovo census data from "Jugoslavia 1918–1988, statisticki godisnjak" (1989), 42–43, and "Statisticki godisnjak Jugoslavije za 1992. godinu" (1992), 62–63, cited in Vickovic and Nikolic 1996, 108–9.

19. For a good history of Kosovo, see Malcolm 1999. For an analysis of the conflict in Kosovo as part of a wider history of the role of the United States in international affairs in the second half of the twentieth century, see Power 2002. For an international legal perspective, see Matheson 2001.

20. See Mertus 2004. Mertus also argues that the international administration failed to capitalize on the "human rights culture" that had developed in the Kosovar Albanian community since the 1980s. Instead of cultivating it by encouraging respect for Serbs as an essential part of a Kosovo human rights culture, the internationals ignored its potential, and it has languished in a stunted form, configured in oppositional terms to Serbs. See also Mertus 1999 for a compelling account of how stories told on both sides perpetuated old animosities and were used for political ends.

21. See United Nations 1999b, paragraphs 1–2.

22. See United Nations 1999a. The UN secretary-general's reports on UN-MIK are available online at www.un.org/peace/kosovo/pages/kosovo1.htm (accessed Sept. 9, 2004).

2. Theoretical Background

1. See Sherif et al. 1961 for an account of an experiment where two previously rival teams of boys in a summer camp were enjoined to cooperate on the basis of working together toward the superordinate goal of defeating a team of boys from a rival camp.

2. Thanks to Professor Lynne Zucker, Department of Sociology, UCLA, for coining this phrase.

3. See Weber 1947; Taylor 1911; Simon [1947] 1976; March and Simon 1958.

4. The idea that an organization must properly be viewed as a social system and not just as a formal system for the division and coordination of labor had its origins in the famous Hawthorne Studies conducted at the Western Electric Company. See Mayo 1945 and Roethlisberger and Dickson 1939 for detailed accounts of this group of studies. See also Homans 1950.

5. Lawrence and Dyer 1983, 295.

6. On the interaction between the organization and its environment, see Davis and Powell 1992 for the argument of resource dependency theorists who regard organizations as loosely linked coalitions of shifting interest, and Hannan and Freeman 1977 for that of population ecologists who stress the selection by the environment of certain kinds of organizations over others.

7. Meyer, Scott, and Deal 1981; Powell and DiMaggio 1991.

8. See Bourdieu 1977 and Bourdieu and Wacquant 1992 on situations where organized groups of actors gather and frame their actions vis-à-vis one another.

9. On the development of the theory of institutionalization, see Zucker 1977, 1986, and 1987. See also Roy 1997 and Fligstein 1985 and 1990. The institutional claim that social and cultural pressures lead to organized conformity derives from German idealist philosophers and phenomenologists as described, e.g., in Berger and Luckmann 1966. Social reality is a human construct and a by-product of repetitive interactions. Thus organizational activities become institutionalized, taking the form of "rationalized myths" when repeated over a period of time. See Meyer and Rowan 1977. The idea that the formal structure may be embraced as myth and ceremony in order to signal legitimacy lies at the very heart of the new institutional perspective. Indeed, once a threshold of firms adopt an innovation, most future adoption, especially in an uncertain environment, is more likely to result from mimetic, coercive, or normative isomorphism than from competition. See DiMaggio and Powell 1983.

10. Fligstein 2001.

11. Burt 1987.

12. See Coleman, Katz, and Menzel 1966; Mizruchi 1989.

13. Granovetter 1985; Powell and Smith-Doerr 1994.

14. See Saxenian 1994 and Chapter 1 n. 10 above.

15. Castells 1996.

16. Arquilla and Ronfeldt 2001, 311.

17. Burns and Stalker 1961, 121.

18. Perrow 1986; Miles and Snow 1986.

19. Powell 1990, 296, 301.

20. Nohria and Eccles 1992; Wasserman and Faust 1994.

21. As in Granovetter 1985.

22. See the claim by Burt 1992 that the key to network dynamics, and social structure in general is the links that do not exit. Networks that are high in nonredundant (i.e., that provide unique information), additive contacts are the most efficient transmitters or sources of information. Structural holes occur when a player fails to have such nonredundant contacts and therefore cannot efficiently gain access to needed information.

23. Granovetter 1985; Perrow 1986.

24. See Doug McAdam, "Beyond Structural Analysis: Toward a More Dynamic Understanding of Social Movements," and Mario Diani, "Networks and Social Movements: A Research Programme," in Diani and McAdam 2003.

25. Arquilla and Ronfeldt 2001.

26. Hasenfeld 1992 has used them to explore the work of human service or-

ganizations, but at the level of institutions such as schools and hospitals—traditional human service needs providers. In Haiti and Kosovo, the military unexpectedly became such a human services provider.

27. Piore and Sabel 1984.
28. Scott Morton 1991; Rockart and Short 1991.
29. Larson 1992; Nohria and Eccles 1992.
30. Powell 1990.
31. Granovetter 1985.
32. See Uzzi 1997.
33. Ibid.
34. Zucker 1986.
35. See Jarillo 1988.
36. Ronfeldt and Arquilla 2001.
37. Fligstein 2001.
38. Castells 1996.
39. Evaristo and van Fenema 1999.
40. DeSanctis and Fulk 1999.
41. Meyerson, Weick, and Kramer 1996.
42. Preiss, Goldman, and Nagel 1997.
43. See Nonaka and Takeuchi 1995.
44. Ibid.
45. Szulanski 1996.
46. Grant 1996.
47. Appleyard 1996, 138.
48. Kodama 1994.
49. As initially proposed in Polanyi 1966.
50. Walsh and Dewar 1987.
51. Weick and Westley 1996.
52. Nelson and Winter 1982.
53. March and Simon 1958, 142.
54. Tyre and Hippel 1997.
55. Weick and Westley 1996.
56. Nohria and Berkley 1994, 367.
57. Nohria and Eccles 1992.
58. Diemers 2000.
59. Schutz 1964.
60. Diemers 2000.
61. For examples of such studies, see Smith and Kollock 1999.
62. Handy 1995.
63. Although dated owing to rapid recent change, for insights into the management of international organizations, see Kay 1980; Lister 1984; McLaren 1980. More recently, see Pitt and Weiss 1986 and Dijkzeul and Beigbeder 2003.
64. Betram 1995: 389.
65. Betram 1995, 405.
66. Weber 1947.

67. Empirical work on ICTs in this area has concentrated on online communities. See Smith and Kollock 1999.

68. Handy 1995.

69. See n. 9 above.

70. See Fligstein 2001.

3. Leadership in Networks

1. See Arquilla and Ronfeldt 2001 on all-channel, hub-and-spokes, and chain networks.

2. See key works in the development of organizational theory for the bureaucratic organization: Weber 1947; Taylor 1911; Simon [1947] 1976; March and Simon 1958.

3. See Baker 1993.

4. See Fligstein 2001.

5. See Ganz 2000.

6. See Arquilla and Ronfeldt 2001, which argues that as hierarchies become flatter, flexible, and responsive, and as network organizations grow and require some structure, in practice what we are seeing is the emergence of hybrids of networks and hierarchies.

7. See Fligstein 2001.

8. Arquilla and Ronfeldt 2001.

9. See Ganz 2000.

10. Zaltman, Duncan, and Holbeck 1973.

11. See Morris 1984.

12. See Granovetter 1973.

13. In an international intervention like UNMIK or KFOR, "strong ties" are forged with individuals who are part of a small international community, rather than being related by family or ethnic ties. The term is appropriate, because they are in practice one another's family in that situation.

14. See Gamson 1990; Rogers 1995.

15. See Chandler 1962; Mansbridge 1986.

16. Powell 1988. See also Alexander 1998.

17. Produktion was one of many state-owned enterprises in Kosovo. Industry had been organized under the state socialist system of the FRY, which had not changed in Kosovo. The EU has plans under way for privatization, but for the moment such enterprises remain state-owned.

18. See Fligstein 2001.

19. Lévi-Strauss 1966.

20. See Campbell 1960; Simonton 1988.

21. See DiMaggio 1997.

22. Each municipality was given a boilerplate municipal statute, which could be altered slightly on certain issues.

23. See Zucker 1986.

4. Formality, Social Embeddedness, and Accountability

1. See Schutz 1964.
2. See Zucker 1986; Zucker et al. 1995.
3. Zucker and Darby 1995, 153.
4. As Granovetter 1985 claims.
5. See Burns and Stalker 1961 on the suitability of "organic" or flexible organizations akin to networks for turbulent environments and the unsuitability of traditional hierarchies for such environments. See also Nohria and Eccles 1992.
6. Dill 1958; Perrow 1986.
7. Cf. Max Weber's idea of the modern organization's impersonality.
8. See Kanter 1983, 1989; Peters and Waterman 1982.
9. Schein, 1985, 11–12.
10. Hofstede [1981] 2001, 91.
11. Barley and Kunda 1992; Van Maanen and Barley 1984.
12. See Morand 1995 for a comprehensive analysis of formal and informal interactions orders within organizations.
13. Flexner 1984; Hudson 1980.
14. Brown and Levinson 1987; Levin, Long, and Shaffer 1981.
15. See Jefferson 1973, 1979; Sacks and Jefferson 1974; Schegloff 1968; Tannen, 1993.
16. Atkinson 1982.
17. Hall [1959] 1969.
18. See Uzzi 1997 for a discussion of trust and social embeddedness.
19. Giampiero (now in Banshik, on Daniel): "I used to work with him in Previca. He promises everything to people. 'You want to work in Yugobanca [popular name for a building the UN occupies in Previca]? I get you a job in Yugobanca.' I tell you something funny [in elongated Italian accent—Giampiero is Italian]. Daniel was in charge of the winterization program last year, and we were up in Zvecan organizing the unloading of coal. Daniel was there and he says to the Serbians, 'You only get paid this much for such hard work? You should get more!' Of course, these are Serbians, when they hear this, they start an immediate strike for more pay. Neil Cameron [head of restructuring], when he heard, was [gestures with hands for bulging eyes and rage like a bull], and Daniel was sent to Thezren. Thezren is where people are sent . . . [laughs]. They used to have very few people out there. Now there are more."
20. A program funded and run by the UN to ensure adequate accommodation, fuel, and food for the people of Kosovo.
21. See Selznick 1949.

5. The Use and Misuse of Information and Communication Technologies

1. Bockowski 2001.
2. Simon 1962.
3. See Galbraith 1973.

4. For example, Katz and Kahn 1978.

5. See Davidow and Malone 1992; Drucker 1992; Malone and Rockart 1991; Snow, Miles, and Coleman 1992.

6. See, e.g., Jarvenpaa and Ives, 1994; Rockhart and Short 1991.

7. See Castells 1996.

8. See Burns and Stalker 1961; Ring and Van de Ven 1992.

9. See Rockart and Short 1991, 191.

10. See Nohria and Eccles 1992: 289.

11. See Zack and MacKenney 1995.

12. See Ronfeldt and Arquilla 2001

13. See Orlikowski 1992.

14. See Lea, O'Shea, and Fung 1995: 214.

15. See Finholt and Sproull 1990; Huber 1990; Markus 1990, 1994; Sproull and Kiesler 1986; Lea, O'Shea, and Fung 1995; Zack and McKenny 1995.

16. See Wellman et al. 1996.

17. See Fulk and DeSanctis 1995; Kling and Jewett 1994; Koppel, Appelbaum, and Albin 1988; Weick, 1993; Wellman et al. 1996.

18. See Applegate, Cash, and Mills 1988; Jarvanpaa and Ives 1994.

19. An intranet is a private organizational network, based in the UN case on the proprietary Internet tool of Lotus Notes, an example of what is known as "groupware": software that enables all members of a bounded social network to receive and read e-mail messages from anyone in the network. See Johnson-Lenz and Johnson-Lenz 1994.

20. Wellman et al. 1996.

21. The concept of "organizational imperialism" captures each hierarchical organization's desire to control its environment for its own benefit and at the same time to protect its own interests.

22. Rockart and Short 1991.

23. Applegate, Cash, and Mills 1988; Lucas and Baroudi 1994; Rockart and Short 1991.

24. Handy 1995.

25. See Rockart and Short 1991; W.W. Powell 1988; Peters 1992.

26. The difference between the two is that the former is employed by KFOR and the latter is a UNMIK employee, one of the famed "blue berets." KFOR personnel do not wear the blue berets of the traditional UN peacekeeping units.

27. Wellman et al. 1996.

28. Hiltz, Johnson, and Turoff 1986; Kiesler, Siegel, and McGuire 1984; Rice 1987; Adrianson and Hjelmquist 1991; Weisband, Schneider, and Connolly 1995.

29. Kanter 1989.

30. Huber 1990.

31. The LCOs were responsible for the welfare of the inhabitants of the Serb enclaves in each municipality.

32. Fulk and Boyd 1991.

33. Although many researchers use the term "virtual" to describe geographically or temporally distributed groups, no one definition has yet gained acceptance (Mowshowitz 1997). Virtuality is thus far a complex and continuum-based

concept. Much of the computer-mediated communications research's emphasis is on the dichotomy of face-to-face versus virtual communication, yet the reality in organizations is that hybrid groups meet face-to-face as well as virtually. See Nunamaker et al. 1998; Griffith and Neale 1999.

34. The EU worked differently from the UN Civil Administration and the OSCE; they did not have local or municipal offices, as their implementing partners at the local level were NGOs, who were not part of the EU's bureaucratic structure.

35. Drucker 1992; Jarvenpaa and Ives 1994; Powell 1988.

36. Huber 1990.

37. Jarvenpaa and Ives 1994.

38. See Davidow and Malone 1992; Drucker 1992; Eccles and Crane 1987; Huber 1990, 1991; Jarvenpaa and Ives 1994.

39. Finholt and Sproull 1990; Huber 1990; Sproull and Kiesler 1986.

40. Huber 1990; Jarvenpaa and Ives 1994.

41. See Handy 1995.

6. Transactive Memory

1. Huber 1990.

2. Huber 1990, 1991.

3. Simon 1962.

4. Piore 1993, 431.

5. Contingency theory seeks to "understand and explain how organizations function under different conditions" (Lawrence and Lorsch 1967, 186).

6. See Daft and Lengel 1984, 1986; Daft, Lengel, and Trevino 1987.

7. Nohria and Eccles 1992.

8. Fish et al. 1992, 37–48.

9. Social information and cues increase involvement and comprehension. See Kraut et al. 1992; Siegal et al. 1986.

10. Hinds and Kiesler 1995.

11. Garton and Wellman 1993; Haythornthwaite, Wellman, and Mantei 1993.

12. Carley and Wendt 1991.

13. Granovetter, 1985.

14. Nohria and Eccles 1992.

15. Zmud 1990.

16. Finholt and Sproull 1990; Kraut et al. 1992.

17. Barry and Bateman 1992.

18. Watson 1982.

19. Feldman 1987; Finholt and Sproull 1990; Eveland and Bikson 1988; Sproull and Kiesler 1986.

20. See Brehm and Cohen 1962.

21. Wenger and Synder 2000, 139.

22. Wegner 1995.

23. To adapt Clifford Geertz's concept of "thick description" (Geertz 1973).

24. Griffith, Sawyer, and Neale 2000.

7. The UN Civil Administration and KFOR

1. In the literature on organizational change in business, traditional business models assume that each organization is responsible for a well-defined and complete portion of the supply chain. This relative independence is being transformed to a web of firms that are strongly connected. Market opportunities trigger combinatorial processes that result in ad hoc forms of cooperation (Meyerson, Weick, and Kramer 1996). Each organization contributes interactively to a coherent aggregate performance that individual organizations could not achieve (Preiss, Goldman, and Nagel 1997). This intricate connectivity implies exchange of valuable resources like knowledge and information and an increased formation of quasi organizations comprising individual organizations that have overlapping interests. However, this doesn't preclude them from also having interests that are partially divergent (ibid.).

2. Simon 1962.

3. Rockart and Short 1991.

4. The UN recognizes the need to improve the efficiency of its staff. The secretary-general's 1997 report entitled "Renewing the United Nations: A Programme for Reform" called for "a simplified structure that avoids duplication and achieves greater impact; empowered and responsible staff and managers; a leaner and more efficient United Nations Secretariat; and an organization that fosters management excellence and is accountable for achieving results determined by the Member States" (A/51/950, para. 224).

5. The Catholic Church, another great hierarchy, dealt similarly with "problem priests" by moving them from parish to parish.

6. See United Nations 1998b.

7. In 2000, the Report of the Panel on United Nations Peace Operations, an independent panel of international experts, urged the UN Department of Peacekeeping Operations (DPKO) to increase its use of UN volunteers, following eight years of "dedicated and competent" UNV performance in crisis zones around the world. According to the report, more than 4,000 UNVs recruited and fielded by the Bonn-based UNV program have served in nineteen different peacekeeping missions since 1992. See the report at www.un.org/peace/reports/peace_operations (accessed Sept. 13, 2004).

8. For a discussion of how economics has supplanted politics in international relations see Charles A. Schmitz, "Changing the Way We Do Business in International Relations," United States Institute of Peace Virtual Diplomacy Conference Paper, www.usip.org/virtualdiplomacy/publications/papers/schmitz.html (accessed Oct. 2004).

9. Over 50 percent of the population of Kosovo is under the age of 25.

10. "Reconstructing Kosovo," *The Economist*, print edition, May 16, 2000.

11. See www.nato.int/kosovo/docu/a990609a.htm (accessed Sept. 14, 2004).

12. The other four brigades are led by Germany, Britain, the United States, and Italy.

13. See Moskos 2000.

14. See, e.g., Snow, Miles, and Coleman 1992.

15. See Eccles and Crane 1987; Lawrence and Lorsch 1967.

8. The OSCE, the International Police, and NGOs

1. OSCE 2000.

2. An exception to the rule of consensus provides that decisions could be taken in the absence of the state concerned in cases of clear, gross, and uncorrected violations of CSCE (now OSCE) commitments relating to the human rights and fundamental freedoms—"consensus minus one"—which was invoked in July 1992 to suspend Yugoslavia from the CSCE.

3. OSCE 2000.

4. Ibid.

5. The LDK is the moderate party; it has an overall majority in Kosovo and won the majority of seats in Banshik in the 2000 elections.

6. Except for the Pakistani Special Unit used for security in Previca.

7. NGOs increasingly obtain their money from UN funds and programs as well as donor government assistance. Private funding comes primarily from mass media appeals and direct mail. Natsios 1995b.

8. A 1995 UN report on global governance suggested that nearly 29,000 international NGOs existed.

9. For example, the International Campaign to Ban Landmines, which won a Noble Peace Prize in 1997, is based on an interactive networking strategy. See www.icbl.org (accessed Sept. 14, 2004).

10. See Bach and Stark 2001b.

11. Ibid., 7.

12. Donini 1995.

13. Sanyal 1994, 37.

Conclusion

1. Hamida Ghafour, "Afghan Villages Locked in Grip of Taliban Forces," *Los Angeles Times*, Mar. 5, 2004.

2. Ibid.

3. See the argument of Hirst and Thompson 1996 that the hyperbole about globalization is not new and that there was a similar phenomenon in the late nineteenth century.

4. For an excellent analysis of the history and theoretical framing of networks of activists that coalesce and operate across national frontiers, see Keck and Sikkink 1998. See also Dartnell 2003 for an account of how the Web has been used by the Revolutionary Association of Women of Afghanistan (RAWA) to wage a worldwide struggle for hearts and minds.

5. Saxenian 1994.

6. Jackson 2003 argues for a more comprehensive analysis of warlords and their governance systems as a means to better understand the construction of peace and stability in countries as diverse as Afghanistan and Sierra Leone.

7. Rubin 2003 argues that in Afghanistan, the full process of seeking justice will have to wait until peace is fully established, in part because after twenty-five years of war, all groups have suffered or been victimized in one way or another. Any attempt at peace and reconciliation must take this into account.

8. See Zakaria 2003. He warns that rushing to hold elections in a security vacuum or highly unstable environment displays a lack of understanding of political processes. Democratization is often understood to be as simple as organizing free and fair elections or importing prefabricated constitutions and made-to-order parliaments. As Fareed Zakaria argues, however, the focus on elections as the sine qua non of democracy misses the fact that the liberal institutions underpinning electoral systems—the rule of law and civil liberties—are what makes democracy work, because democracy rests on civil society and citizenship. Without the institutions of constitutional democracy and civic society, democracy, as universal suffrage, can produce conflict and authoritarianism. Zakaria notes that in Austria, Italy, and the Weimar Republic in Germany in the early part of the twentieth century, against a background of weak liberal institutions, the direct result of the expansion of the vote to all adults was the rise of national socialism and communism, because peasants supported nationalist parties and workers supported communist parties. More recently, the numerous elections held immediately after the collapse of communism were won in the Soviet Union and Yugoslavia by nationalist separatists. This resulted in rapid secessions without guarantees, institutions, or political power for the many minorities in the new countries that emerged. The outcome was frequently rebellion, repression, and war. Without a background of constitutional liberalism, the introduction of democracy in divided societies such as Kosovo, Afghanistan, and Iraq merely foments nationalism, ethnic or religious conflict, and even war.

Appendix: Background and Methods

1. Berger and Luckmann 1966.
2. Garfinkel 1967, 1.
3. Barley 1986; Giddens 1984.
4. Granovetter 1985.

References

Adrianson, L., and E. Hjelmquist. 1991. "Group Processes in Face-to-Face and Computer-Mediated Communication." *Behavior and Information Technology* 10, no. 4: 281–96.

Aldrich, H. 1979. *Organizations and Environments*. Englewood Cliffs, N.J.: Prentice-Hall.

Alexander, V. D. 1998. "Environmental Constraints and Organizational Strategies: Complexity, Conflict and Coping in the Non Profit Sector." In *Private Action and the Public Good*, ed. Walter W. Powell and Elisabeth Clemens. New Haven, Conn.: JAI.

American Institute of Physics. 1995. *AIP Study of Multi-Institutional Collaborations, Phase II: Space Science and Geophysics*, Report No. 2: *Documenting Collaborations in Space Science and Geophysics*. New York: Center for History of Physics, American Institute of Physics.

Applegate, L. M., J. I. Cash, and D. Q. Mills. 1988. "Information Technology and Tomorrow's Manager." *Harvard Business Review* 66, no. 6 (Nov.–Dec.): 128–36.

Appleyard, M. M. 1996. "How Does Knowledge Flow? Inter-firm Patterns in the Semiconductor Industry." *Strategic Management Journal* 17 (Winter): 137–54.

Arquilla, John, and David F. Ronfeldt. 2001. *Networks and Netwars: The Future of Terror, Crime, and Militancy*. Document No. MR-1382-OSD. Santa Monica, Calif.: Rand Corporation.

Atkinson, J. M. 1982. "Understanding Formality: The Categorization and Production of 'Formal' Interaction." *British Journal of Sociology* 33, no. 1: 86–117.

Back, J., and D. Stark. 2001. "Link, Search, Interact: The Co-evolution of NGOs and Interactive Technology." Center on Organizational Innovation: Columbia University, New York.

Baker, W. E. 1990. "Market Networks and Corporate Behavior." *American Journal of Sociology* 101, no. 6: 589–625.

———. 1993. "The Network Organization in Theory and Practice. In *Networks and Organizations: Structure, Form, and Action,* ed. N. Nohria and R. G. Eccles, 397–429. Boston: Harvard Business School Press.

Barber, B. 2001. *Jihad vs. McWorld.* New York: Ballantine Books.

Barley, S. R. 1986. "Technology as an Occasion for Structuring: Evidence from Observations of CT Scanners and the Social Order of a Radiology Department." *Administrative Science Quarterly* 31: 78–108.

Barley, S. R., and G. Kunda. 1992. "Design and Devotion: Surges of Rational and Normative Ideologies of Control in Managerial Discourse." *Administrative Science Quarterly* 37: 363–99.

Barry, B., and T. S. Bateman. 1992. "Perceptions of Influence in Managerial Dyads: The Role of Hierarchy, Media and Tactics." *Human Relations* 45, no. 6: 555–74.

Bell, Daniel. 1973. *The Coming of Post-Industrial Society: A Venture in Social Forecasting.* New York: Basic Books. New ed., 1999.

Berger, Peter L., and Thomas Luckmann. 1966. *The Social Construction of Reality: A Treatise in the Sociology of Knowledge.* Garden City, N.Y.: Doubleday.

Bergman, J. 1979. "Energy Levels: An Important Factor in Identifying and Facilitating the Development of Giftedness in Young Children." *Creative Child and Adult Quarterly* 4: 181–88.

Betram, Eve. 1995. "Reinventing Governments: The Promise and Perils of United Nations Peace Building." *Journal of Conflict Resolution* 39, no. 3: 387–418.

Blumer, Herbert. 1969. *Symbolic Interactionism: Perspective and Method.* Englewood Cliffs, N.J.: Prentice-Hall.

Bockowski, Pablo. 2001. "Affording Flexibility: Transforming Information Practices in Online Newspapers." PhD diss., Cornell University.

Bourdieu, Pierre. 1977. *Outline of a Theory of Practice.* Translated by Richard Nice. New York: Cambridge University Press.

Bourdieu, Pierre, and Loïc J. D. Wacquant. 1992. *An Invitation to Reflexive Sociology.* Chicago: University of Chicago Press.

Brandenburger, A. M., and B. J. Nalebuff. 1996. *Co-opetition: A Revolutionary Mindset That Combines Competition and Co-operation: The Game Theory Strategy That's Changing the Game of Business.* Garden City, N.Y.: Doubleday.

Brehm, J. W., and A. R. Cohen. 1962. *Explorations in Cognitive Dissonance.* New York: Wiley.

Brown, P., and S. Levinson. 1987. *Politeness: Some Universals in Language Usage.* Cambridge: Cambridge University Press.

Buenger, V., R. L. Daft, E. J. Conlon, and J. Austin. 1996. "Competing Values in Organizations: Contextual Influences and Structural Consequences." *Organization Science* 7, no. 5: 557–76.

Burns Tom, and G. M. Stalker. 1961. *The Management of Innovation.* London: Tavistock Publications.

Burt, Ronald. 1987. "Social Contagion and Innovation: Cohesion and Structural Equivalence." *American Journal of Sociology* 92, no. 6: 1287–1335.

———. 1992. *Structural Holes.* Chicago: University of Chicago Press.

————. 1993. "The Social Structure of Competition." In *Networks and Organizations: Structure, Form, and Action,* ed. N. Nohria and R. G. Eccles, 57–91. Boston: Harvard Business School Press.

Campbell, D. T. 1960. "Blind Variation and Selective Retention in Creative Thought as in Other Knowledge Processes." *Psychological Review* 67: 380–400.

Campbell, J. L., J. Rogers Hollingsworth, and L. N. Lindberg, eds. 1991. *Governance of the American Economy.* New York: Cambridge University Press.

Carley, K., and K. Wendt. 1991. "Electronic Mail and Scientific Communication." *Knowledge* 12, no. 4: 406–40.

Castells, Manuel. 1996. *The Information Age: Economy, Society and Culture,* vol. 1: *The Rise of the Network Society.* Oxford: Blackwell.

Chandler, A. D. 1962. *Strategy and Structure: Chapters in the History of the American Industrial Enterprise.* Cambridge, Mass.: MIT Press.

Chomsky, Noam. 1972. *Language and Mind.* New York: Harcourt, Brace, Jovanovich.

————. 1999. *The New Military Humanism: Lessons from Kosovo.* London: Pluto Press.

Coleman, J. S., E. Katz, and H. Menzel. 1966. *Medical Innovation: A Diffusion Study.* Indianapolis: Bobbs-Merrill.

Conti, R., T. M. Amabile, and S. Pollak. 1995. "Problem Solving Among Computer Science Students: The Effects of Skill, Evaluation Expectation and Personality on Solution Quality." Paper presented at the Annual Meeting of the Eastern Psychological Association, Boston.

Daft, R. L., and R. H. Lengel. 1984. "Information Richness: A New Approach to Managerial Information Processing and Organization Design." In *Research in Organizational Behavior*, ed. B. Staw and L. Cummings, 191–233. Greenwich, Conn.: JAI Press.

————. 1986. "A Proposed Integration Among Organizational Information Requirements, Media Richness, and Structural Design." *Management Science* 32, no. 5: 554–71.

Daft, R. L., R. H. Lengel, and L. Klebe Trevino. 1987. "Message Equivocality, Media Selection, and Manager Performance: Implications for Information Systems." *MIS Quarterly* 11, no. 3: 355–66.

Dartnell, M. 2003. "Post-Territorial Insurgency: The Online Activism of the Revolutionary Association of Women of Afghanistan." *Small Wars and Insurgencies* 14, no. 2: 151–76.

Davidow, W. H., and M. S. Malone. 1992. *The Virtual Corporation: Structuring and Revitalizing the Corporation for the 21st Century.* New York: Harper-Business.

Davis, G. F., and W. W. Powell. 1992. "Organization-Environment Relations." In *Handbook of Industrial and Organizational Psychology*, ed. Marvin D. Dunnette and Leatta M. Hough, 3: 315–75. 2d ed. Palo Alto, Calif.: Consulting Psychologists Press.

Denzin, Norman K. 1989. *Interpretive Interactionism.* 2d ed. Thousand Oaks, Calif.: Sage Publications, 2001.

DeSanctis, G., and J. Fulk. 1999. *Shaping Organizational Form: Communication, Connection and Community*. Walnut Creek, Calif.: AltaMira.

DeSanctis, G., and M. S. Poole. 1994. "Capturing the Complexity in Advanced Technology Use: Adaptive Structuration Theory." *Organization Science*, 5, no. 2: 121–47.

Diani, Mario, and Douglas McAdam. 2003. *Social Movements and Networks: Relational Approaches to Collective Action*. Oxford: Oxford University Press.

Diemers, Daniel. 2000. "Information Quality and its Interpretive Reconfiguration." In *Knowledge Management and Virtual Organizations*, ed. Yogesh Malhotra. Hershey, Pa.: Idea Group Publishing.

Dijkzeul, Dennis, and Yves Beigbeder. 2003. *Rethinking International Organizations: Pathology and Promise*. New York: Berghahn Books.

Dill, W. R. 1958. "Environment as an Influence on Managerial Autonomy." *Administrative Science Quarterly* 2: 409–43.

DiMaggio, Paul. 1997. "Culture and Cognition." *Annual Review of Sociology* 23: 263–87.

DiMaggio, P. J., and H. Anheier. 1990. "The Sociology of NonProfit Organizations and Sectors." *Annual Review of Sociology* 16: 137–59.

DiMaggio, P. J., and W. W. Powell. 1983. "The Iron Cage Revisited: Institutional Isomorphism and Collective Rationality in Organizational Fields." *American Sociological Review* 48: 147–60.

Donini, Antonio. 1995. "The Bureaucracy and the Free Spirits: Stagnation and Innovation in the Relationship Between the UN and NGOs." *Third World Quarterly* 16, no. 3.

Drucker, Peter. 1988. "The Coming of the New Organization" *Harvard Business Review* 66, no. 1 (Jan.–Feb.) 45–53.

———. 1992. "The New Society of Organizations." *Harvard Business Review* 70, no. 5 (Sept.–Oct.): 95–104.

Dyer, W. G., Jr. 1982. "Culture in Organizations: A Case Study." MIT Sloan School of Management Working Paper.

Eccles, R. G., and D. B. Crane. 1987. "Managing Through Networks in Investment Banking." *California Management Review* 30, no. 1: 176–95.

Evaristo, R., and P. C. van Fenema. 1999. "A Typology of Project Management: Emergence and Evolution of New Forms." *International Journal of Project Management* 17, no. 5: 275–81.

Eveland, J. D., and T. K. Bikson. 1988. "Evolving Electronic Communications Networks: An Empirical Assessment." *Office, Technology and People* 3: 103–28.

Feldman, M. S. 1987. "Electronic Mail and Weak Ties in Organizations." *Office, Technology and People* 3: 83–101.

Finholt, T., and L. S. Sproull. 1990. "Electronic Groups at Work." *Organizational Science* 1, no. 1: 41–64.

Fish, R. S., R. E. Kraut, R. W. Root, and R. E. Rice. 1992. "Evaluating Video as a Technology for Informal Communication." In *CHI '92 Conference Proceedings: ACM Conference on Human Factors in Computing Systems: Striking a Balance, May 3-7, 1992, Monterey, California*, ed. Penny Bauersfeld,

John Bennett, and Gene Lynch, 37–48. New York: Association for Computing Machinery.

Fishman, J. 1965. "Who Speaks What Language to Whom and When." *La Linguistique* 2: 67–68.

Flexner, Stuart B. 1984. *Dictionary of American Slang*. New York: Crowell.

Fligstein, Neil. 1985. "The Spread of the Multidivisional Form Among Large Firms, 1919–1979." *American Sociological Review* 50, no. 3: 377–91.

———. 1990. *The Transformation of Corporate Control*. Cambridge, Mass.: Harvard University Press.

———. 2001. "Social Skill and the Theory of Fields." *Sociological Theory* 19, no. 2: 105–25.

Fulk, J., and B. Boyd. 1991. "Emerging Theories of Communication in Organizations." *Journal of Management* 17, no. 2: 407–46.

Fulk, J., and G. DeSanctis. 1995. "Electronic Communication and Changing Organizational Forms." *Organization Science* 6, no. 4: 337–49.

Galaskiewicz, J. 1985. "Interorganizational Relations." *Annual Review of Sociology* 11: 281–304.

Galbraith, J. R. 1973. *Strategies of Organizational Design*. Reading, Mass.: Addison-Wesley.

Gamson, William. 1990. *The Strategy of Social Protest*. Belmont, Calif.: Wadsworth Publishing.

Ganz, Marshall. 2000. "Resources and Resourcefulness: Strategic Capacity in the Unionization of California Agriculture, 1959–1966." *American Journal of Sociology* 105, no. 4: 1003–62.

Garfinkel, Harold. 1967. *Studies in Ethnomethodology*. Englewood Cliffs, N.J.: Prentice-Hall.

Garton, L., and B. Wellman. 1993. "Social Impacts of Electronic Mail in Organizations: A Review of the Research Literature." Technical Report No. OTP-93-13. Toronto: Ontario Telepresence Project.

Geertz, Clifford. 1973. *The Interpretation of Cultures*. New York: Basic Books.

Giddens, Anthony. 1984. *The Constitution of Society: Outline of the Theory of Structuration*. Cambridge: Cambridge University Press.

Glaser, B. G., and A. L. Strauss. 1967. *The Discovery of Grounded Theory: Strategies for Qualitative Research*. Chicago: Aldine.

Glover, J. A., and F. Sautter. 1977. "Relations of Four Components of Creativity to Risk-Taking Preferences." *Psychological Reports* 41: 227–30.

Goffman, E. 1958. *The Presentation of Self in Everyday Life*. Edinburgh: University of Edinburgh, Social Sciences Research Center.

Goodenough, W. 1971. *Culture, Language and Society*. Modular Publication No. 7. Reading, Mass: Addison-Wesley.

Granovetter, Mark. 1973. "The Strength of Weak Ties." *American Journal of Sociology* 78: 1360–80.

———. 1982. "Alienation Reconsidered: The Strength of Weak Ties." *Connections* 5 (Summer): 4–16.

———. 1983. "The Strength of Weak Ties: A Network Theory Revisited." *Sociological Theory* 1: 201–33.

———. 1985. "Economic Action and Social Structure: The Problem of Embeddedness." *American Journal of Sociology* 91: 481–510.

Grant, R. M. 1996. "Toward a Knowledge-Based Theory of the Firm." *Strategic Management Journal* 17: 109–22.

Greco, Thomas. 1998. "How Military Planners Can Better Integrate Non-Military Agencies into Campaign Planning. Two Case Studies: Bosnia and Somalia." MA thesis, Fort Leavenworth, Kans.

Griffith, T., and M. A. Neale. 1999. "Information Processing and Performance in Traditional and Virtual Teams: The Role of Transactive Memory." Research Paper No. 1613. Graduate School of Business, Stanford University.

Griffith, T., J. Sawyer, and M. A. Neale. 2000. "Information Technology as a Jealous Mistress: Competition for Knowledge Between Individuals and Organizations." Research Paper No. 1611. Graduate School of Business, Stanford University.

Hall, E. T. [1959] 1969. *The Silent Language.* Garden City, N.Y.: Doubleday.

Handy, Charles. 1995. "Trust and the Virtual Organization." *Harvard Business Review* 73: 40–50.

Hannan, M., and J. Freeman. 1977. "The Population Ecology of Organizations." *American Journal of Sociology* 82: 929–64.

Hasenfeld, Yaheskel, ed. 1992. *Human Services as Complex Organizations.* Thousand Oaks, Calif.: Sage Publications.

Hayek, F. A. 1945. "The Use of Knowledge in Society." *American Economic Review* 35, no. 4: 3–17.

Haythornthwaite, C., B. Wellman, and M. Mantei. 1993. "Putting Computerized Communications in Perspective: Media Use and Content in a Research Group." Working Paper, Ontario Telepresence Project.

Hiltz, S. R., K. Johnson, and M. Turoff. 1986. "Experiments in Group Decision-Making: Communication Process and Outcome in Face-to-Face Versus Computerized Conferences." *Human Communication Resources* 13, no. 2: 225–52.

Hinds, P., and S. Kiesler. 1995. "Communication Across Boundaries: Work, Structure and Use of Communication Technologies in a Large Organization?" *Organization Science* 6, no. 4: 373–93.

Hinds, P., and J. Pfeffer. 2001. "Why Organizations Don't Know 'What They Know': Cognitive and Motivational Factors Affecting the Transfer of Expertise." Research Paper No. 1697. Graduate School of Business, Stanford University.

Hirst, Paul, and Grahame Thompson. 1996. *Globalization in Question: The International Economy and the Possibilities of Governance.* Cambridge: Polity Press; Cambridge, Mass.: Blackwell.

Hofstede, Geert. [1981] 2001. *Culture's Consequences: Comparing Values, Behaviors, Institutions and Organizations Across Nations.* Thousand Oaks, Calif.: Sage Publications.

Holohan, Anne. 2003. "Haiti 1990–6: Older and Younger Journalists in the Post–Cold War World." *Media, Culture and Society* 25: 691–709.

Homans, G. C. 1950. *The Human Group.* New York: Harcourt, Brace & World.

Huber, G. P. 1990. "A Theory of the Effects of Advanced Information Technologies on Organizational Design, Intelligence, and Decision Making." *Academy of Management Review* 15: 47–71.

———. 1991. "Organizational Learning: The Contributing Processes and the Literatures." In *Organization Science* 2, no. 1, special issue, *Organizational Learning: Papers in Honor of (and by) James G. March*: 88–115.

Hudson, R. A. 1980. *Sociolinguistics*. Cambridge: Cambridge University Press.

Hughes, E. C. 1936. "The Ecological Aspect of Institutions." *American Sociological Review* 1: 180–89.

———. 1971. *The Sociological Eye*. Chicago: Aldine.

Jackson, Paul. 2003. "Warlords as Alternative Forms of Governance." *Small Wars and Insurgencies* 14, no. 2: 131–50.

Janowitz, M. 1960. *The Professional Soldier*. Glencoe, Ill.: Free Press.

Jarillo, C. 1988. "On Strategic Networks." *Strategic Management Journal* 9: 31–41.

Jarvenpaa, S. L., and B. Ives. 1994. "The Global Network Organization of the Future: Information Management Opportunities and Challenges." *Journal of Information Management Systems* 10, no. 4: 25–57.

Jarvenpaa, S. L., K. Knoll, and D. E. Leidner. 1998. "Is Anybody Out There? Antecedents of Trust in Global Virtual Teams." *Journal of Management Information Systems* 14, no. 4: 29–64.

Jefferson, G. 1973. "A Case of Precision-Timing in Ordinary Conversation." *Semiotica* 9, no. 1: 47–96.

———. 1979. "A Technique for Inviting Laughter and Its Subsequent Acceptance-Declination." In *Everyday Language: Studies in Ethnomethodology*, ed. George Psathas. New York: Irvington Publishers.

Johnson-Lenz, P., and T. Johnson-Lenz. 1994. "Groupware for a Small Planet." In *Groupware in the 21st Century: Computer-Supported Cooperative Working Toward the Millennium*, ed. Peter Lloyd. Westport, Conn.: Praeger.

Jorgensen, D. L. 1989. *Participant Observation: A Methodology for Human Studies*. Thousand Oaks, Calif.: Sage Publications.

Kanter, Rosabeth Moss. 1977. *Men and Women of the Corporation*. New York: Basic Books.

———. 1983. *The Change Masters: Innovation for Productivity in American Corporations*. New York: Simon & Schuster.

———. 1989. "The New Managerial Work." *Harvard Business Review* 67, no. 6 (Nov.–Dec.): 85–92.

Katz, D., and R. Kahn. 1978. *The Social Psychology of Organizations*. New York: Wiley.

Kay, D. A. 1980. *The Functioning and Effectiveness of Selected United Nations System Programs*. St. Paul: West Publishing Co.

Keck, M. E., and K. Sikkink. 1998. *Activists Beyond Borders: Advocacy Networks in International Politics*. Ithaca, N.Y.: Cornell University Press.

Kiesler, S., J. Siegel, and T. McGuire. 1984. "Social Psychological Aspects of Computer-Mediated Communication." *American Psychologist* 39: 1123–34.

Kling, R., and T. Jewett. 1994. "The Social Design of Worklife with Computers and Networks: An Open Natural Systems Perspective." *Advanced Computers* 39: 239–93.

Kodama, F. 1994. "Technology Fusion and the New R&D." In *The Product Development Challenge: Competing Through Speed, Quality, and Creativity,* ed. K. B. Clark and S. C. Wheelwright. Boston: Harvard Business School Press.

Koppel, R., E. Appelbaum, and P. Albin. 1988. "Implications of Workplace Information Technology: Control, Organization of Work and the Occupational Structure." *Research in the Sociology of Work* 4: 125–52.

Kozaryn, L. D. 1999. "Serb Terror, Ethnic Cleansing Reach New Heights." American Forces Press Service. www.defenselink.mil/news/Mar1999/n03301999_9903304.html (accessed Sept. 9, 2004).

Kraut, R. E., J. Galegher, R. Fish, and B. Chalfonte. 1992. "Requirements and Media Choice in Collaborative Writing." *Human-Computer Interaction* 7: 375–407.

Larson, A. 1992. "Network Dyads in Entrepreneurial Settings: A Study of the Governance of Exchange Processes." *Administrative Science Quarterly* 37: 76–104.

Lawrence, P., and D. Dyer. 1983. *Renewing American Industry.* New York: Free Press.

Lawrence, P. R., and J. W. Lorsch. 1967. *Organization and Environment: Managing Differentiation and Integration.* Boston: Division of Research, Graduate School of Business Administration, Harvard University. Reprint, Harvard Business School Press, 1986.

Lea, M., T. O'Shea, and P. Fung. 1995. "Constructing the Networked Organization." *Organizational Science* 6, no. 4: 462–78.

Lévi-Strauss, Claude. 1966. *The Savage Mind.* Chicago: University of Chicago Press. Originally published as *La Pensée sauvage* (Paris: Plon, 1962).

Levin, H., S. Long, and C. Shaffer. 1981. "The Formality of Latinate Lexicon in English." *Language and Speech* 24: 161–71.

Lipnack, J., and J. Stamps. 1997. *Virtual Teams: Reaching Across Space, Time, and Organizations with Technology.* New York: Wiley.

Lister, F. K. 1984. *Decision Making Strategies for International Organizations: The IMF Model.* Denver: Graduate School of International Studies, University of Denver.

Loebbecke, C., and P. C. van Fenema. 2000. "Virtual Organizations That Cooperate and Compete: Managing the Risks of Knowledge Exchange." In *Knowledge Management and Virtual Organizations,* ed. Yogesh Malhotra. Hershey, Pa.: Idea Group Publishing.

Lucas, H. C., and J. Baroudi. 1994. "The Role of Information Technology in Organizational Design." *Journal of Management Information Systems* 10, no. 4: 9–23.

Malcolm, Noel. 1999. *Kosovo: A Short History.* New York: Harper Perennial.

Malone, T. W. 1987. "Modeling Coordination in Organizations and Markets." *Management Science* 33, no. 10: 1317–32.

Malone, T. W., and J. F. Rockart. 1991. "Computers, Networks and the Corporation." *Scientific American* 265, no. 3: 128-36.

Malone, T., J. Yates, and R. Benjamin. 1987. "Electronic Markets and Electronic Hierarchies." *Communications of the ACM* 30, no. 6: 484–97.

Mansbridge, J. 1986. *Why We Lost the ERA.* Chicago: University of Chicago Press.

March, J. G., and H. A. Simon. 1958. *Organizations.* New York: Wiley.

Markus, M. L. 1990. "Toward a 'Critical Mass' Theory of Interactive Media." In *Organizations and Communication Technology,* ed. Janet Fulk and Charles W. Steinfeld. Thousand Oaks, Calif.: Sage Publications.

———. 1994. "Electronic Mail as the Medium of Managerial Choice." *Organizational Science* 5: 502–27.

Matheson, M. J. 2001. "United Nations Governance of Post Conflict Societies." *American Journal of International Law* 95, no. 1: 76–85.

Mayo, Elton. [1933] 1992. *The Human Problems of an Industrial Civilization.* Salem, N.H.: Ayer.

———. 1945. *The Social Problems of an Industrial Civilization.* Boston: Division of Research, Graduate School of Business Administration, Harvard University.

McLaren, R. I. 1980. *Civil Servants and Public Policy: A Comparative Study of International Secretariats.* Waterloo, Ontario: Wilfred Laurier University Press.

Mertus, Julie. 1999. *Kosovo: How Myths and Truths Started a War.* Berkeley: University of California Press.

———. 2004. "Improving International Peacebuilding Efforts: The Example of Human Rights Culture in Kosovo." *Global Governance* 10, no. 3: 333-52.

Meyer, J. W., and B. Rowan. 1977. "Institutionalized Organizations: Formal Structure as Myth and Ceremony." *American Journal of Sociology* 83: 340–63.

Meyer, J. W., W. R. Scott, and T. E. Deal. 1981. "Institutional and Technical Sources of Organizational Structure." In *Organization and the Human Services,* ed. H. D. Stein. Philadelphia: Temple University Press.

Meyer, Marshall W., and Lynne G. Zucker. 1989. *Permanently Failing Organizations.* Thousand Oaks, Calif.: Sage Publications.

Meyerson, D., K. E. Weick, and R. M. Kramer. 1996. "Swift Trust and Temporary Groups." In *Trust in Organizations: Frontiers of Theory and Research,* ed. R. M. Kramer and T. R. Tyler. Thousand Oaks, Calif.: Sage Publications.

Miles M., and M. Huberman. 1984. *Qualitative Data Analysis.* Thousand Oaks, Calif.: Sage Publications.

Miles, R. E., and C. C. Snow. 1986. "Network Organizations: New Concepts for New Forms." *California Management Review* 28: 62–73.

Miller, L. L. 1999. "From Adversaries to Allies: Relief Workers' Attitudes Toward the US Military." *Qualitative Sociology* 22, no. 3: 181–97.

Mizruchi, M. S. 1989. "Similarity of Political Behavior Among Large American Corporations." *American Journal of Sociology* 95, no. 2: 401–24.

Morand, D. A. 1995. "The Role of Behavioral Formality and Informality in the Enactment of Bureaucratic Versus Organic Organizations." *Academy of Management Review* 20, no. 4: 831–72.

Morris, A. D. 1984. *Origins of the Civil Rights Movement: Black Communities Organizing for Change.* New York: Free Press.

208 *References*
Moskos, Charles. 2000. *The Media and the Military in Peace and Humanitarian Operations*. Chicago: Robert R. McCormick Tribune Foundation.

Mowshowitz, A. 1994. "Virtual Organization: A Vision of Management in the Information Age." *Information Society* 10: 267–88.

———. 1997. "Introduction to Special Issue on Virtual Organization." *Communications of the ACM* 40, no. 9: 30–37.

Natsios, A. 1995a. "The International Response System." *Parameters*, Spring 1995, 68–91.

———. 1995b. "NGOs and the UN System in Complex Humanitarian Emergencies: Conflict or Cooperation?" *Third World Quarterly* 16, no. 3: 405–19.

Nelson, R. R., and S. G. Winter. 1982. *An Evolutionary Theory of Economic Change*. Cambridge, Mass.: Belknap Press.

Nohria, N., and J. D. Berkley. 1994. "The Virtual Organization: Bureaucracy, Technology and the Implosion of Control." In *The Post-Bureaucratic Organization: New Perspectives on Organizational Change*, ed. C. von Heckscher and A. Donellon. Thousand Oaks, Calif.: Sage Publications.

Nohria, Nitin, and R. G. Eccles. 1992. *Networks and Organizations: Structure, Form, and Action*. Boston: Harvard Business School Press.

Nonaka, Ikujiro, and Hirotaka Takeuchi. 1995. *The Knowledge-Creating Company. How Japanese Companies Create the Dynamics of Innovation*. New York: Oxford University Press.

Nunamaker, J. F., R. O. Briggs, N. C. Romano, and D. D. Mittleman. 1998. "The Virtual Office Work-Space: Group Systems Web and Case Studies." In *Groupware: Collaborative Strategies for Corporate LANs and Intranets*, ed. D. Coleman. New York: Prentice-Hall.

Orlikowski, W. J. 1992. "The Duality of Technology: Rethinking the Concept of Technology in Organizations." *Organization Science* 3, no. 3: 398–427.

OSCE [Organization for Security and Cooperation in Europe]. 2000. *OSCE, 1975–2000 Handbook*. Vienna: OSCE.

Ouchi, W., and A. L. Wilkins. 1985. "Organizational Culture." *Annual Review of Sociology* 11: 457–83.

Perrow, C. 1986. *Complex Organizations: A Critical Essay*. New York: McGraw-Hill.

———. 1993. "Small Firm Networks." In *Networks and Organizations: Structure, Form, and Action,* ed. N. Nohria and R. G. Eccles. Boston: Harvard Business School Press.

Peters, Tom. 1992. *Liberation Management: Necessary Disorganization for the Nanosecond Nineties*. New York: Knopf.

Peters, T. J., and R. H. Waterman Jr. 1982. *In Search of Excellence*. New York: Harper & Row.

Piore, M. J. 1993. "Fragments of a Cognitive Theory of Technological Change and Organizational Structure." In *Networks and Organizations: Structure, Form, and Action*, ed. N. Nohria and R. G. Eccles. Boston: Harvard Business School Press.

Piore, M. J., and C. F. Sabel. 1984. *The Second Industrial Divide*. New York: Basic Books.

Pitt, D., and T. G. Weiss. 1986. *The Nature of United Nations Bureaucracies.* Boulder, Colo.: Westview Press.

Polanyi, Michael. 1966. *The Tacit Dimension.* Garden City, N.Y.: Doubleday.

Powell, Walter W. 1988. "Institutional Effects on Organizational Structure and Performance." In *Institutional Patterns and Organizations*, ed. L. Zucker. Cambridge, Mass.: Ballinger.

―――. 1990. "Neither Market Nor Hierarchy: Network Forms of Organization." *Research in Organizational Behavior*, ed. Barry Staw and L. L. Cummings, 12: 295–336.

Powell, Walter W., and P. DiMaggio. 1991. *The New Institutionalism in Organizational Analysis.* Chicago: University of Chicago Press.

Powell, Walter W., and L. Smith-Doerr. 1994. "Networks and Economic Life." In *The Handbook of Economic Sociology*, ed. N. J. Smelser and R. Swedberg. Princeton, N.J.: Princeton University Press; New York: Russell Sage Foundation.

Power, Samantha. 2002. *A Problem from Hell: America and the Age of Genocide.* New York: Basic Books.

Preiss, K., S. L. Goldman, and R. N. Nagel. 1997. *Cooperate to Compete: Building Agile Business Relationships.* New York: Wiley.

Prentky, R. A. 1980. *Creativity and Psychopathology.* New York: Praeger.

Ragin, C. C., and H. S. Becker. 1992. *What Is a Case? Exploring the Foundations of Social Inquiry.* Cambridge: Cambridge University Press.

"Reconstructing Kosovo." *Economist*, May 16, 2000.

Rice, R. 1987. "Computer-mediated Communication and Organizational Innovation." *Journal of Communications* 37, no. 4: 65–95.

Ring, S. P., and A. H. Van de Ven. 1992. "Structuring Cooperative Relationships Between Organizations." *Strategic Management Journal* 13, no. 7: 483–98.

Rocco, E. 1996. "Cooperative Efforts in Electronic Contexts: the Relevance of Prior Face-to-Face Interactions." http://hsb.baylor.edu/ramsower/ais.ac.96/papers/rocco.htm (accessed Mar. 2002).

Rockhart, J. F., and J. E. Short. 1991. "The Networked Organization and the Management of Interdependence." In *The Corporation of the 1990s: Information Technology and Organizational Transformation*, ed. M. S. Scott Morton, 189–219. New York: Oxford University Press.

Roethlisberger, F. J., and W. Dickson. 1939. *Management and the Worker.* Cambridge, Mass.: Harvard University Press.

Rogers, E. 1995. *Diffusion of Innovations.* New York: Free Press.

Roy, William. 1997. *Socializing Capital: The Rise of the Large Industrial Corporation in America.* Princeton, N.J.: Princeton University Press.

Rubin, Barnett R. 2003. "Transnational Justice and Human Rights in Afghanistan." *International Affairs* 79, no. 3: 567–81.

Sacks, H. E., and G. Jefferson. 1974. "A Simplest Systematics for the Organization of Turntaking for Conversation." *Language* 50: 696–735.

Salancik, G. R., and J. Pfeffer. 1977. "Who Gets Power—and How They Hold On to It: A Strategic Contingency Model of Power." *Organizational Dynamics* 2, no. 21: 2–21.

Sanyal, Bishwapriya. 1994. *Cooperative Autonomy: The Dialectic of State-NGOs Relationship in Developing Countries.* Research Series, no. 100. Geneva: International Institute for Labour Studies.

Saxenian, Annalee. 1994. *Regional Advantage: Culture and Competition in the Silicon Valley.* Cambridge: Cambridge University Press.

Schegloff, E. A. 1968. "Sequencing in Conversational Openings." *American Anthropologist* 70: 1075–95.

Schein, E. H. 1985. *Organizational Culture and Leadership.* San Francisco: Jossey-Bass.

Schmitz, Charles A. 1997. "Changing the Way We Do Business in International Relations." United States Institute of Peace Virtual Diplomacy Conference Paper. www.usip.org/virtualdiplomacy/publications/papers/schmitz.html (accessed Oct. 2004).

Schutz, Alfred. 1964. *Collected Papers II: Studies in Social Theory.* Edited by Arvid Brodersen. The Hague: Martinus Nijhoff.

Scott Morton, Michael S. 1991. "The Corporation of the 1990s: Information Technology and Organizational Transformation." In *The Corporation of the 1990s,* ed. id. New York: Oxford University Press.

cott, W. R. 1992. *Organizations: Rational, Natural and Open Systems.* 3d ed. Englewood Cliffs, N.J.: Prentice-Hall.

Selznick, Philip. 1949. *TVA and the Grass Roots: A Study in the Sociology of Formal Organization.* Berkeley: University of California Press.

Shawcross, William. 2000. *Deliver Us from Evil: Warlords and Peacekeepers in a World of Endless Conflict.* London: Bloomsbury.

Sherif, M., O. J. Harvey, B. J. White, W. R. Hood, and C. W. Sherif. 1961. *Intergroup Conflict and Cooperation: The Robbers Cave Experiment.* Norman, Okla.: Institute of Group Relations.

Shiras, Peter. 1996. "Big Problems, Small Print: A Guide to the Complexity of Humanitarian Emergencies and the Media." In *From Massacres to Genocide,* ed. R. Rotberg and T. Weiss. Cambridge, Mass.: World Peace Foundation.

Siegal, J., V. Dubrovsky, S. Kiesler, and T.W. McGuire. 1986. "Group Processes in Computer-Mediated Communication." *Organizational Behavior and Human Decision Making Processes* 37: 157–87.

Simon, H. [1947] 1976. *Administrative Behavior: A Study of Decision-making Processes in Administrative Organization.* 3d ed. New York: Free Press.

Simonton, D. K. 1988. "Creativity, Leadership and Chance." In *The Nature of Creativity: Contemporary Psychological Perspectives,* ed. R. J. Sternberg. Cambridge: Cambridge University Press.

Skocpol, Theda. 1984. "Emerging Agendas and Recurrent Strategies in Historical Sociology." In *Vision and Method in Historical Sociology,* ed. id. Cambridge: Cambridge University Press.

Smith, M., and P. Kollock. 1999. *Communities in Cyberspace.* London: Routledge.

Snow, C. C., R. E. Miles, and H. J. Coleman. 1992. "Managing 21st Century Network Organizations." *Organizational Dynamics* 20, no. 3: 5–20.

Sproull, Lee, and Sara Kiesler. 1986. "Reducing Social Context Cues: Electronic Mail." *Organizational Communication in Management Science* 32, no. 11: 1492–1512.

———. 1991. *Connections: New Ways of Working in the Networked Organization.* Cambridge, Mass.: MIT Press.

Stark, D. 2001. "Ambiguous Assets for Uncertain Environments: Heterarchy in PostSocialist Firms." In *The 21st Century Firm: Changing Economic Organization in International Perspective,* ed. P. DiMaggio, W. Powell, D. Stark, and E. Westney. Princeton, N.J.: Princeton University Press.

Stark, F. M. 1996. *Communicative Interaction, Power and the State: A Method.* Toronto: University of Toronto Press.

Stasser, G., and W. Titus. 1985. "Pooling of Unshared Information in Group Decision Making: Biased Information Sampling During Group Discussion." *Journal of Personality and Social Psychology* 48: 1467–78.

———. 1987. "Effects of Information Load and Percentage of Shared Information on the Dissemination of Unshared Information During Group Discussion." *Journal of Personality and Social Psychology* 53: 81–93.

Stinchcombe, A. 1959. "Bureaucratic and Craft Administration of Production." *Administration Science Quarterly* 4: 168–87.

———. 1990. *Information and Organizations.* Berkeley: University of California Press.

Szulanski, G. 1996. "Exploring Internal Stickiness: Impediments to the Transfer of Best Practice with the Firm." *Strategic Management Journal* 17: 77–91.

Tannen, D. 1993. "The Relativity of Linguistic Strategies: Rethinking Power and Solidarity in Gender and Dominance." In *Gender and Conversational Interaction,* ed. id. New York: Oxford University Press.

Taylor, F. W. 1911. *The Principles of Scientific Management.* New York: Norton.

Tyre, M. J., and E. von Hippel. 1997. "The Situated Nature of Adaptive Learning in Organizations." *Organization Science* 8, no. 1: 71–83.

United Nations. 1997. Report of the Secretary General on Renewing the United Nations: A Programme for Reform. A/51/950. www.un.org/reform/refdoc.htm (accessed Oct. 7, 2004).

———. 1998a. "OAS Peace-Building Experiences: Progress Achieved, Lessons Learned, and Future Possibilities." OAS/UN International Civilian Mission in Haiti (MICIVIH). www.un.org/rights/micivih/rapports/peace-bu.htm (accessed Oct. 7, 2004).

———. 1998b. Report to the Secretary-General on Human Resources Management Reform. A/53/414. www.un.org/reform/a53414.pdf (accessed Oct. 3, 2004).

———. 1999a. Report of the Secretary-General on the United Nations Interim Administration Mission in Kosovo, UN Doc. S/1999/779, paragraphs 8–9. July 12, 1999. www.un.org/peace/kosovo/pages/kosovo1.htm (accessed Sept. 9, 2004).

———. 1999b. Security Council Resolution 1244, S/RES/1244. June 10, 1999. www.un.org/Docs/scres/1999/sc99.htm ods-dds-ny.un.org/doc/UNDOC/GEN/N99/172/89/PDF/N9917289.pdf (accessed Sept. 9, 2004).

———. 2001. *Report of the Office of Internal Oversight Services on the Audit of the Policies and Procedures of the Department of Peacekeeping Operations for Recruiting International Civilian Staff for Field Missions.* A/56/202/ (2001).www.un.org/Depts/oios/reports/a56_202.pdf (accessed Oct. 3, 2004).

Urquhart, B. 1992. "The United Nations in 1992: Problems and Opportunities." *International Affairs* 68, no. 2: 311–19.

Uzzi, Brian. 1996. "The Sources and Consequences of Embeddedness for the Economic Performance of Organizations: The Network Effect." *American Sociological Review* 61, no. 4: 674–98.

———. 1997. "Social Structure and Competition in Interfirm Networks: The Paradox of Embeddedness." *Administrative Science Quarterly* 42, no. 1: 35–67.

Van Maanen, J. 1973. "Observations on the Making of Policemen." *Human Organization* 32: 407–18.

Van Maanen, J., and S. Barley. 1984. "Occupational Communities: Culture and Control in Organizations." In *Research in Organizational Behavior*, ed. B. M. Staw and L. L. Cummings, 6: 287–365. Greenwich, Conn.: JAI Press.

Van Maanen, J., and G. Kunda, G. 1989. "Real Feelings: Emotional Expression and Organizational Culture." In *Research in Organizational Behavior*, ed. B. M. Staw and L. L. Cummings, 11: 43–103. Greenwich, Conn.: JAI Press.

Vickovic, Milan, and Goran Nikolic. 1996. *Stanovnistvo Kosva u razdoblju od 1918. do 1991. godine.* Munich: Slavica Verlag.

Walberg, H. J. 1971. "Varieties of Adolescent Creativity and the High School Environment." *Exceptional Children* 38: 111–16.

Walton, J. 1992. "Making the Theoretical Case." In *What Is a Case? Exploring the Foundations of Social Inquiry*, ed. C. Ragin and H. Becker. Cambridge: Cambridge University Press.

Walsh, J. P., and R. D. Dewar. 1987. "Formalization and the Organizational Life Cycle." *Journal of Management Studies* 24, no. 3: 215–31.

Wasserman, S., and K. Faust. 1994. *Social Network Analysis: Methods and Applications.* New York: Cambridge University Press.

Watson, K. M. 1982. "An Analysis of Communication Patterns: A Method for Discriminating Leader and Subordinate Roles." *Academy of Management Journal* 25, no. 1: 107–20.

Weber, Max. 1947. *The Theory of Social and Economic Organization.* Translated by A. M. Henderson and Talcott Parsons. New York: Free Press.

Wegner, D. M. 1987. "Transactive Memory: A Contemporary Analysis of the Group Mind." In *Theories of Group Behavior*, ed. B. Mullen and G. R. Goethals. New York: Springer.

———. 1995. "A Computer Network Model of Human Transactive Memory." *Social Cognition* 13: 319–39.

Weick, K. E. 1979. *The Social Psychology of Organizing.* 2d ed. Reading, Mass.: Addison-Wesley.

———. 1993. "Sensemaking in Organizations: Small Structures with Large Consequences." In *Social Psychology in Organizations*, ed. J. K. Murnighan. New York: Prentice-Hall.

Weick, K. E., and F. Westley. 1996. "Organizational Learning." In *Handbook of*

Organizational Studies, ed. S. R. Clegg, C. Hardy, and W. R. Nord. London: Sage.

Weisband, S. P., S. K. Schneider, and T. Connolly. 1995. "Computer-mediated Communication and Social Information: Status Salience and Status Difference." *Academy of Management Journal* 38, no. 4: 1124–51.

Weiss, R. 2000. "Governance, Good Governance and Global Governance: Conceptual and Actual Challenges." *Third World Quarterly* 21, no. 5: 795–814.

Wellman, B., J. Salaff, D. Dimitrova, L. Garton, M. Gulia, and C. Haythornthwaite. 1996. "Computer Networks as Social Networks: Collaborative Work, Telework and Virtual Community." *Annual Review of Sociology* 22: 213–38.

Wenger, E., and W. Synder. 2000. "Communities of Practice: The Organizational Frontier." *Harvard Business Review* 78, no. 1 (Jan.–Feb.): 139–45.

White, H. 1992. *Identity and Control: A Structural Theory of Social Action.* Princeton, N.J.: Princeton University Press.

———. 1993. "Agency as Control in Formal Networks" In *Networks and Organizations: Structure, Form, and Action,* ed. N. Nohria and R. G. Eccles, 92–117. Boston: Harvard Business School Press.

Williamson, O. 1975. *Markets and Hierarchies.* New York: Free Press.

———. 1994. "Transaction Costs Economics and Organization Theory." In *The Handbook of Economic Sociology,* ed. N. J. Smelser and R. Swedberg. Princeton, N.J.: Princeton University Press; New York: Russell Sage Foundation.

Whyte, W. 1943. *Street Corner Society.* Chicago, Illinois: University of Chicago Press.

Whyte, W., and K. K. Whyte. 1984. *Learning from the Field: A Guide from Experience.* Thousand Oaks, Calif.: Sage Publications.

Zack, M. H., and J. L. MacKenney. 1995. "Social Context and Interaction in Ongoing Computer Supported Management Groups." *Organizational Science* 6, no. 4: 394–422.

Zakaria, Fareed. 2003. *The Future of Freedom: Illiberal Democracy at Home and Abroad.* New York: Norton.

Zaltman, G., R. Duncan, and J. Holbeck. 1973. *Innovations and Organizations.* New York: Wiley.

Zmud, R. W. 1990. "Opportunities for Strategic Information Manipulation Through New Information Technology." In *Organizations and Communication Technology,* ed. Janet Fulk and Charles W. Steinfield. Thousand Oaks, Calif.: Sage Publications.

Zucker, Lynne G. 1977. "The Role of Institutionalization in Cultural Persistence." *American Sociology Review* 42: 726–43.

———. 1986. "Production of Trust: Institutional Sources of Economic Structure, 1840 to 1920." *Research in Organizational Behavior* 8: 53–111.

———. 1987. "Institutional Theories of Organization." *Annual Review of Sociology* 13: 443–64.

Zucker, Lynne G., and Michael R. Darby. 1995. "Social Construction of Trust to Protect Ideas and Data in Space Science and Geophysics." NBER Working Paper No. w5373. http://papers.nber.org/papers/w5373 (accessed Sept. 3, 2004).

Zucker, Lynne G., Michael R. Darby, Marilynn B. Brewer, and Yusheng Peng, 1995. "Collaboration Structure and Information Dilemmas in Biotechnology: Organizational Boundaries as Trust Production." NBER Working Paper No. w5199. www.nber.org/papers/w5199 (accessed Sept. 3, 2004).

Index

In this index an "f" after a number indicates a separate reference on the next page, and an "ff" indicates separate references on the next two pages. A continuous discussion over two or more pages is indicated by a span of page numbers, e.g., "57–59." *Passim* is used for a cluster of references in close but not consecutive sequence.